DATE DUE

2/4/20 1			
DEC 2 7 2012			
12/16/2015			

GAYLORD | | | PRINTED IN U.S.A.

The Usborne
Essential
Atlas
of the World

Stephanie Turnbull

Designers: Stephen Moncrieff and Helen Wood
Consultant cartographic editor: Craig Asquith

Cartography by European Map Graphics Ltd
Map design by Laura Fearn
and Keith Newell

Usborne Quicklinks

The Usborne Quicklinks Website is packed with links to all the best websites on the internet. For links to over 50 recommended websites for this book, go to www.usborne-quicklinks.com and enter the keywords "essential atlas".

There you will find links to websites where you can:
- explore interactive maps of the Earth
- discover how satellite images can show the way land and weather can change over time
- take virtual tours of countries around the world
- try quizzes to test your general knowledge of countries across the globe
- find out about some of the world's wildlife and habitats

Internet safety
When using the internet, make sure you follow these internet safety guidelines which are also displayed on the Usborne Quicklinks Website.

- Children should ask their parent's or guardian's permission before using the internet.
- Never give details of your full name, address, telephone number or school, or any other personal information.
- If a website asks you to log in or register by typing your name or email address, children should ask an adult's permission first.

CONTENTS

MAPS AND ATLASES

A map is an image that represents a particular area of the Earth's surface, usually from above and at a reduced size. A map can show the whole world or just a street. An atlas is a collection of maps, along with useful information about the areas shown.

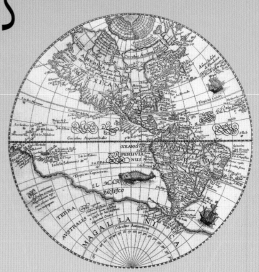

This map was drawn in 1584. Although people at this time knew much less about the shapes and locations of countries, they still created many maps of the world.

What maps show

Unlike an aerial photograph, which shows exactly what an area looks like from above, a map can show features of the area in a clearer, simplified way. There can be many kinds of maps of a place, each giving different kinds of information. For example, maps can show the names of places, the position of borders between countries, or the types of crops that grow.

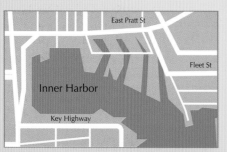

On the left is a simple map of Baltimore Harbor, U.S.A. It just shows the area's main streets.

On this aerial photograph of the same area it's difficult to see the streets.

Internet links

For links to websites where you can find out more about maps and map-making, see physical and political maps of different countries, and find street maps of towns and cities around the world, go to **www.usborne-quicklinks.com**.

Map features

Maps are designed to be clear, so most of them use conventions to help us recognize certain features. Land is often shown as green, and seas, rivers and lakes are usually shown as blue. Symbols can also be used to represent features. The meanings of the symbols are usually explained in a key.

- Mountain vegetation
- Coniferous forest
- Deciduous forest
- Grassland
- Scrubland

This is a thematic map that shows Europe's natural vegetation. The key above indicates the type of land that the different shading represents.

Kinds of maps

There are many different kinds of maps. Physical maps focus on natural features such as mountains, rivers and lakes. Political maps focus on the division of the Earth's surface into separate states*.

Some maps are thematic. This means that only certain information, such as climate types or population, is represented. You can find out more about thematic maps on pages 14 and 15.

Which way is up?

Although the Earth doesn't have a top and a bottom, north is usually at the top of maps. But it is sometimes more convenient to reposition a map, so north might not necessarily be at the top. Some maps have a compass symbol that indicates where north lies.

Scale

The size of a map in relation to the area it shows is called its scale. Some maps have a scale bar, which is a rule with measurements. It tells you how many miles or km are represented by a certain distance on the map. Other maps show this ratio in numbers. The figure 1:100 may mean, for example, that 1cm on the map represents 100cm on the Earth's surface. The scale of a map depends on its purpose. A map showing the whole world is on a very small scale, but a town plan is on a much larger scale so that features, such as roads and buildings, can be shown clearly.

1:80,000,000

| 0 | 1,000 | 2,000 | 3,000km |

| 0 | | 1,000 | 2,000 miles |

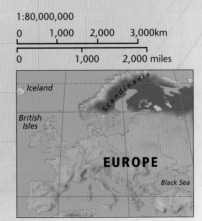

This map of Europe is on a small scale so that it all fits onto one small map.

1:7,000,000

| 0 | 100 | 200 | 300km |

| 0 | | 100 | 200 miles |

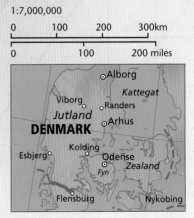

This map of Denmark is on a larger scale to show more detail.

DIVIDING LINES

Map-makers divide up the Earth with imaginary lines that help us measure distances and find where places are. There are two sets of lines, called latitude and longitude.

This Arctic fox lives in northern Canada, very near the Arctic Circle line of latitude.

Latitude lines

Lines of latitude run around the globe. They are parallel to each other and get shorter the closer they are to the two poles. The latitude line that runs around the middle of the Earth is called the Equator. It is the most important line of latitude as all other lines are measured north or south of it.

Latitude lines   Longitude lines

Longitude lines

Lines of longitude run from the North Pole to the South Pole. All the lines are the same length, and they all meet at the North and South Poles.

The most important line of longitude is the Prime Meridian Line, which runs through Greenwich, in England. All other lines of longitude are measured east or west of this line.

Other lines

The Equator is not the only named latitude line. The Tropic of Cancer is a line north of the Equator, and the Tropic of Capricorn is at the same distance south of the Equator. Between these lines is the hottest, stormiest part of the world. It is called the tropics.

The Arctic Circle is a latitude line far north of the Equator. The area north of this includes the North Pole and is called the Arctic. On the other side of the globe is the Antarctic Circle. The area south of this includes the South Pole and is known as the Antarctic.

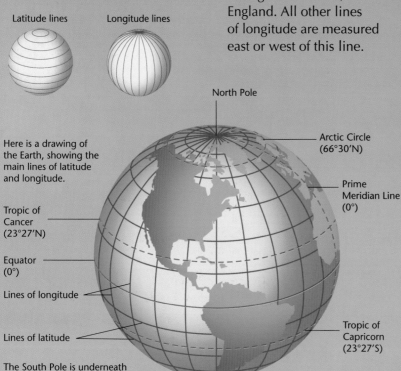

Here is a drawing of the Earth, showing the main lines of latitude and longitude.

North Pole

Arctic Circle (66°30'N)

Prime Meridian Line (0°)

Tropic of Cancer (23°27'N)

Equator (0°)

Lines of longitude

Lines of latitude

Tropic of Capricorn (23°27'S)

The South Pole is underneath the globe, so you can't see it here.

Internet links

For links to websites where you can find out more about maps and map-making and how lines of latitude and longitude are used in GPS, go to **www.usborne-quicklinks.com**

Using the lines

Lines of latitude and longitude are measured in degrees (°). We describe the positions of places according to which lines of latitude and longitude are nearest to them. For example, a place with a location of 50°S and 100°E has a latitude 50 degrees south of the Equator, and a longitude 100 degrees east of the Prime Meridian Line.

Exact locations

The distance between degrees is divided up to give even more precise measurements. Each degree is divided into 60 minutes ('), and each minute is divided into 60 seconds ("). The subdivisions allow us to locate any place on Earth. For example, the city of New York, U.S.A., is at 40°42'51"N and 74°00'23"W.

The steamy rainforests of Malaysia lie near the Equator. Many orangutans, like the one shown here, live in these rainforests.

Using a grid

This is a map of New Zealand, with a grid formed by lines of latitude and longitude.

Lines of latitude and longitude form grids on maps. The maps in this book look similar to the one on the left. The vertical columns formed by lines of longitude are marked with letters, and the horizontal rows formed by lines of latitude are numbered.

All the places listed in the map index on page 98 have a letter and a number reference that tell you where to find them on a particular page. For example, on the map on the left, the city of Christchurch would have a grid reference of C3.

LOOKING AT THE EARTH

Modern technology has enabled scientists to make more accurate maps of the world than ever before. Even remote places, such as deserts, ocean floors and mountain ranges, have been mapped in detail using information from satellites that observe the Earth from space.

What is a satellite?

Artificial satellites are machines that orbit, or travel around, the Earth. They observe the Earth using a technique called remote sensing. Instruments on the satellite monitor the Earth without touching it, and send back pictures of its surface. Satellites also monitor moons and other planets.

This satellite monitors the Earth 24 hours a day. It uses powerful radar that pierces through clouds. This means that the satellite can provide images of the Earth in all weather conditions.

Satellite movement

Some satellites orbit the Earth at a height of between 5km (3 miles) and 1,500km (930 miles), providing views of different parts of the planet. Others stay above the same place all the time, moving at the same speed as the Earth rotates to give a constant view of a particular area. These are called geostationary satellites. They travel at a height of around 36,000km (22,370 miles).

Internet links

For links to websites where you can find out more about maps and map-making and see detailed satellite images of the Earth, go to **www.usborne-quicklinks.com**

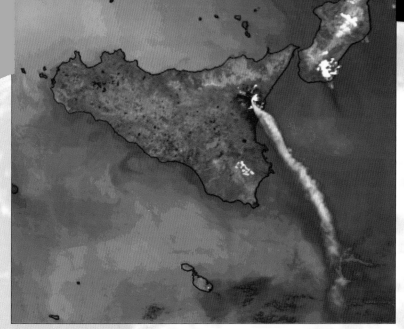

This satellite image of Sicily was taken in July 2001. It shows the volcano Mount Etna erupting. You can see smoke from the volcano on the right of the picture.

Satellite uses

The information provided by satellites helps scientists to produce accurate maps. Satellite pictures can also be used to help predict and monitor natural hazards such as volcanic eruptions or earthquakes. Some satellites monitor the weather. Satellite images can also show the effects that people have on their environment, for example the destruction of rainforests in South America.

Remote sensing

Satellites use a range of remote sensing techniques. One type is radar, which can provide images of the Earth even when it is dark or cloudy. Radar works by reflecting radio waves off a target object. The time it takes for a wave to bounce back indicates how far away the object is.

Powerful cameras provide pictures of the Earth's surface. Often, infrared cameras are used. Different surfaces reflect the infrared rays differently, so infrared images of the Earth are able to show its various types of land surfaces, such as deserts, grasslands and forests.

This satellite image of the Earth shows different types of land. Deserts and other dry regions are red, and areas with lots of vegetation are orange and yellow.

HOW MAPS ARE MADE

The process of making maps is called cartography. Map-makers, or cartographers, compile each map by gathering information about the area and then representing it as an image as accurately as possible.

Internet links

For links to websites where you can find out more about maps and map-making, go to **www.usborne-quicklinks.com**

Creating maps

Many sources are used to create maps. These include satellite images and aerial photographs. Cartographers often visit the area to be mapped, where they take many extra measurements.

In addition, cartographers use statistics, such as population figures, from censuses and other documents. As the maps are being made, many people check them to make sure they are accurate and up-to-date.

Map projections

Cartographers can't draw maps that show the world exactly as it is, because it is impossible to show a curved surface on a flat map without distorting (stretching or squashing) some areas. A representation of the Earth on a map is called a projection. Projections are worked out using complex mathematics.

There are three basic types of projections – cylindrical, conical and azimuthal, but there are also variations on these. They all distort the Earth's surface in some way, either by altering the shapes or sizes of areas of land or the distance between places.

A cartographer uses an electronic distance measurer to check the measurements of an area of land.

10

Cylindrical projections

A cylindrical projection is similar to what you would get if you wrapped a piece of paper around a globe to form a cylinder and then shone a light inside the globe. The shapes of countries would be projected onto the paper. Near the middle they would be accurate, but farther away they would be distorted.

Cartographers often alter the basic cylindrical projection to make the distortion less obvious in certain areas, but they can never make a map that is completely accurate.

This picture of a piece of paper wrapped around a globe illustrates how a cylindrical projection is made.

Below is a type of cylindrical projection called the Mercator Projection, which was invented in 1596 by a cartographer named Gerardus Mercator. It makes countries the right shape, but makes those near the poles too big.

This cylindrical projection makes countries the right size in relation to each other, but some parts are too long. The projection was created in 1973 by Arno Peters. It is called the Peters Projection.

Conical projections

A conical projection is similar to the image you would get if you wrapped a cone of paper around part of a globe, then shone a light inside the globe. Where the cone touches the globe, the projection will be most accurate.

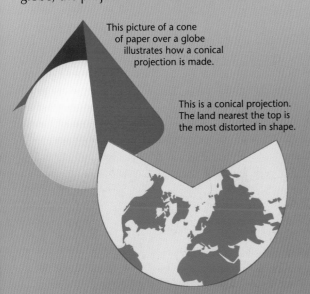

This picture of a cone of paper over a globe illustrates how a conical projection is made.

This is a conical projection. The land nearest the top is the most distorted in shape.

Azimuthal projections

An azimuthal projection is like an image made by holding paper in front of a globe, and shining a light through it. Land projected onto the middle of the paper would be accurate, but areas farther away would be distorted.

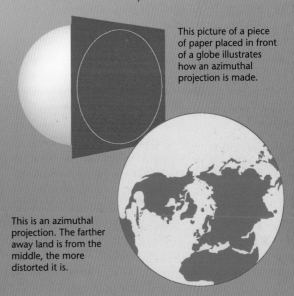

This picture of a piece of paper placed in front of a globe illustrates how an azimuthal projection is made.

This is an azimuthal projection. The farther away land is from the middle, the more distorted it is.

STATES AND BORDERS

The world's main land masses, which are called continents, are divided into independent states and dependent territories. The different areas are separated by borders.

What is a state?

A state is an area of land that has its own government* and is fully independent. Independent states are also known as countries.

Some large countries, such as the U.S.A., are split into several regions. Each region has its own government, which is responsible for the affairs of that region. In the U.S.A. these regions are also known as states.

Changing states

States don't always stay the same. They can divide or merge. For example, Germany was split into two states after the Second World War, and was then reunited as one state in 1990. Sometimes an area becomes independent and a new state is formed. For example, Croatia and Slovenia were once part of Yugoslavia, but are now separate states.

The picture above shows people sitting on the Berlin Wall. The wall formed a border between East and West Berlin when East and West Germany were separate states. It has now been pulled down.

What is a territory?

A dependent territory is an area of land that has a very limited government or no government at all. Instead, the land is owned and governed by a separate, independent state. For example, French Guiana in South America is a dependent territory of France.

*Governments, 83

Border disputes

Sometimes states disagree about where the border between them should be. This can lead to long conflicts, such as the war between Eritrea and Ethiopia. Eritrea was once part of Ethiopia but became an independent state in 1993. The two countries are still disputing the position of the border between them. Thousands of people have been killed in the conflict.

Borders often follow natural features such as rivers or mountain ranges. The Danube River separates several countries. Above, it is shown separating Serbia (left) and Romania (right).

Internet links

For links to websites where you can find flags, facts, maps, and try quizzes to test your knowledge of different countries around the world, go to **www.usborne-quicklinks.com**

Some borders are marked by barriers. Guards check that anyone crossing from one state to another is permitted to do so. This barrier marks the border between Belarus and Poland.

THEMATIC MAPS

Maps that represent information on particular themes, like the ones on these pages, are known as thematic maps. They help you to identify patterns and make comparisons between the features of different areas.

Earth's resources

The Earth contains all kinds of useful resources. Rocks and minerals can be used as building materials, and fuels such as coal, oil and gas contain energy that can be turned into heat and electricity.

Countries with large amounts of natural resources can become very rich. For example, Saudi Arabia, in western Asia, has large oil and gas reserves, which it exports all over the world.

This is an oil field, where oil is extracted from the ground using pumps. It is then piped to refineries and turned into products such as motor fuel.

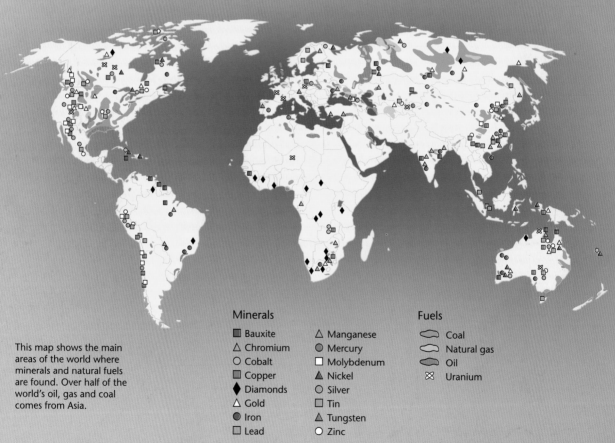

This map shows the main areas of the world where minerals and natural fuels are found. Over half of the world's oil, gas and coal comes from Asia.

Minerals

▨ Bauxite	△ Manganese
△ Chromium	● Mercury
○ Cobalt	▢ Molybdenum
▢ Copper	▲ Nickel
◆ Diamonds	○ Silver
△ Gold	▢ Tin
● Iron	△ Tungsten
▢ Lead	○ Zinc

Fuels

◠ Coal
◠ Natural gas
◠ Oil
⊠ Uranium

Different climates

The long-term or typical pattern of weather in a particular area is known as its climate. Climates vary across the world and depend largely on each area's latitude. The hottest parts of the world are those closest to the Equator.

Climate is also affected by other factors, such as wind and the height of the land. Oceans influence climate too – places near the sea normally have a milder, wetter climate than areas farther inland.

On this map, land is divided into five climate types. Dry areas are generally hot, but temperatures there can fall very low too. Some dry places, such as the Gobi Desert in eastern Asia, are extremely cold in winter.

- ☐ Polar
- ☐ Cold
- ☐ Temperate
- ☐ Dry
- ◼ Tropical

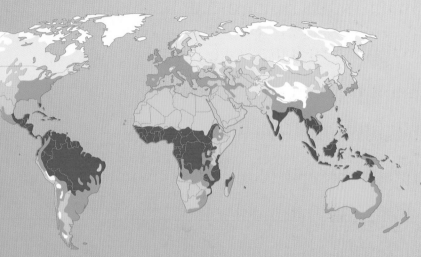

World population

There are more than six billion people in the world, and the population is still growing. Experts think it may reach more than nine billion by 2050. The number of people living in a given area is known as its population density. Europe and Asia are the most densely populated continents in the world. About a third of the world's population lives in China and India alone.

Internet link

For links to websites where you can find out more about maps and map-making and the population of the world, go to **www.usborne-quicklinks.com**

This map shows the average population density by country. The shading indicates the number of people per sq km (0.386 sq miles).

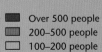

- ◼ Over 500 people
- ▨ 200–500 people
- ☐ 100–200 people
- ☐ 50–100 people
- ☐ 10–50 people
- ☐ Fewer than 10 people

HOW TO USE THE MAPS

The maps in this atlas cover the whole world and are grouped by continent. At the beginning of each section there is a political map showing the whole continent. The rest of the maps are larger scale maps showing more detailed views of the region.

Political maps

The shading on the political maps in this book is there to help you see clearly the different states, or countries, that make up each continent. The main purpose of these maps is to show country borders and capital cities. Alongside them there are facts and figures about the continents and their features.

This is a section of the political map of South America. You can see the whole map on pages 30–31.

Environmental maps

The majority of the maps in this book are environmental maps, like the one on the right. The shading on these maps shows different types of land, or environments, such as desert, mountain or wetland.

The main key on the opposite page shows what the different shading means. It also shows the symbols used to represent towns, cities and other features. There is a smaller key on each environmental map repeating the most important information from this key.

Finding places

To find a particular place or feature on the environmental maps, look up its name in the index on pages 98–111. Its page number and grid reference is given next to the name. You can find out how to use the grid on page 7.

The map on the right is part of the environmental map of the U.S.A. The numbered labels at the top explain some important features of these maps.

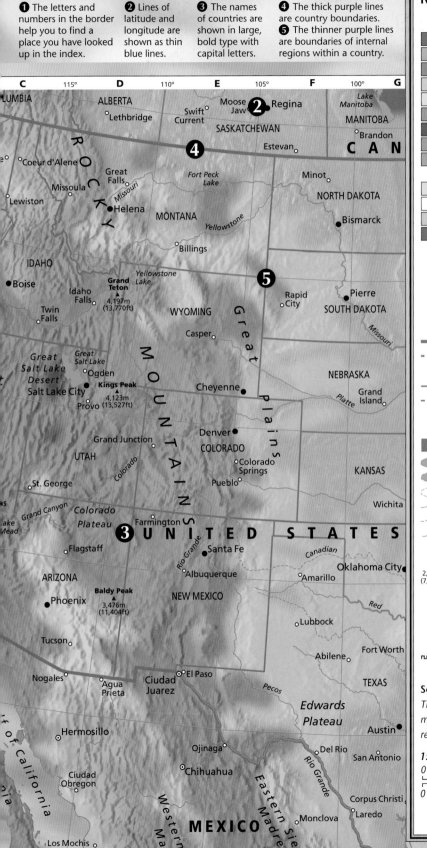

① The letters and numbers in the border help you to find a place you have looked up in the index.

② Lines of latitude and longitude are shown as thin blue lines.

③ The names of countries are shown in large, bold type with capital letters.

④ The thick purple lines are country boundaries.

⑤ The thinner purple lines are boundaries of internal regions within a country.

Main key

Land cover:

- Boreal forest
- Temperate forest
- Tropical forest
- Temperate grassland
- Savanna
- Semi-desert and scrub
- Hot desert
- Wetland
- Mountain (Only high mountains are marked.)
- Tundra
- Ice
- Cultivation
- Urban

Cities and towns:

- ■ National capital
- ● Internal capital
- ⊙ Major city or town
- ○ Other town

Boundaries:

- International boundary
- International boundary through water
- Internal boundary
- Internal boundary through water

Water features:

- Sea
- Lake or reservoir
- Seasonal lake
- Dry lake/salt pan
- River
- Seasonal river
- Waterfall/dam

Other features:

- 2,490m (7,988ft) Height above or below sea level (Only a selection of elevation points are given. Places below sea level have a minus sign in front of the height.)
- ∴ Ruin or other place of interest
- ⌐⌐⌐⌐ Ancient wall

Scale:

This tells you the size of the map in relation to the area it represents. For example:

1:10,900,000

| 0 | 200 | 400km |

| 0 | 100 | 200 | 300 miles |

160° 140° 120° 100° 80° 60° 40° 20° W

80°

GREENLAND
(Denmark)

Arctic Circle

ALASKA
(U.S.A.)

60°

ICELAND

CANADA

IRELAND UNITED
KINGDOM

40°

**UNITED STATES
OF AMERICA**

FF

SPAIN

Azores
(Portugal)

PORTUGAL

MOROCCO

Canary Islands
(Spain)

Tropic of Cancer

THE BAHAMAS

WESTERN SAHARA
(Morocco)

AL G

20°
N

MEXICO

CUBA

HAITI

DOMINICAN
REPUBLIC

MAURITANIA

MALI

Hawaiian
Islands
(U.S.A.)

BELIZE
GUATEMALA HONDURAS
EL SALVADOR NICARAGUA

JAMAICA

DOMINICA

Caribbean Sea

CAPE VERDE

SENEGAL

THE GAMBIA
GUINEA-BISSAU

BURKINA
FASO

TOG

PACIFIC

COSTA RICA
PANAMA

TRINIDAD AND TOBAGO

VENEZUELA

GUYANA
SURINAME

SIERRA LEONE
LIBERIA

GUINEA

IVORY
COAST

GHANA

COLOMBIA

FRENCH GUIANA
(France)

EQ

OCEAN

0° Equator

KIRIBATI

Galapagos Islands
(Ecuador)

ECUADOR

SAO TOME AN
PRINCIPE

A T L A N T I C

PERU

B R A Z I L

O C E A N

Cook
Islands
(New Zealand)

French
Polynesia
(France)

BOLIVIA

20°
S

Tropic of Capricorn

Pitcairn
Islands
(U.K.)

PARAGUAY

40°

1:72,700,000

0 1,000 2,000 3,000 4,000 5,000km

0 1,000 2,000 3,000 miles

CHILE

URUGUAY

ARGENTINA

60°

Antarctic Circle

Falkland Islands
(U.K.)

South Georgia
(U.K.)

W e d d e l l
S e a

80°

160° 140° 120° 100° 80° 60° 40° 20° W

CTIC OCEAN

80°

Arctic Circle

FINLAND

RUSSIA

60°

ESTONIA
LATVIA
LITHUANIA
BELARUS
ND
KAZAKHSTAN
MONGOLIA
40°
AKIA
GARY
ROMANIA
ERB
MOLDOVA
UKRAINE

Black Sea
Caspian
Sea
UZBEKISTAN
KYRGYZSTAN
NORTH
KOREA
KOS BULGARIA
MAC.
GEORGIA
ARM.   AZER.

GREECE
TURKEY
TURKMENISTAN
TAJIKISTAN
CHINA
SOUTH
KOREA
JAPAN

PACIFIC

CYPRUS
LEB.
SYRIA
ISRAEL
JORDAN
IRAQ
IRAN
AFGHANISTAN
OCEAN

anean Sea
KUWAIT

EGYPT
BAHRAIN
QATAR
U.A.E.
PAKISTAN
NEPAL
BHUTAN
Tropic of Cancer

SAUDI
ARABIA
OMAN
INDIA
BANGLA-
DESH
BURMA
(MYANMAR)
20°
N

AD
LAOS

SUDAN
ERITREA
YEMEN
THAILAND
VIETNAM
Northern
Mariana
Islands
(U.S.A.)
MARSHALL
ISLANDS

DJIBOUTI
CAMBODIA
PHILIPPINES

ENTRAL
AFRICAN
PUBLIC
N
ETHIOPIA
SRI LANKA

SOMALIA
BRUNEI
PALAU
FEDERATED STATES
OF MICRONESIA
Equator
0°

UGANDA
RWANDA
KENYA
MALDIVES
MALAYSIA
SINGAPORE

CONGO
EMOCRATIC
REPUBLIC)
BURUNDI
SEYCHELLES
NAURU
KIRIBATI

TANZANIA
INDIAN
INDONESIA
PAPUA
NEW GUINEA
SOLOMON
ISLANDS
TUVALU

LA
ZAMBIA
MALAWI
COMOROS
OCEAN
EAST TIMOR
SAMOA

ZIMBABWE
MADAGASCAR
MAURITIUS
Coral Sea
Islands
Territory
(Australia)
VANUATU
FIJI   TONGA
20°
S

BOTSWANA
MOZAMBIQUE
Reunion
(France)
New
Caledonia
(France)
Tropic of Capricorn

SWAZILAND
AUSTRALIA

LESOTHO
OUTH AFRICA

NEW
ZEALAND
40°

Kerguelen Islands
(France)

OUTHERN OCEAN
60°

Antarctic Circle

The shading on this map is there to help
you see the different countries clearly.

NTARCTICA
80°

Abbreviations used on map:

ALB.   ALBANIA
ARM.   ARMENIA
AUST.   AUSTRIA
AZER.   AZERBAIJAN
BELG.   BELGIUM
B.H.   BOSNIA AND HERZEGOVINA
CRO.   CROATIA
CZECH REP. CZECH REPUBLIC
KOS.   KOSOVO
LEB.   LEBANON
LUX.   LUXEMBOURG
MAC.   MACEDONIA
MONT.   MONTENEGRO
NETH.   NETHERLANDS
SERB.   SERBIA
SLOV.   SLOVENIA
SWITZ.   SWITZERLAND
U.A.E.   UNITED ARAB EMIRATES
YUG.   YUGOSLAVIA

160°   140°   120°   100°   80°   60°   40°   20° W

80°

*Beaufort
Sea*

**Queen
Elizabeth
Islands**

Ellesmere
Island

*Greenland
Sea*

Victoria
Island

Greenland

Baffin
Bay

Baffin
Island

Iceland

Arctic Circle

Alaska
Mount McKinley
▲
6,194m
(20,321ft)

Yukon

Hudson
Bay

*Labrador
Sea*

60°

British
Isles

Aleutian Islands

Gulf of Alaska

**NORTH
AMERICA**

Newfoundland

Rocky Mountains

Great Plains

Great
Lakes

Appalachian Mountains

Azores

40°

Mississippi

Canary
Islands

Atlas Mo

Tropic of Cancer

Gulf of
Mexico

West Indies

Cuba

20°
N

*Hawaiian
Islands*

Greater Antilles

*Lesser
Antilles*

Cape Verde
Islands

**Caribbean
Sea**

0°   Equator

Guiana
Highlands

P o l y n e s i a

PACIFIC

Galapagos
Islands

*Amazon
Basin*

Amazon

A T L A N T I C

OCEAN

Selvas

O C E A N

**SOUTH
AMERICA**

20°
S

Tahiti

A n d e s

Tropic of Capricorn

Easter Island

Atacama Desert

40°

Aconcagua
▲
6,959m
(22,831ft)

Pampas

Patagonia

1:72,700,000

0   1,000   2,000   3,000   4,000   5,000km

Falkland Islands

0   1,000   2,000   3,000 miles

Cape Horn

South Georgia

60°

Antarctic Circle

80°

Antarctic
Peninsula

*Weddell
Sea*

160°   140°   120°   100°   80°   60°   40°   20° W

RCTIC OCEAN

Severnaya
Zemlya
Laptev Sea
New Siberia
Islands
East Siberian Sea
80°

albard
Kara Sea
Arctic Circle

Novaya
Zemlya

Cape
Barents Sea

Verkhoyansk Range
60°

navia

Ob
Yenisey
Siberia

Ural Mountains
Sea
of
Okhotsk
Kamchatka
Peninsula

European Plain

ASIA
Lake
Baikal

Volga
Altai Mountains

ROPE
Aral
Sea
Gobi
Desert
Hokkaido
40°

Danube
Mount
Elbrus
Caspian
Sea
Huang He
(Yellow)
Sea
of
Japan

Black Sea
5,642m
(18,510ft)

Zagros Mountains
Himalayas
Chang Jiang (Yangtze)
Yellow
Sea
Honshu

rranean Sea

Nile
Mount Everest
8,850m
(29,035ft)
East
China
Sea
Chang Jiang
Tropic of Cancer

a
Red Sea
Ganges
Taiwan
20°
N

Arabian
Peninsula
Deccan
Plateau
Bay
of
Bengal
Micronesia
PACIFIC

RICA
Ethiopian
Highlands
Arabian
Sea
Mekong
Philippine
Islands
OCEAN

Lake
Victoria
South
China
Sea

Congo
Basin
Kilimanjaro
Sri Lanka
Celebes
Sea

5,895m
(19,340ft)
Seychelles
Sumatra
Borneo
New Guinea
Mount Wilhelm
4,509m
(14,793ft)
Melanesia
Equator
0°

Rift Valley
INDIAN
Greater Sunda Islands
Java
Arafura
Sea
Solomon
Islands

Comoro
Islands
OCEAN
Lesser Sunda Islands

Madagascar
Coral
Sea
New
Caledonia
Fiji
Islands

Mauritius
Reunion
Great Sandy
Desert
Great Barrier Reef
Tropic of Capricorn
20°
S

Kalahari
Desert
AUSTRALASIA AND OCEANIA

Drakensberg
Good Hope
Great Victoria
Desert
Great Dividing Range
Tasman
Sea
North
Island
40°

Kerguelen
Islands
Tasmania
South
Island

OUTHERN OCEAN
60°

Antarctic Circle

ANTARCTICA
See page 17 for key.
80°

40°   60°   80°   100°   120°   140°   160°   180°

NORTH AMERICA

The name "North America" can be used to mean different things. In this atlas, North America includes Greenland, Canada, the U.S.A., the Caribbean, and the countries of Central America, the narrow strip of land between the U.S.A. and South America. This continent contains over 20 countries, ranging from Canada, the world's second largest state, to tiny islands such as Grenada and Saint Lucia.

These are columns of rock called hoodoos in Bryce Canyon National Park, U.S.A.

Arctic Circle

ARCTIC OCEAN

Bering Sea

Beaufort Sea

Yukon

ALASKA (U.S.A.)

Anchorage

Victoria Island

CANAD

Vancouver

Columbia

PACIFIC OCEAN

Hawaiian Islands (U.S.A.)

UNITED STAT

Colorado

Los Angeles

Rio Grande

Tropic of Cancer

MEXICO

Mexico C

The shading on this map is there to help you see clearly the different countries that make up the continent.

Internet links

For links to websites where you can find out more about the countries in North America, go to www.usborne-quicklinks.com

Facts

Total land area 24,709,000 sq km (9,540,000 sq miles)

Total population 528 million

Biggest city Mexico City, Mexico

Biggest country Canada 9,984,670 sq km (3,855,103 sq miles)

Smallest country Saint Kitts and Nevis 261 sq km (101 sq miles)

Highest mountain Mount McKinley, Alaska, U.S.A. 6,194m (20,321ft)

Longest river Mississippi/Missouri, U.S.A. 6,019km (3,741 miles)

Biggest lake Lake Superior, between the U.S.A. and Canada 82,414 sq km (31,820 sq miles)

Highest waterfall Yosemite Falls, on the Yosemite Creek, California, U.S.A. 739m (2,425ft)

Biggest desert Great Basin Desert, U.S.A. 518,000 sq km (200,000 sq miles)

Biggest island Greenland 2,166,086 sq km (836,330 sq miles)

Main mineral deposits Silver, gold, copper, lead, zinc, graphite, molybdenum, nickel

Main fuel deposits Oil, coal, natural gas, uranium

The bald eagle is the national bird of the U.S.A. It is not really bald, but has white feathers on its head.

Arctic Circle

GREENLAND
(Denmark)

mere
d

n
beth
s

Baffin
Island

Nuuk

Hudson
Bay

Newfoundland

St. Lawrence

Great
Lakes

Montreal
Ottawa

New York

Chicago

Washington D.C.

AMERICA

Mississippi

Houston

Gulf of
Mexico

ATLANTIC

OCEAN

Bermuda
(U.K.)

Tropic of Cancer

THE
BAHAMAS
Nassau

Havana
CUBA
Port-au-
Prince
Santo
Domingo
HAITI
Kingston
JAMAICA

DOMINICAN
REP.

Guadeloupe
(France)

Puerto
Rico
(U.S.A.)

DOMINICA
Martinique (France)

BARBADOS

BELIZE
Belmopan
HONDURAS
Tegucigalpa
GUATEMALA
temala City

Caribbean Sea

Port-of-Spain
TRINIDAD
AND TOBAGO

an Salvador
EL SALVADOR

NICARAGUA
Managua

San Jose
COSTA RICA
PANAMA

Panama City

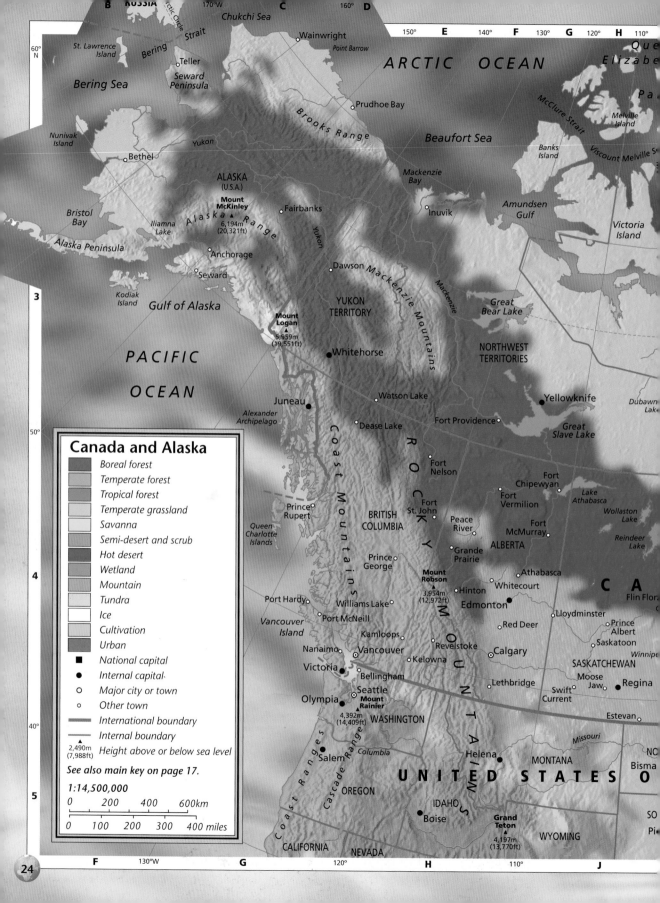

Canada and Alaska

Legend:
- Boreal forest
- Temperate forest
- Tropical forest
- Temperate grassland
- Savanna
- Semi-desert and scrub
- Hot desert
- Wetland
- Mountain
- Tundra
- Ice
- Cultivation
- Urban
- ■ National capital
- ● Internal capital
- ○ Major city or town
- ○ Other town
- ▬ International boundary
- ▬ Internal boundary
- ▲ 2,490m (7,988ft) Height above or below sea level

See also main key on page 17.

1:14,500,000

0   200   400   600km

0   100   200   300   400 miles

Map labels:

RUSSIA

Chukchi Sea

Bering Strait

Wainwright

Point Barrow

ARCTIC OCEAN

Queen Elizabe...

St. Lawrence Island

Teller

Seward Peninsula

Bering Sea

Prudhoe Bay

McClure Strait

Melville Island

Banks Island

Viscount Melville S...

Beaufort Sea

Nunivak Island

Bethel

Yukon

ALASKA (U.S.A.)

Mount McKinley ▲ 6,194m (20,321ft)

Fairbanks

Mackenzie Bay

Inuvik

Amundsen Gulf

Victoria Island

Bristol Bay

Iliamna Lake

Alaska Range

Yukon

Anchorage

Alaska Peninsula

Seward

Kodiak Island

Gulf of Alaska

Dawson

Mackenzie Mountains

Mackenzie

Great Bear Lake

Dubawn... Lak...

PACIFIC OCEAN

Mount Logan ▲ 5,959m (19,551ft)

YUKON TERRITORY

Whitehorse

NORTHWEST TERRITORIES

Yellowknife

Juneau

Alexander Archipelago

Watson Lake

Dease Lake

Fort Providence

Great Slave Lake

R O C K Y

Fort Nelson

Fort Chipewyan

Lake Athabasca

Wollaston Lake

Prince Rupert

Queen Charlotte Islands

Coast Mountains

BRITISH COLUMBIA

Fort St. John

Fort Vermilion

Fort McMurray

Reindeer Lake

Prince George

Mount Robson ▲ 3,954m (12,972ft)

Peace River

Grande Prairie

ALBERTA

Athabasca

C A

Port Hardy

Port McNeill

Williams Lake

Hinton

Whitecourt

Edmonton

Flin Flor...

Vancouver Island

Kamloops

Red Deer

Lloydminster

Prince Albert

Saskatoon

Nanaimo

Vancouver

Revelstoke

Kelowna

Calgary

SASKATCHEWAN

Winnipe...

Victoria

Bellingham

Lethbridge

Moose Jaw

Regina

Olympia

Seattle

Mount Rainier ▲ 4,392m (14,409ft)

Swift Current

Estevan

WASHINGTON

M O U N T A I N S

Coast Ranges

Columbia

Missouri

Salem

Cascade Range

Helena

MONTANA

NO...

Bisma...

OREGON

U N I T E D   S T A T E S

Pi...

IDAHO

Boise

Grand Teton ▲ 4,197m (13,770ft)

WYOMING

SO...

CALIFORNIA

NEVADA

60°N

50°

40°

130°W

120°

110°

170°W

160°

150°

140°

130°

120°

110°

B   C   D   E   F   G   H

F   G   H   J

3   4   5

90° **L** 80° **M** 70° **N** 60° **P** 50° **Q** 40° **R** 30° **S** 60°

1

Ellesmere
Island

Devon Island

Lancaster Sound

Baffin

Bay

Somerset
Island

Gulf of
Boothia
Boothia
Peninsula

*Baffin
Island*

Melville
Peninsula

Foxe
Basin

Foxe
Peninsula

Nettilling
Lake

Amadjuak
Lake

Iqaluit

Cumberland
Peninsula

70°
N

A 180° **B** 170°W **C** 160°

Bering Sea

Shishaldin
Volcano
2,857m
(9,372ft)   Unimak
Island

55°N

3   Attu
Island
Near
Islands

A l e u t i a n   I s l a n d s

Fox Islands

Unalaska
Island

3

55°N

Rat
Islands

Andreanof Islands

Atka
Island

Umnak
Island

A 180° **B** 170°W **C**

Same scale as main map

3

NUNAVUT

Southampton
Island

Ivujivik

Davis Strait

2   **GREENLAND**
(Denmark)

Cape Farewell

Labrador Sea

ATLANTIC

OCEAN

Cape Chidley

Nain

Makkovik

Cartwright

50°

Hudson Strait

Ungava
Peninsula

*Ungava
Bay*

Kuujjuaq

NEWFOUNDLAND

Happy Valley-
Goose Bay

All islands within Hudson Bay,
James Bay and Ungava Bay lie
within Nunavut.

Inukjuak

Smallwood
Reservoir

Churchill Falls

Gander

St. John's

Newfoundland

Hudson Bay

Churchill

Belcher
Islands

La Grande
Reservoir

Labrador
City

Corner Brook

MANITOBA

Thompson

Fort Severn

*James
Bay*

Radisson

Manicouagan
Reservoir

QUEBEC

Anticosti
Island

St. Pierre
and Miquelon
(France)

4

Lake
Winnipeg

Fort Albany

Waskaganish

Lake
Mistassini

Baie-
Comeau

Gaspe

Gulf of
St. Lawrence

Sydney

ONTARIO

Dryden

Kenora

Lake
Nipigon

Kirkland Lake

Val-d'Or

Trois-Rivieres

Chicoutimi

Bathurst

PRINCE
EDWARD
ISLAND

Edmundston   NEW
BRUNSWICK

Moncton

Charlottetown

Winnipeg

Lake
of the
Woods

Marathon

Quebec

St. Lawrence

Fredericton

Saint
John

Halifax

NOVA
SCOTIA

Thunder Bay

Montreal

Ottawa   Montpelier

MAINE

Augusta

Yarmouth

40°

MINNESOTA

Lake Superior

Sudbury

Sault
Ste. Marie

North Bay

Huntsville
Kingston

VERMONT

NEW
HAMPSHIRE

Concord

Boston

AMERICA

St. Paul

Minneapolis

MICHIGAN

Lake Huron

Owen
Sound

*Lake
Ontario*

Toronto

Albany

NEW YORK

MASSACHUSETTS
Providence
RHODE ISLAND

Hartford

CONNECTICUT

5

Mississippi

WISCONSIN

Madison

Lansing

Hamilton

Lake Michigan

London
Detroit

Niagara
Falls

Buffalo

Lake Erie
Erie

New York
Trenton

NEW JERSEY

Windsor

PENNSYLVANIA

Harrisburg

Philadelphia

Dover

70°   **N**

Chicago

ILLINOIS

INDIANA

90°

Cleveland

Pittsburgh

OHIO

Columbus

80°

Annapolis

Washington D.C.

DELAWARE

Copyright © Usborne Publishing Ltd.

K

25

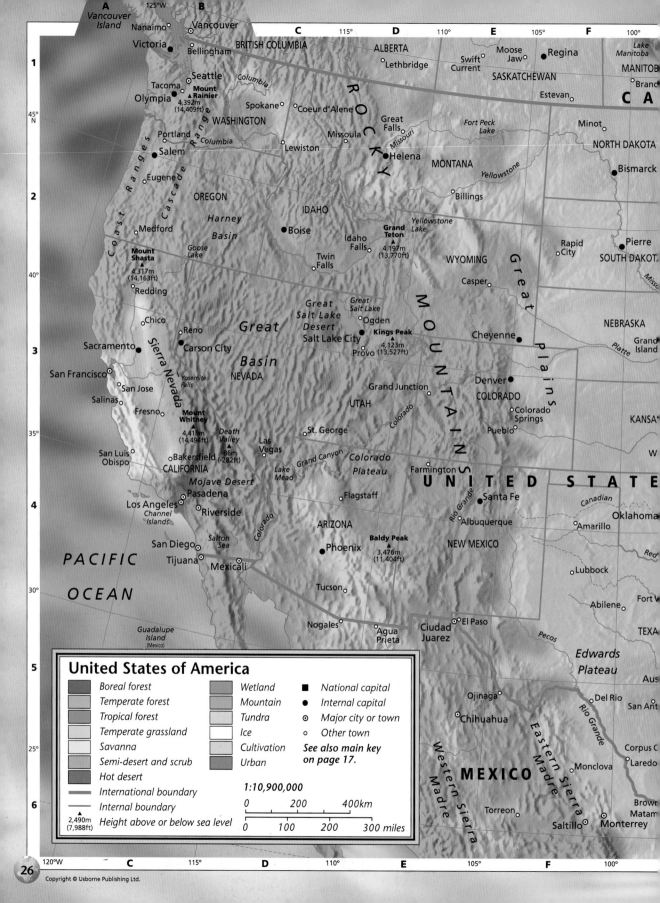

95°   H   90°   J   85°   K   80°   L   75°   M   70°   N   65°

CANADA

Winnipeg
Kenora   Dryden
Lake of
the Woods   Lake
Nipigon   ONTARIO   Chicoutimi   Bathurst
Edmundston   **NEW
BRUNSWICK**
Marathon   Val-d'Or   QUEBEC   Quebec   Fredericton
MAINE   Saint
John
Forks   Thunder Bay   Kirkland
Lake   Cabonga
Reservoir   Trois-Rivieres   St. Stephen
Duluth   Sault
Ste. Marie   Sudbury   North Bay   **Ottawa**   Montreal   Bangor
MINNESOTA   Huntsville   Kingston   Montpelier   VERMONT   Augusta
**Gulf of
Maine**
Minneapolis   St. Paul   MICHIGAN   Owen Sound   Toronto   **NEW
YORK**   Concord   NEW
HAMPSHIRE   Portland
Green Bay   Lake Ontario   Albany   MASSACHUSETTS   Boston   Cape Cod
WISCONSIN   Grand
Rapids   Hamilton   Niagara
Falls   Rochester   Syracuse   Springfield   Providence
Madison   Milwaukee   Lansing   London   Buffalo   Hartford   RHODE
ISLAND
Sioux City   Rockford   South
Bend   Detroit
Windsor   Lake Erie   Jamestown   CONNECTICUT
Cedar Rapids   Chicago   Fort
Wayne   Toledo   Cleveland   Erie   PENNSYLVANIA   Newark   New York
IOWA   Des Moines   Peoria   Pittsburgh   Harrisburg   Trenton
Philadelphia   NEW JERSEY
Omaha   ILLINOIS   INDIANA   OHIO   Columbus   Baltimore   Dover   Atlantic
City
Lincoln   Springfield   Indianapolis   Cincinnati   WEST
VIRGINIA   MARYLAND   Annapolis   DELAWARE
Quincy   **Washington D.C.**
Kansas City   Jefferson
City   St. Louis   Evansville   Frankfort   Charleston   Charlottesville
Topeka   MISSOURI   Ohio   Lexington   KENTUCKY   VIRGINIA   Richmond
Springfield   Cape
Girardeau   Kentucky
Lake   Nashville   Knoxville   Roanoke   Virginia Beach   Cape Hatteras
OF   A M E R I C A   Plateau   Greensboro   Raleigh
Tulsa   Ozark   Jonesboro   TENNESSEE   Tennessee   NORTH CAROLINA   **ATLANTIC**
Arkansas   Jackson   Chattanooga   Charlotte
Little
Rock   Memphis   Huntsville   Clark Hill
Lake   Columbia   **OCEAN**
OKLAHOMA   ARKANSAS   Tupelo   Atlanta   SOUTH
CAROLINA   160°W   Same scale as main map
Texarkana   Greenville   Birmingham   Charleston   *Hawaiian Islands*
Dallas   MISSISSIPPI   Tuscaloosa   ALABAMA   GEORGIA   Macon   7   Kauai   Oahu   Molokai   7   30°
Shreveport   Meridian   Montgomery   Columbus   Savannah   Honolulu   Kahului
Vicksburg   Jackson   Albany   HAWAII
(U.S.A.)   Maui
LOUISIANA   Hattiesburg   Mobile   Valdosta   Jacksonville   20°N   4,205m
(13,796ft)▲   20°N
Beaumont   Toledo
Bend
Reservoir   Pensacola   Tallahassee   160°W   **PACIFIC OCEAN**   Hilo
Sam
Rayburn
Reservoir   Baton
Rouge   8   P   *Hawaii*   155°   8
Houston   New Orleans   Orlando   Cape Canaveral
Galveston   Mississippi
Delta   Apalachee
Bay   FLORIDA   Daytona
Beach
St. Petersburg   Tampa   Grand
Bahama   Abaco   Tropic of Cancer
Lake
Okeechobee   Freeport
City   **THE BAHAMAS**
Gulf of Mexico   Fort
Lauderdale   Eleuthera
The
Everglades   Miami   **Nassau**   Cat Island
Key West   Florida Keys   Andros   Long Island
Straits of Florida   Acklins Island
Havana   Matanzas   Santa
Clara   Ciego de Avila
95°   H   90°   J   Cienfuegos   **CUBA**   Camaguey
Pinar del Rio   85°   80°   75°

1
45°
N
2
40°
3
35°
4
30°
5
25°
6

Mississippi
Lake Superior
Lake Michigan
Lake Huron
MICHIGAN
Appalachian Mountains

120°W   A   115°   B   110°   C   105°   D   100°   E   95°   F   90°

CALIFORNIA

San Diego
Tijuana
Mexicali
Phoenix
ARIZONA
NEW MEXICO
OKLAHOMA
Little Rock
ARKANSAS
MISSISSIPPI
Tupe
1
30°N
Tucson
UNITED STATES OF AMERICA
Lubbock
Fort Worth
Dallas
Texarkana
Shreveport
Jacks
Hattiesbur
Nogales
Agua Prieta
El Paso
Abilene
TEXAS
Waco
LOUISIANA
Guadalupe Island (Mexico)
Ciudad Juarez
Pecos
Red
Mississippi

Hermosillo
Ojinaga
Austin
Houston
Baton Rouge
New Orle
2
Cedros Island
Chihuahua
San Antonio
Galveston
Missis De
Point Eugenia
Ciudad Obregon
Rio Grande

Lower California
Gulf of California
Western Sierra Madre
25°
Laredo
Corpus Christi
Gulf of Mexic

Los Mochis
Plateau of Mexico
Torreon
Saltillo
Monterrey
Brownsville
Matamoros
Tropic of Cancer
La Paz
Durango
4,054m (13,300ft)
Ciudad Victoria
3
Cape San Lucas
Mazatlan
Matehuala
Eastern Sierra Madre
20°
MEXICO
San Luis Potosi
Tampico
Aguascalientes
Leon
Merida
Yuca Penin
Puerto Vallarta
Guadalajara
Celaya
Bay of Campeche
Campec
Revillagigedo Islands (Mexico)
Colima
Morelia
Teotihuacan
4
Uruapan
Mexico City
Veracruz
Ciudad del Carm
Puebla
Orizaba 5,610m (18,405ft)
Tehuacan
Coatzacoalcos
Villahermosa
15°
Acapulco
Southern Sierra Madre
Oaxaca
Isthmus of Tehuantepec
Tuxtla Gutierrez
Tikal
Belmopan
Ba

Gulf of Tehuantepec
Tajumulco 4,220m (13,845ft)
GUATEMAL
5
San Juan
Tapachula
Quetzalten
Guatemala City
San Salvador
EL SALVA

ATLANTIC OCEAN

L   65°W   M   60°   N

Virgin Islands (U.K.)
Anguilla (U.K.)
Leeward Islands
Puerto Rico (U.S.A.)
Virgin Islands (U.S.A.)
St. Martin (France and Netherlands)
ANTIGUA AND BARBUDA
St. John's
Basseterre
ST. KITTS AND NEVIS
Montserrat (U.K.)
4
1:7,300,000
Guadeloupe (France)
Windward Islands
Basse-Terre
0   100   200km
0   50   100 miles
DOMINICA
6
Roseau
15° N
PACIFIC OCEAN
15° N
Martinique (France)
Caribbean Sea
Fort-de-France
5° N
Castries
ST. LUCIA
BARBADOS
Kingstown
ST. VINCENT AND THE GRENADINES
Bridgetown
7
Lesser Antilles
St. George's
GRENADA
0°
Margarita Island
Tobago
Equator
Galapagos Islands (Ecuador)
Porlamar
Port-of-Spain
TRINIDAD AND TOBAGO
8
Cumana
VENEZUELA
Trinidad
Puerto Ayora
L   65°W   M   60°   N

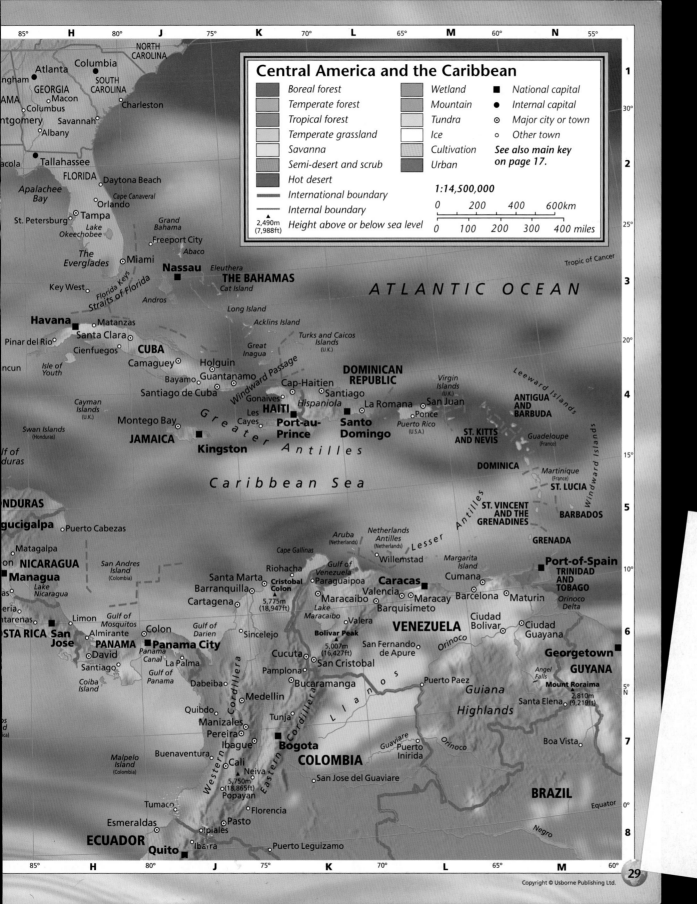

Central America and the Caribbean

SOUTH AMERICA

Triangle-shaped South America is made up of only 12 independent countries, along with French Guiana, which belongs to France. A huge part of this continent is taken up with the Amazon rainforest, which contains over a third of the world's trees. South America also has dusty deserts, towering mountains and, in Venezuela, the world's highest waterfall – Angel Falls.

This is a guanaco. Guanacos are members of the camel family that live in South America. Guanaco hair is used to make textiles.

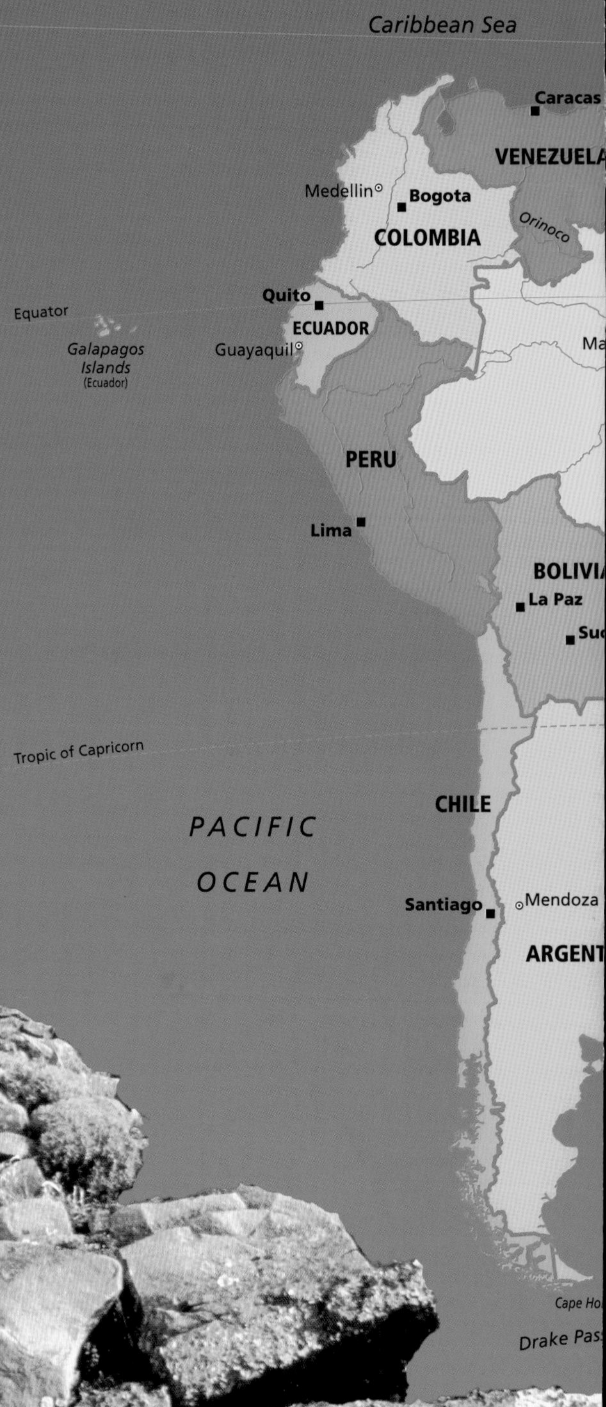

Caribbean Sea

Caracas

VENEZUELA

Medellin° Bogota

Orinoco

COLOMBIA

Equator

Quito

ECUADOR

Galapagos
Islands
(Ecuador)

Guayaquil°

Ma

PERU

Lima

BOLIVI

La Paz

Su

Tropic of Capricorn

CHILE

PACIFIC

OCEAN

Santiago °Mendoza

ARGENT

Cape Ho

Drake Pas

The shading on this map is there to help you see clearly the different countries that make up the continent.

orgetown
■ Paramaribo
A   ■ Cayenne
NAME FRENCH
      GUIANA
      (France)

n

Equator

°Recife

B R A Z I L

■ Brasilia

Parana

Belo Horizonte

AGUAY   Sao Paulo   Rio de Janeiro
suncion   Tropic of Capricorn

Porto Alegre

ATLANTIC

JGUAY
Montevideo   OCEAN
nos Aires

kland Islands
(U.K.)

This is a red-eyed tree frog. These frogs live in rainforests in South and Central America.

Facts

Total land area 17,840,000 sq km (6,888,062 sq miles)

Total population 382 million

Biggest city Sao Paulo, Brazil

Biggest country Brazil *8,547,400 sq km (3,287,612 sq miles)*

Smallest country Suriname *163,270 sq km (63,252 sq miles)*

Highest mountain Aconcagua, Argentina *6,962m (22,841ft)*

Longest river Amazon, mainly in Brazil *6,437km (4,000 miles)*

Biggest lake Lake Maracaibo, Venezuela *13,210 sq km (5,100 sq miles)*

Highest waterfall Angel Falls, on the Churun River, Venezuela *979m (3,212ft)*

Biggest desert Patagonian Desert, Argentina *673,000 sq km (260,000 sq miles)*

Biggest island Tierra del Fuego *46,360 sq km (17,900 sq miles)*

Main mineral deposits Copper, tin, molybdenum, bauxite, emeralds

Main fuel deposits Oil, coal

Internet links

For links to websites where you can find out more about the countries in South America, go to **www.usborne-quicklinks.com**

A 85°W   B   80°   C

1
Liberia
Puntarenas
Limon
San Jose
COSTA
RICA
David
Almirante
Puerto
Armuelles
Santiago
Penonome
Colon
Panama City
Panama
Canal
Coiba
Island
PANAMA
Gulf of
Panama
La Palma
Turbo
Dabeiba
Cartagena
Sincelejo
Magangue
Caceres
Cape Gallinas
Riohacha
Santa Marta
Barranquilla
Cristobal
Colon
5,775m
(18,947ft)
Gulf of
Darien
Gulf of
Mosquitos
Coro
Maracaibo
Paraguaipoa
Lake
Maracaibo
Lagunillas
Valera
Araure
Bolivar Peak
5,007m
(16,427ft)
Barinas
San Fernando
de Apure
San Cristobal
Pamplona
Cucuta
Bucaramanga
Cravo
Norteo
Llanos
Puerto
Paez
Aruba 70°
(Netherlands)
Willemstad
Netherlands Antilles
(Netherlands)
Lesser Antilles
Maracay
Valencia
Caracas
Barcelona
Cumana
Guiria
Maturin
Tucupita
Ciudad
Bolivar
Ciudad
Guayan
Orinoco
Caicara
Guiana
Highlands
Angel
Falls
Mount Ror
2,810r
(9,219
Santa Elena
Boa V
GRENADA
TRINIDAD
AND TOBAGO
Port
Spa
VENEZUELA
Zaraza
Barquisimeto

2
PANAMA
Gulf of
Panama

Nuqui
Quibdo
Medellin
Duitama
Tunja
Pereira
Manizales
Buga
Ibague
Cali
Neiva
5,750m
(18,865ft)
Popayan
Tumaco
Florencia
Esmeraldas
Cape
San Francisco
Ipiales
Pasto
Ibarra
Quito
Santo Domingo de los Colorados
Manta
Quevedo
Ambato
6,310m
(20,702ft)
Babahoyo
Montalvo
Guayaquil
La Libertad
Cuenca
Gulf of
Guayaquil
Tumbes
Machala
Loja
Talara
Zumba
Sullana
Maranon
Piura
Chulucanas
Cape Negro
Yurimaguas
Chiclayo
Moyobamba
Pacasmayo
Cajamarca
Trujillo
Huacrachuco
Chimbote
Mount Huascaran
6,746m
(22,132ft)
Huanuco
Cerro de Pasco
La Oroya
Lima
Huancayo
Mala
Chincha Alta
Ica
Nazca
Chala
Mount
Coropuna
6,425m
(21,079ft)
Mollendo
Tacna
Arica
Gulf of
Arica
CHILE
Potosi
Sucre
Charagua
Camiri
BOLIVIA
Cochabamba
La Paz
Mount Illimani
6,402m
(21,004ft)
Oruro
Santa
Cruz
San Jos
Chiqu
Concepcion
Magdalena
Trinidad
Rurrenabaque
Cobija
Riberalta
Porto Velho
Rio Branco
Cruzeiro do Sul
Pucallpa
Leticia
Atalaia do Norte
Iquitos
La Chorrera
Puerto Leguizamo
Nueva Loja
San Jose del Guaviare
Puerto
Inirida
Guaviare
Orinoco
Negro
Japura
Amazon
Amazon
Selvas
Jurua
Purus
Madeira
Ucayali

COLOMBIA
Bogota
Buenaventura
Western Cordillera
Eastern Cordillera

ECUADOR
Equator

PERU
Central Cordillera
ANDES
Western Cordillera
Eastern Cordillera

Machu Picchu
Quillabamba
Ayacucho
Cusco
Sicuani
Juliaca
Puno
Lake
Titicaca
Arequipa
Lake
Poopo
Challapata
Puerto
Maldonado

3
4
5°
N
0°
4
5°
S
5
6
7
10°
15°
20°

PACIFIC
OCEAN

Malpelo Island
(Colombia)

N   90°W   P
Same scale as main map
9   9
Galapagos Islands
(Ecuador)
0° Equator   0°
Fernandina   San Salvador
Isabela   Santa Cruz
10   Puerto   10
Ayora   San Cristobal
PACIFIC OCEAN
N   90°W   P

32

A   85°W   B   80°   C   75°   D   70°   E   65°   F

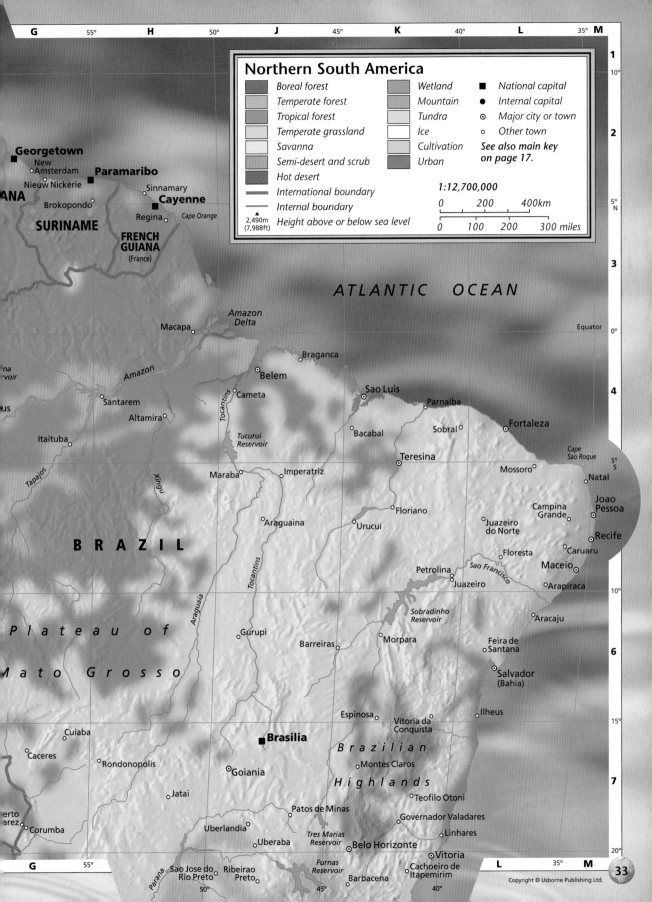

Northern South America

Legend	
Boreal forest	Wetland
Temperate forest	Mountain
Tropical forest	Tundra
Temperate grassland	Ice
Savanna	Cultivation
Semi-desert and scrub	Urban
Hot desert	

■ National capital
● Internal capital
⊙ Major city or town
○ Other town

See also main key on page 17.

—— International boundary
—— Internal boundary
▲ 2,490m (7,988ft) Height above or below sea level

1:12,700,000

0 200 400km
0 100 200 300 miles

Georgetown
New Amsterdam
Nieuw Nickerie
Brokopondo
GUYANA
SURINAME
Paramaribo
Sinnamary
Cayenne
Regina
Cape Orange
FRENCH GUIANA (France)

ATLANTIC OCEAN

Macapa
Amazon Delta
Braganca
Belem
Cameta
Sao Luis
Parnaiba
Sobral
Fortaleza
Cape Sao Roque

Amazon
Santarem
Altamira
Itaituba
Tapajos
Xingu
Tocantins

Maraba
Imperatriz
Bacabal
Teresina
Mossoro
Natal
Joao Pessoa

Floriano
Urucui
Juazeiro do Norte
Campina Grande
Recife
Caruaru

B R A Z I L

Araguaina
Floresta
Petrolina
Sao Francisco
Juazeiro
Maceio
Arapiraca

Tocantins
Araguaia

Gurupi
Barreiras
Morpara
Sobradinho Reservoir
Aracaju

P l a t e a u   o f
M a t o   G r o s s o

Feira de Santana
Salvador (Bahia)

Cuiaba
Caceres
Rondonopolis
Jatai

Espinosa
Vitoria da Conquista
Ilheus

Brasilia
B r a z i l i a n

Goiania
Montes Claros
H i g h l a n d s

Teofilo Otoni

Corumba
Patos de Minas
Governador Valadares
Linhares

Uberlandia
Tres Marias Reservoir
Uberaba
Belo Horizonte
Vitoria

Sao Jose do Rio Preto
Ribeirao Preto
Furnas Reservoir
Barbacena
Cachoeiro de Itapemirim
Parana

Equator
5°N
0°
5°S
10°
15°
20°

Sobradinho Reservoir

Feira de Santana
Morpara
Barreiras
Espinosa
Montes Claros
Ilheus
Vitoria da Conquista
Teofilo Otoni
Governador Valadares
Linhares
Belo Horizonte
Vitoria
Cachoeiro de Itapemirim
Barbacena
Campos
Juiz de Fora
Macae
Nova Iguacu
Rio de Janeiro

Brazilian Highlands

Patos de Minas
Tres Marias Reservoir
Furnas Reservoir
Mount Aguihas Negras 2,787m (9,144ft)
Sao Paulo

Brasilia
Goiania
Uberlandia
Uberaba
Ribeirao Preto
Pocos de Caldas
Campinas
Araraquara
Marilia
Presidente Prudente
Itapetininga
Curitiba
Paranagua
Itajai
Florianopolis
Criciuma
Caxias do Sul
Porto Alegre
Rio Grande
Patos Lagoon

BRAZIL

Gurupi
Jatai
Sao Jose do Rio Preto
Londrina
Guarapuava
Passo Fundo
Santa Maria
Bage
Pelotas
Melo
Mirim Lake

Plateau of Mato Grosso

Rondonopolis
Campo Grande
Dourados
Ponta Pora
Cascavel
Foz do Iguacu
Iguacu Falls
Eldorado
Posadas
Uruguaiana
Rivera
Tacuarembo
Durazno
URUGUAY

Cuiaba
Caceres
Corumba
Puerto Suarez
Concepcion
Pedro Juan Caballero
Ciudad del Este
Villarrica
Encarnacion
Reconquista
Concordia
Salto
Paysandu
Gualeguaychu

Asuncion
PARAGUAY
Paraguay
Gran Chaco
Pilcomayo
Formosa
Corrientes
Santa Fe
San Nicolas
Venado
Rosario
Parana

Magdalena
Trinidad
Concepcion
Santa Cruz
San Jose de Chiquitos
Camiri
Charagua
Tartagal
Salado
San Francisco
Villa Maria
Rio Cuarto

BOLIVIA
Cochabamba
Sucre
Tarija
San Salvador de Jujuy
San Miguel de Tucuman
Santiago del Estero
Catamarca
Cordoba
San Luis

Rurrenabaque
Riberalta
Cobija
Rio Branco
Puerto Maldonado

PERU
Juliaca
Puno
Tacna
Arica
Iquique
Antofagasta
Chanaral
Copiapo
Vallenar
Coquimbo
Ovalle
Illapel
Valparaiso
Santiago

La Paz
Mount Illimani 5,402m (21,004ft)
Lake Titicaca
Oruro
Challapata
Lake Poopo
Potosi
Uyuni
Tupiza
Ollague
Calama
San Pedro de Atacama
Pica
La Rioja
Merlo
San Juan
Mendoza
Mount Aconcagua 6,959m (22,831ft)
Mount Ojos del Salado 6,908m (22,664ft)

Atacama Desert
Tropic of Capricorn
Talcal
Andes
CHILE

Salta

Tocantins
Araguaia
Parana

Rio Branco

Tropic of Capricorn

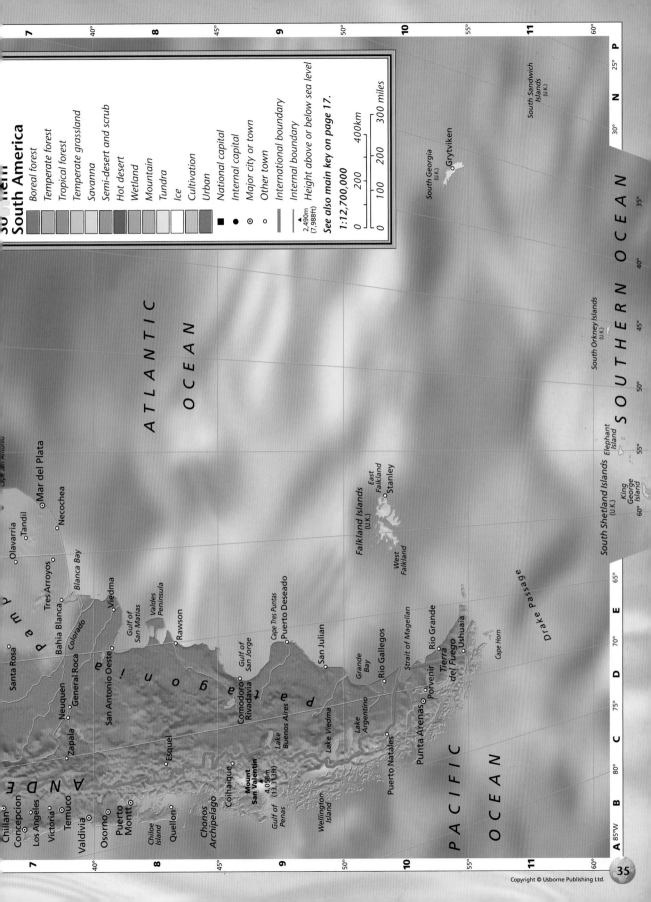

Southern South America

Legend:
- Boreal forest
- Temperate forest
- Tropical forest
- Temperate grassland
- Savanna
- Semi-desert and scrub
- Hot desert
- Wetland
- Mountain
- Tundra
- Ice
- Cultivation
- Urban
- ■ National capital
- ● Internal capital
- ◉ Major city or town
- ○ Other town
- International boundary
- Internal boundary
- ▲ 2,490m (7,988ft) Height above or below sea level

See also main key on page 17.

1:12,700,000

0 100 200 300 miles
0 200 400km

Copyright © Usborne Publishing Ltd.

35

AUSTRALASIA AND OCEANIA

Australasia is made up of Australia, New Zealand and Papua New Guinea. Oceania is a collection of over 20,000 islands stretching out into the Pacific Ocean.

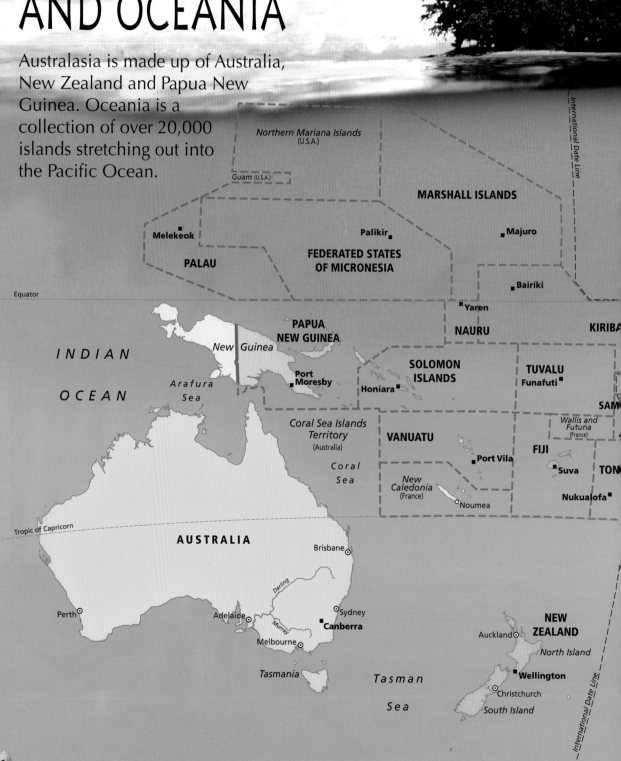

Northern Mariana Islands (U.S.A.)

International Date Line

Guam (U.S.A.)

MARSHALL ISLANDS

• Melekeok

Palikir •

• Majuro

PALAU

FEDERATED STATES OF MICRONESIA

• Bairiki

Equator

• Yaren

KIRIBA

PAPUA NEW GUINEA

NAURU

INDIAN

New Guinea

Arafura Sea

Port Moresby

SOLOMON ISLANDS

TUVALU
Funafuti ▪

OCEAN

Honiara ▪

SAM

Coral Sea Islands Territory (Australia)

VANUATU

Wallis and Futuna (France)

Coral Sea

Port Vila ▪

FIJI

TON

New Caledonia (France)

▪ Suva

○ Noumea

Nukualofa ▪

Tropic of Capricorn

AUSTRALIA

Brisbane ○

Darling

NEW ZEALAND

Perth ○

Adelaide ○

○ Sydney
▪ **Canberra**

Auckland ○

North Island

Murray

Melbourne ○

▪ Wellington

Tasmania

Tasman Sea

○ Christchurch

South Island

International Date Line

36

This small island is part of Papua New Guinea.

The shading on this map is there to help you see clearly the different countries that make up the continent.

PACIFIC OCEAN

Line Islands

Equator

'lau
aland)

:an
a
)

ue
ealand)

Cook Islands
(New Zealand)

Tokelau

Society
Islands

Marquesas
Islands

French
Polynesia
(France)

Pitcairn Islands
(U.K.)

Tropic of Capricorn

Facts

Total land area 9,008,458 sq km (3,478,185 sq miles)

Total population 32 million

Biggest city Sydney, Australia

Biggest country Australia 7,686,850 sq km (2,967,909 sq miles)

Smallest country Nauru 21 sq km (8 sq miles)

Highest mountain Mount Wilhelm, Papua New Guinea 4,509m (14,793ft)

Longest river Murray/Darling River, Australia 3,718km (2,310 miles)

Biggest lake Lake Eyre, Australia 9,500 sq km (3,668 sq miles)

Highest waterfall Sutherland Falls, on the Arthur River, New Zealand 580m (1,904ft)

Biggest desert Great Victoria Desert, Australia 424,400 sq km (163,862 sq miles)

Biggest island New Guinea 786,000 sq km (303,500 sq miles) (Australia is counted as a continental land mass and not as an island.)

Main mineral deposits Iron, nickel, precious stones, lead, bauxite

Main fuel deposits Oil, coal, uranium

The Moorish idol fish is found in shallow waters throughout the Pacific. It has a long, distinctive dorsal fin.

Internet links

For links to websites where you can find out more about Australia and New Zealand, go to **www.usborne-quicklinks.com**

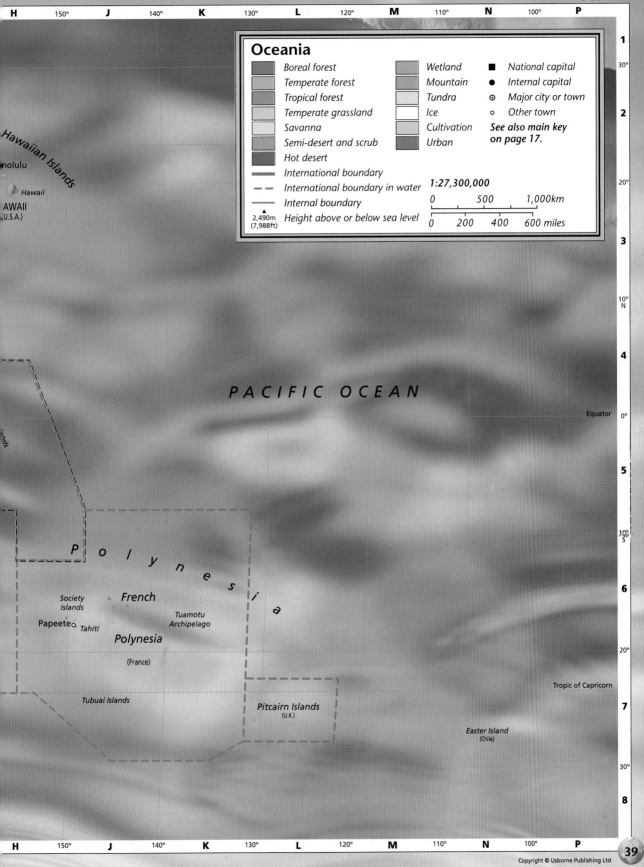

Oceania

- Boreal forest
- Temperate forest
- Tropical forest
- Temperate grassland
- Savanna
- Semi-desert and scrub
- Hot desert
- Wetland
- Mountain
- Tundra
- Ice
- Cultivation
- Urban

- ■ National capital
- ● Internal capital
- ⊙ Major city or town
- ○ Other town

See also main key on page 17.

International boundary
International boundary in water
Internal boundary

▲ 2,490m (7,988ft) Height above or below sea level

1:27,300,000

0   500   1,000km
0   200   400   600 miles

PACIFIC OCEAN

Equator

Hawaiian Islands

Honolulu

Hawaii

HAWAII (U.S.A.)

Polynesia

Society Islands

French Polynesia

Papeete   Tahiti

Tuamotu Archipelago

(France)

Tubuai Islands

Pitcairn Islands (U.K.)

Easter Island (Chile)

Tropic of Capricorn

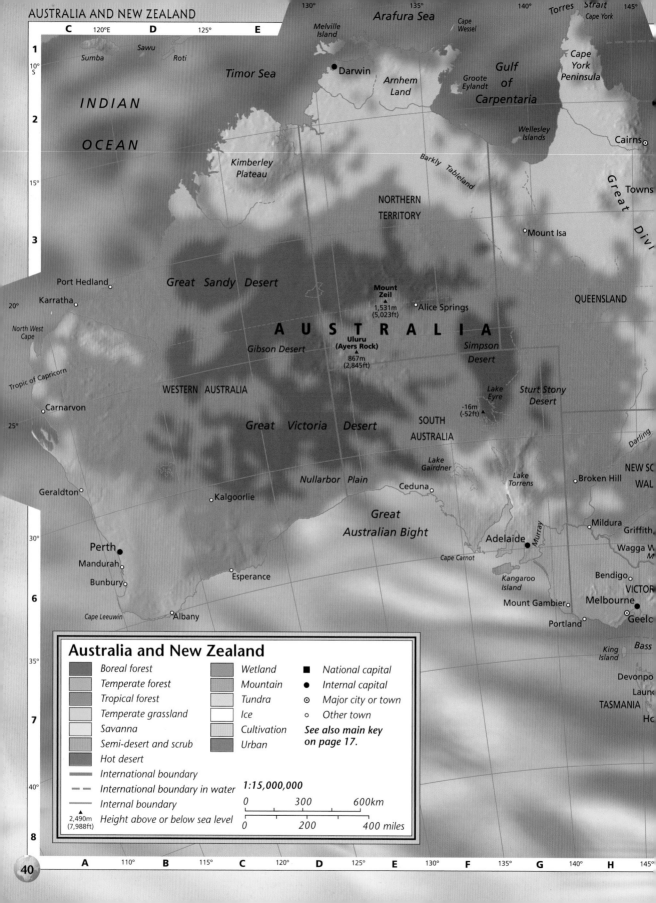

130° 135° 140° 145°

Arafura Sea

Cape Wessel

Torres Strait

Cape York

C 120°E D 125° E

1

10° S

Sumba Sawu Roti

Melville Island

Timor Sea

Darwin

Arnhem Land

Cape York Peninsula

INDIAN

Groote Eylandt

Gulf of Carpentaria

2

OCEAN

Wellesley Islands

Cairns

Kimberley Plateau

Barkly Tableland

Great Divi

15°

NORTHERN

TERRITORY

Towns

3

Mount Isa

QUEENSLAND

Great Sandy Desert

Port Hedland

Mount Zeil

Alice Springs

20°

Karratha

1,531m (5,023ft)

North West Cape

AUSTRALIA

Gibson Desert

Uluru (Ayers Rock)

Simpson Desert

Tropic of Capricorn

867m (2,845ft)

WESTERN AUSTRALIA

Lake Eyre

Sturt Stony Desert

Carnarvon

-16m (-52ft)

25°

Great Victoria Desert

SOUTH

AUSTRALIA

Lake Gairdner

NEW SC

Lake Torrens

Broken Hill

WAL

Geraldton

Kalgoorlie

Nullarbor Plain

Ceduna

Mildura

Griffith

30°

Great

Australian Bight

Adelaide

Murray

Wagga W

M

Perth

Cape Carnot

Bendigo

Mandurah

Kangaroo Island

VICTOR

Bunbury

Esperance

Mount Gambier

Melbourne

Geelc

6

Cape Leeuwin

Albany

Portland

King Island

Bass

35°

Devonpo

Laun

TASMANIA

Ho

7

Australia and New Zealand

▮ Boreal forest	▮ Wetland	■ National capital
▮ Temperate forest	▮ Mountain	● Internal capital
▮ Tropical forest	▮ Tundra	⊙ Major city or town
▮ Temperate grassland	□ Ice	○ Other town
▮ Savanna	▮ Cultivation	*See also main key*
▮ Semi-desert and scrub	▮ Urban	*on page 17.*
▮ Hot desert		

— International boundary

-- International boundary in water

— Internal boundary

▲ 2,490m (7,988ft) Height above or below sea level

1:15,000,000

0 300 600km

0 200 400 miles

8

40°

A 110° B 115° C 120° D 125° E 130° F 135° G 140° H 145°

150°   K   155°   L   160°   M   165°   N   170°   P   175°   Q

1   10°S
2

SOLOMON ISLANDS

Rennell Island

Santa Cruz Islands

TUVALU

Coral Sea

Coral Sea Islands Territory
(Australia)

VANUATU

Espiritu Santo

Banks Islands

•Luganville

Malakula

Efate   ■ **Port Vila**   15°

FIJI

Vanua Levu

Lautoka•

Viti Levu   ■ **Suva**

Chesterfield Islands

New Caledonia
(France)

Noumea•   *Loyalty Islands*   20°

rrier

Reef

•Mackay

mpton°

Gladstone

Bundaberg

Fraser Island

Gympie

oowoomba°   •Brisbane
          ⊙Gold Coast   4

PACIFIC OCEAN

Tropic of Capricorn

ee°

Great Dividing Range

•Grafton   25°

Norfolk Island
(Australia)

bbo°

•Port Macquarie

Lord Howe Island
(Australia)

•Newcastle   5

•Sydney
•Wollongong

Canberra
AUSTRALIAN CAPITAL
TERRITORY   30°

unt
uszko

Kermadec Islands
(New Zealand)

ers
d

North Cape   6

Tasman Sea

•Whangarei

⊙Auckland   *North Island*   35°

Hamilton⊙

East Cape

•Rotorua
Lake Taupo

New Plymouth•

Cape Farewell

•Napier   7

Nelson•

Cook Strait   ■ **Wellington**

South Island

NEW ZEALAND

Aoraki
(Mount Cook)
3,754m
(12,316ft)   ⊙Christchurch   40°

Sutherland Falls

Cape Providence

Invercargill•   •Dunedin

Stewart Island   *South West Cape*   *Chatham Islands*
(New Zealand)   8

50°   K   155°   L   160°   M   165°   N   170°   P   175°E   Q   180°   R   175°W   S   170°

Copyright © Usborne Publishing Ltd.

ASIA

Asia is the largest continent and has over 40 countries, including Russia, the biggest country in the world. As well as large land masses, it has thousands of islands and inlets, giving it over 160,000km (100,000 miles) of coastline. Asia also contains the Himalayas, the world's highest mountain range. Turkey and Russia are part in Europe and part in Asia, but both are shown in full on this map.

The shading on this map is there to help you see clearly the different countries that make up the continent.

Internet links

For links to websites where you can find out more about the countries in Asia, go to
www.usborne-quicklinks.com

ARCTIC OCEAN

Franz Josef Land

Novaya Zemlya

Barents Sea

Kara

■ Moscow

R U S

Ob

Volga

Black Sea

■ Ankara

TURKEY

GEORGIA

Caspian Sea

■ Astana

KAZAKHSTAN

CYPRUS

ARMENIA

AZERBAIJAN

Aral Sea

UZBEKISTAN

■ Bishkek

LEBANON

SYRIA

Beirut■ ■Damascus

Jerusalem■ ■Amman

ISRAEL

JORDAN

TURKMENISTAN

Ashgabat ■

Tashkent■

KYRGYZSTAN

■ Baghdad

■ Tehran

Dushanbe■

TAJIKISTAN

IRAQ

IRAN

Tropic of Cancer

KUWAIT

Kabul■

AFGHANISTAN

■Islamabad

SAUDI ARABIA

BAHRAIN

QATAR

PAKISTAN

Riyadh ■

Doha■

■ Abu Dhabi

UNITED ARAB EMIRATES

Indus

■New Delhi

NEPAL

■Kathmandu

Thir

BANGLA

■ Muscat

■Sana

YEMEN

OMAN

Arabian Sea

INDIA

Ganges

Socotra (Yemen)

Bay Beng

INDIAN OCEAN

Equator

Sri Jayewardenepura Kotte ■

SRI LANK

■Colombo

MALDIVES

■Male

A type of Chinese sailing boat called a junk in the port at Singapore

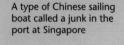

Map labels:

Wrangel Island

New Siberia Islands

East Siberian Sea

Bering Sea

ernaya mlya

Laptev Sea

Lena

Sea of Okhotsk

A

Lake Baikal

Hokkaido

Ulan Bator ■

MONGOLIA

Sea of Japan

NORTH KOREA

JAPAN

Tokyo ■

Pyongyang ■

Beijing ■

Seoul ■

Honshu

SOUTH KOREA

Huang He (Yellow)

East China Sea

C H I N A

Chang Jiang (Yangtze)

Tropic of Cancer

Taiwan

PACIFIC OCEAN

(Irrawaddy)

N

BURMA (MYANMAR)

Hanoi ■

LAOS

South China Sea

PHILIPPINES

idaw

Vientiane ■

Mekong

Manila ■

Philippine Sea

oon

THAILAND

VIETNAM

Bangkok ■

CAMBODIA

ndaman slands (India)

Phnom Penh ■

Nicobar Islands (India)

Equator

MALAYSIA

BRUNEI

Kuala Lumpur ■

New Guinea

Putrajaya ■

SINGAPORE

Borneo

Celebes

Sumatra

INDONESIA

Dili ■

EAST TIMOR

Arafura Sea

Jakarta ■

Java

Facts

Total land area 44,537,920 sq km (17,196,090 sq miles)

Total population 3.8 billion (including all of Russia)

Biggest city Tokyo, Japan

Biggest country Russia *Total area: 17,075,200 sq km (6,592,735 sq miles) Area of Asiatic Russia: 12,780,800 sq km (4,934,667 sq miles)*

Smallest country Maldives *300 sq km (116 sq miles)*

Highest mountain Mount Everest, Nepal/China border *8,850m (29,035ft)*

Longest river Chang Jiang (Yangtze), China *6,380km (3,964 miles)*

Biggest lake Caspian Sea, western Asia *370,999 sq km (143,243 sq miles)*

Highest waterfall Jog Falls, on the Sharavati River, India *253m (830ft)*

Biggest desert Arabian Desert, in and around Saudi Arabia *2,230,000 sq km (900,000 sq miles)*

Biggest island Borneo *751,100 sq km (290,000 sq miles)*

Main mineral deposits Zinc, mica, tin, chromium, iron, nickel

Main fuel deposits Oil, coal, uranium, natural gas

These are lotus flowers, Asian water lilies known for their beauty. In China they are associated with purity and for Buddhists they are sacred.

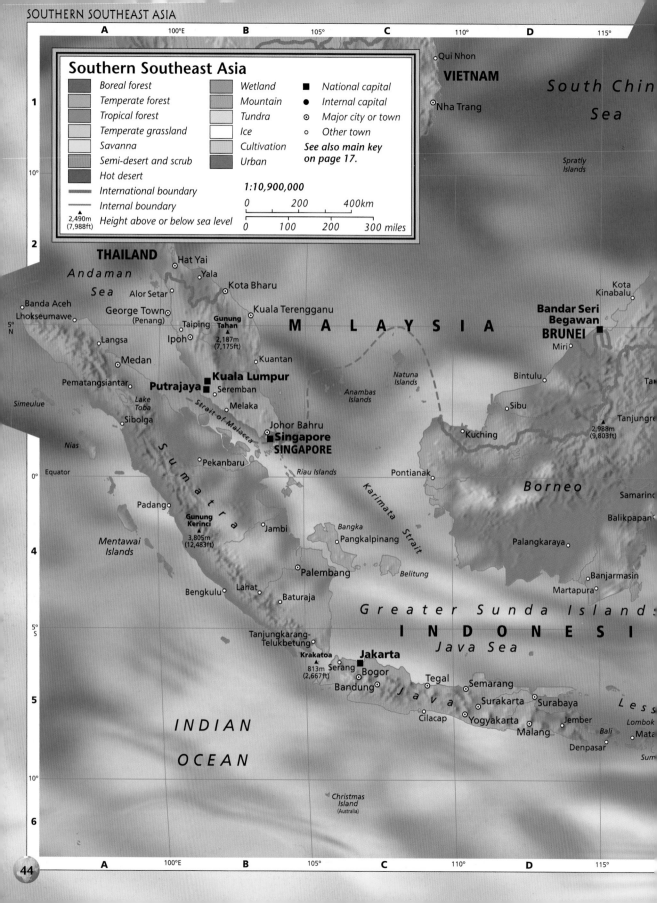

Southern Southeast Asia

Boreal forest		Wetland	■ National capital
Temperate forest		Mountain	● Internal capital
Tropical forest		Tundra	⊙ Major city or town
Temperate grassland		Ice	○ Other town
Savanna		Cultivation	
Semi-desert and scrub		Urban	*See also main key*
Hot desert			*on page 17.*

International boundary

Internal boundary

▲ 2,490m
(7,988ft) Height above or below sea level

1:10,900,000

0   200   400km

0   100   200   300 miles

VIETNAM

Qui Nhon

Nha Trang

South China Sea

Spratly Islands

THAILAND

Hat Yai
Yala
Alor Setar
Kota Bharu
Andaman Sea
Banda Aceh
Lhokseumawe
George Town
(Penang)
Taiping
Gunung Tahan
▲ 2,187m
(7,175ft)
Kuala Terengganu

M A L A Y S I A

Kota Kinabalu

Bandar Seri Begawan
BRUNEI ■
Miri

Langsa
Ipoh
Kuantan

Medan
Kuala Lumpur ■
Putrajaya ■
Seremban

Pematangsiantar
Melaka
Lake Toba

Bintulu
Sibu

Natuna Islands
Anambas Islands

Tanjungre
▲ 2,988m
(9,803ft)

Simeulue
Sibolga

Johor Bahru
Singapore
SINGAPORE ■

Kuching

Nias
Pekanbaru

Pontianak

Borneo

0° Equator

Riau Islands

Samarind

Padang

Strait of Malacca

S u m a t r a

Gunung Kerinci
▲ 3,805m
(12,483ft)

Jambi
Bangka
Pangkalpinang

Karimata Strait

Palangkaraya

Balikpapan

Mentawai Islands

Palembang
Belitung

Banjarmasin
Martapura

Bengkulu
Lahat
Baturaja

G r e a t e r   S u n d a   I s l a n d s

I N D O N E S I

Tanjungkarang-
Telukbetung

Java Sea

Krakatoa
▲ 813m
(2,667ft) Serang
Jakarta ■
Bogor
Bandung

J a v a

Tegal
Semarang
Surakarta
Surabaya
L e s s

Cilacap
Yogyakarta
Jember
Lombok
Mata

Malang
Bali
Denpasar

Sum

INDIAN

OCEAN

Christmas Island
(Australia)

120° · Cabanatuan · 125°
Olongapo · Luzon
· Quezon City
Manila ■ · Naga
Lucena · Legaspi
Calapan
Mindoro
Masbate
Masbate · Calbayog
· Roxas · Samar
Panay · Tacloban
· Taytay · Iloilo · Bacolod
· Cebu
Negros · Surigao
Dumaguete · Bohol
· Butuan
Pagadian · Cagayan de Oro
· Iligan
Mindanao
· Zamboanga · Davao
· Jolo · General Santos
Sulu Sea
Sulu Archipelago
amian roup
uerto Princesa
wan

PHILIPPINES

Philippine Sea

Sulu Sea

Celebes Sea

Talaud Islands

5° N

PACIFIC **PALAU**

OCEAN

Morotai

Manado
Gorontalo
Ternate · Halmahera
Molucca Sea
Palu
Peleng
Celebes · Sula Islands
Palopo
epare · Kendari
Watampone
· Buru
Ujung Pandang
Buton

Ceram Sea

· Sorong
Obi
Misool
· Fakfak
Ceram
· Ambon

Biak

Yapen

Jayapura

Maoke Range
New Guinea
Puncak Jaya
5,030m
(16,502ft)

Banda Sea

Aru Islands

Flores Sea

nda Islands

Wetar

Flores
· Ende
Sawu Sea
Sumba
Sawu
Timor
· Kupang
Roti

Tanimbar Islands

Dolak

Arafura Sea

Torres Strait

Dili ■
EAST TIMOR

Timor Sea

AUSTRALIA

· Darwin **NORTHERN TERRITORY**

Equator 0°

5° S

10°

5° S

10°

120° **F** 125° **G** 130° **H** 135° **J** 140°

45

Inset map:

J 140°E **K** 145° **L** 150° **M** 155° **N**
0° Equator 0°

PACIFIC OCEAN

4
· Jayapura
Admiralty Islands
· Wewak *Bismarck Sea* New Ireland
· Rabaul
Mount Wilhelm
4,509m
(14,793ft)
· Mount Hagen · Madang New Britain
New Guinea · Lae
PAPUA NEW GUINEA
· Kerema
Solomon Sea

5
D'Entrecasteaux Islands
Gulf of Papua

10° **Port Moresby** ■ 1:16,400,000
Torres Strait
Cape York 0 400km

6 Cape York Peninsula
AUSTRALIA 0 200 miles

J 140°E **K** 145° **L** 150° **M** 155° **N**

G 130° **H** 135° **J** 140°

1

2

3

4

5

6

A 90°E B 95° C 100° D 105° E

Brahmaputra Lhasa

H i m a l a y a s

Chengdu

Wanxian

2 ▲ Mount Everest
8,850m
(29,035ft)

Thimphu

Gongga Shan
▲ 7,556m
(24,790ft)

Leshan

Chongqing

Neijiang
Luzhou

C H

NEPAL Darjeeling BHUTAN

Biratnagar

Dibrugarh

INDIA

Xichang

Yibin

Zunyi

Hu

Darbhanga

Brahmaputra

Jorhat

Zhaotong

Rangpur Guwahati

Panzhihua

Guiyang

Bhagalpur Shillong

Anshun

25°N Ganges

Rajshahi Sylhet

Imphal

Myitkyina

Dali

Baoshan

Kunming

Liuzh

Asansol BANGLADESH

Jamshedpur Dhaka

Aizawl

Kaiyuan

Gejiu

Nar

3 Kolkata
(Calcutta)

Khulna

Lashio

Simao

Ha Giang

Phongsali

Lao Cai

Chittagong

Monywa

Mandalay

Red

Thai Nguyen

Qinzhou

Mouths of the Ganges

▲ Mount Victoria
3,053m
(10,016ft)

BURMA
(MYANMAR)

Son La

Hanoi

20° Sittwe

Meiktila

Taunggyi

Hai Phong

Mekong Louangphrabang

Bay of Bengal

Naypyidaw

Saleen

LAOS

Thanh Hoa

Gulf of Tonkin

Pye

Sandoway

Irrawaddy

Chiang Mai

Vientiane

Vinh

Sa

4 Henzada

Pegu

Thaton

Udon Thani

Savannakhet

Pathein

Rangoon

Moulmein

Phitsanulok

Khon Kaen

Hue

Da N

15° *Mouths of the Irrawaddy*

Nakhon Sawan

Ubon Ratchathani

Pakxe

Attapu

INDIAN

THAILAND

Nakhon Ratchasima

VIETN

OCEAN

Tavoy

Bangkok

Angkor ❖

Stoeng Treng

Tonle Sap

Qui Nho

5 *Andaman Islands*
(India)

Andaman Sea

Mergui

Pattaya

Batdambang

CAMBODIA

Buon
Thuot

Port Blair

Prachuap Khiri Khan

Kampong Chhnang

Kampong Cham

Da Lat

Little Andaman

Mergui Archipelago

Krong Kaoh Kong

Phnom Penh

Bien Hoa

10° *Ten Degree Channel*

Chumphon

Kampong Saom

Long Xuyen

Mekong

Ho Chi Minh C
(Saigon)

Gulf of Thailand

Can Tho

Bac Lieu

6 *Nicobar Islands*
(India)

Nakhon Si Thammarat

Con Son

Hat Yai

Yala

7 Banda Aceh

Alor Setar

Kota Bharu

5° Lhokseumawe

George Town
(Penang)

▲ Gunung Tahan
2,187m
(7,175ft)

Kuala Terengganu

Sumatra

Langsa

Taiping

Ipoh

MALAYSIA

Natuna Islands
(Indonesia)

INDONESIA

A 90°E B 95° C 100° D 105° E

Northern Southeast Asia

Boreal forest
Temperate forest
Tropical forest
Temperate grassland
Savanna
Semi-desert and scrub
Hot desert
Wetland
Mountain
Tundra
Ice
Cultivation
Urban

■ National capital
● Internal capital
⊙ Major city or town
○ Other town
▬▬ International boundary
─── Internal boundary
▲ 2,490m
(7,988ft) Height above or below sea level

See also main key on page 17.

1:10,900,000

0   200   400km

0 100 200 300 miles

F   115°   G   120°   Nantong   J   125°   130°   K

Hefei   Nanjing   Wuxi

Luan   Wuhu   Shanghai

Chang Jiang (Yangtze)   Tai Lake

Yichang   Wuhan   Anqing   Hangzhou

Huangshi   Ningbo

Poyang   Quzhou   Jinhua   **East**
Lake

Yueyang   Nanchang   **China**

Dongting   Wenzhou   **Sea**
Lake

A   Changsha   Linchuan   2

Zhuzhou

Shaoyang   Nanping   25°
N

Hengyang   Fuzhou   *Ryukyu Islands*
(Japan)

Chenzhou   Ganzhou   Yongan

Sakishima   3
Islands

Shaoguan   Quanzhou   Taipei   Chilung

Wuzhou   Zhangzhou   Xiamen   Taichung   *Tropic of Cancer*

Xi Jiang   Canton   Changhua   **Taiwan**
(Guangzhou)   Shantou

Macau   Tainan   Yu Shan   3
3,997m
(13,113ft)

Hong Kong   Kaohsiung
(Xianggang)

jiang   20°

Batan
Islands

u   **Luzon   Strait**

Babuyan
nan   *Islands*   4

Laoag   Aparri

Tuguegarao

Ilagan

Mount Pulog   15°
▲
2,930m
(9,613ft)

Dagupan

Cabanatuan

Luzon

Olongapo   Quezon City   *Philippine*

South China   **Manila**   *Sea*   **PACIFIC**

Sea   Lucena   Naga   **OCEAN**   5

Calapan   Legaspi   **PHILIPPINES**

Mindoro   Masbate

Calamian   *Masbate*   Calbayog
Group   Roxas   *Samar*

Panay   Tacloban   10°

Taytay   Iloilo   Bacolod
Cebu

Spratly   *Negros*   Surigao
Islands   Dumaguete   *Bohol*   Butuan

Palawan   Puerto   Cagayan de Oro
Princesa   Iligan   6

Sulu   Sea   Pagadian   *Mindanao*

Davao

Zamboanga   General Santos

MALAYSIA   Jolo   5°

Kota   Sandakan   *Sulu*   7
Kinabalu   *Archipelago*   *Talaud*
Islands

Bandar Seri   *Celebes Sea*
Begawan
BRUNEI

Miri   120°   H   125°   J   130°   K   47

INDONESIA   Tawau

Bintulu   115°   *Borneo*   Tarakan   Copyright © Usborne Publishing Ltd.

A   80°E   B   85°   C   90°   D   95°   E   100°   F   105°   G   110°

KAZAKHSTAN

Bulgan

■ **Ulan Bator**

2   °Almaty   Karamay   Dzungarian   Altay   **MONGOLIA**
    Lake   Yining   Basin
    Issyk   Kuytun   Altai Mountains
KYRGYZSTAN   Shihezi
    ▲Pik Pobedy   °Urumqi   T i e n   S h a n
    7,439m
    (24,406ft)   Turpan
40°   °Aksu   Bosten -154m
N   Korla°   Lake (-505ft)   Hami°
                   Turpan
                   Depression   G o b i   D e s e r t

                   Lop Lake   Mogao Caves   Baotou   Hoh
3   °Hotan   Tarim Basin   Yumen°   Wuhai
    Taklimakan   Altun Mountains   The Great Wall of China
    Desert   5,547m   Yinchuan
                        (18,199ft)
    Kunlun Mountains   Qaidam   Xining   Ta
35°   Basin   Golmud°   Qinghai °Xining
                                           Lake   Lanzhou
                        C H I N A   Huang He (Yellow)
4   Plateau of Tibet
                                                   Baoji   Mount Li
30°   Siling Lake   Yushu°   Chang Jiang (Yangtze)   °Xian (Terracott.
    TIBET   Shiyan°
    Himalayas   Nam Lake   Salween   Xian
         Brahmaputra   Lhasa°   Mekong   Gongga Shan   °Chengdu
5   **NEPAL**   °Lhasa   7,556m   °Yichang°
    ■**Kathmandu**   (24,790ft) °Leshan °Chongqing
    ▲Mount Everest   Darjeeling   **Thimphu**   °Luzhou   Change
    8,850m   °Biratnagar   **BHUTAN**   Xichang°   °Zunyi   Huaihu
    (29,035ft)   °   °Guiyang   Hen
Darbhanga°   Darjeeling°   Dibrugarh   Panzhihua°
°Patna   Bhagalpur Rangpur° °Guwahati   °Dali
25°   Ganges   °Shillong   Brahmaputra   °Kunming   Guilin°
INDIA   °Rajshahi Sylhet°   Myitkyina°   Liuzhou°
Ranchi° Asansol°   Imphal°   °Wuzhou
Tropic of Cancer **BANGLADESH** Aizawl°   Red   Nanning° °Yulin
6   ■**Dhaka**   Lashio°   Gejiu°
Kolkata° °Khulna   Monywa° Mandalay°   Simao°   °Lao Cai   Thai   °Zhanj
(Calcutta)   **Mount**   °Son La Nguyen
°Cuttack   Chittagong°   **Victoria**   Phongsali°   **Hanoi** °Haikou
    Mouths of the   3,053m   °   Hai   °
    Ganges   (10,016ft) Sittwe°   **BURMA**   Taunggyi° Mekong Phong Gulf of   °Haiku
20°   (MYANMAR)   Louangphrabang° Tonkin
Bay of Bengal   Sandoway° °Pye   Chiang   Thanh Hoa°   Hain
7   **I N D I A N**   Henzada°   **Naypyidaw**■   Mai°   **LAOS** °Vinh
                        Irrawaddy Salween   **THAILAND**   **VIETNAM**
    O C E A N   Pathein° **Pegu** °   ■**Vientiane**   Sanya°
                   ° ■**Rangoon**   Udon Thani°
15°
48   C   90°E   D   Mouths of the   Moulmein°   F   100°   105°   G   110°
              Irrawaddy
              95°

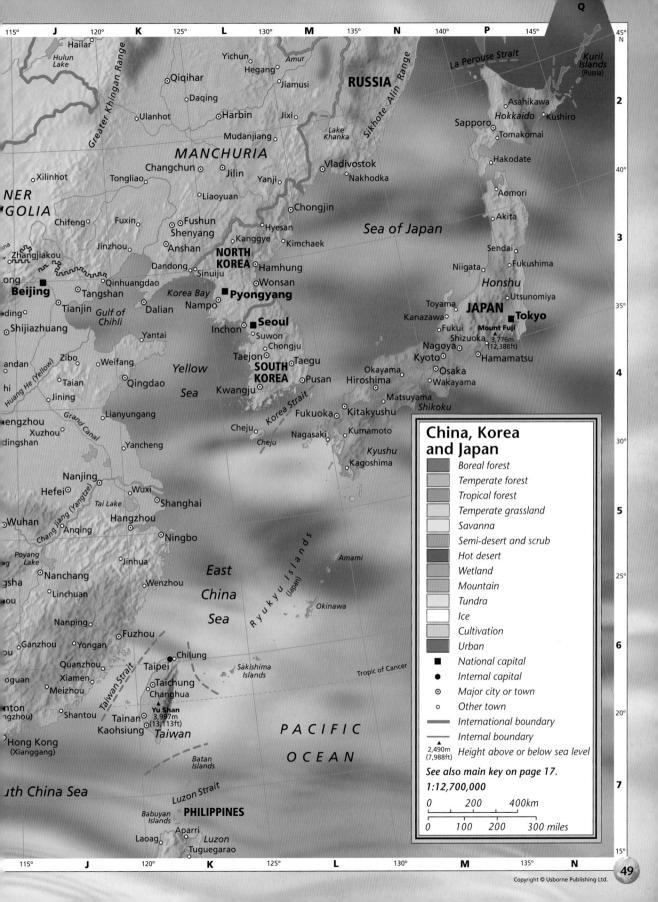

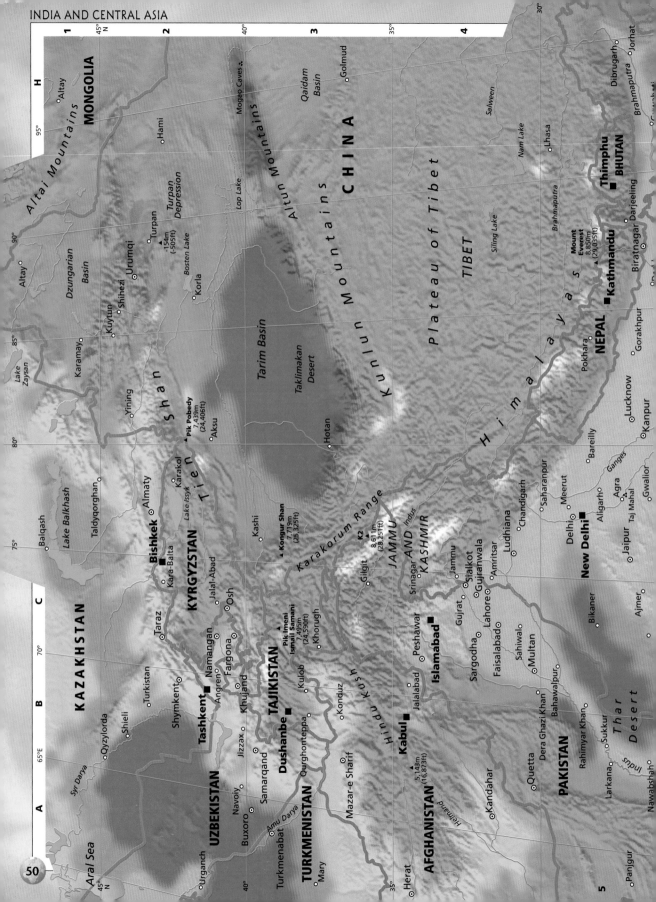

MONGOLIA

Altai Mountains

Altay

Altay

Hami

Mogao Caves

Qaidam Basin

Golmud

Altun Mountains

CHINA

Dzungarian Basin

Turpan
Turpan Depression
-154m (-505ft)

Lop Lake

Salween

Urumqi

Shihezi

Korla

Bosten Lake

Nam Lake

Lhasa

Kuytun

Karamay

Plateau of Tibet

Brahmaputra

Thimphu
BHUTAN

Lake Zaysan

Altay

Yining

Tarim Basin

Kunlun Mountains

Siling Lake

TIBET

Mount Everest
8,850m (29,035ft)

Darjeeling

Pik Pobedy
7,439m (24,406ft)

Taklimakan Desert

Brahmaputra

NEPAL

Pokhara

Birātnagar

Dibrugarh

Jorhat

Balqash

Lake Balkhash

Taldyqorghan

Aksu

Hotan

Kathmandu

Gorakhpur

Brahmaputra

T i e n   S h a n

Karakol

Lake Issyk

Kashi

Kongur Shan
7,719m (25,325ft)

Himalayas

Bareilly

Ganges

Lucknow

Kanpur

KAZAKHSTAN

Oyzylorda

Shieli

Turkistan

Almaty

Bishkek

Kara-Balta

Jalal-Abad

K2
8,611m (28,251ft)

Gilgit

JAMMU

Indus

Srinagar

KASHMIR

Saharanpur

Meerut

Delhi

Aligarho

Agra

Taj Mahal

Gwalior

KYRGYZSTAN

Taraz

Osh

Jammu

Sialkot

Chandigarh

Ludhiana

New Delhi

Jaipur

Tashkent

Namangan

Fargona

Khujand

Pik Imeni
Ismail Samani
7,495m (24,590ft)

Khorugh

Karakorum Range

AND

Gujrat

Lahore

Amritsar

Bikaner

Ajmer

Shymkent

Angren

Jizzax

TAJIKISTAN

Kulob

Peshawar

Sargodha

Gujranwala

Faisalabad

Sahiwal

Ajmer

UZBEKISTAN

Navoiy

Samarqand

Dushanbe

Qurghonteppa

Konduz

Hindu Kush

Jalalabad

Islamabad

PAKISTAN

Multan

Bahawalpur

Dera Ghazi Khan

Buxoro

Syr Darya

Mary

Mazar-e Sharif

Kabul

5,143m (16,873ft)

Quetta

Rahimyar Khan

Thar Desert

Urganch

Turkmenabat

Amu Darya

TURKMENISTAN

AFGHANISTAN

Helmand

Kandahar

Larkana

Sukkur

Indus

Nawabshah

Aral Sea

Herat

Panjgur

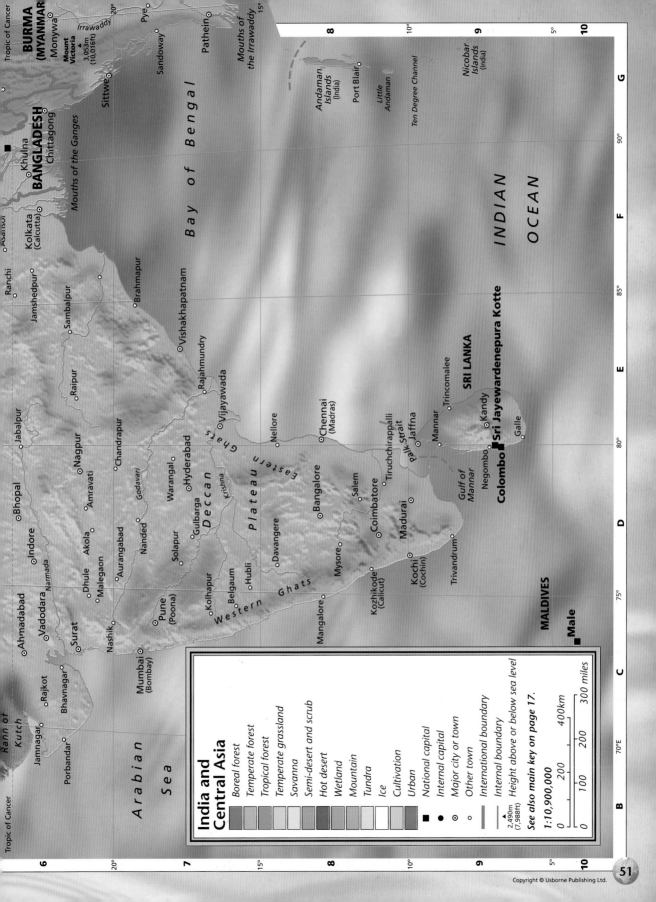

Tropic of Cancer

BURMA
(MYANMAR)

20°

Irrawaddy
Monywa

Mount
Victoria
3,053m
(10,016ft) ▲

15°

Pye

Sandoway

Pathein

Sittwe

Mouths of
the Irrawaddy

8

10°

Andaman
Islands
(India)

Port Blair

Little
Andaman

Ten Degree Channel

5°

Nicobar
Islands
(India)

9

10

G

Khulna ■

BANGLADESH   Chittagong

Kolkata
(Calcutta)

Mouths of the Ganges

B a y   o f   B e n g a l

90°

I N D I A N

O C E A N

F

Ranchi

Jamshedpur

Sambalpur

Brahmapur

Vishakhapatnam

Rajahmundry

85°

SRI LANKA

Sri Jayewardenepura Kotte ■

Trincomalee

E

Jabalpur

Raipur

Vijayawada

Krishna

Nellore

Chennai
(Madras)

Tiruchchirappalli

Palk Strait

Jaffna

Mannar

Kandy

Negombo

Colombo ■

Galle

80°

Bhopal

Nagpur

Chandrapur

Hyderabad

Warangal

Gulbarga

Bangalore

Salem

Coimbatore

Madurai

Gulf of
Mannar

D

Indore

Akola

Amravati

Godavari

Nanded

D e c c a n   P l a t e a u

E a s t e r n   G h a t s

Davangere

Mysore

Kochi
(Cochin)

Trivandrum

75°

Ahmadabad

Vadodara

Surat

Narmada

Dhule

Malegaon

Aurangabad

Solapur

Kolhapur

Belgaum

Hubli

W e s t e r n   G h a t s

Mangalore

Kozhikode
(Calicut)

MALDIVES

Male ■

C

Rajkot

Bhavnagar

Jamnagar

Porbandar

Rann of
Kutch

A r a b i a n

S e a

Nashik

Mumbai
(Bombay)

Pune
(Poona)

70°E

Tropic of Cancer

B

India and
Central Asia

Boreal forest
Temperate forest
Tropical forest
Temperate grassland
Savanna
Semi-desert and scrub
Hot desert
Wetland
Mountain
Tundra
Ice
Cultivation
Urban

■ National capital
● Internal capital
⊙ Major city or town
○ Other town
International boundary
Internal boundary

2,490m
(7,988ft) ▲ Height above or below sea level

See also main key on page 17.

1:10,900,000

0   100   200   300   400km
0   100   200   300 miles

20°

7

15°

8

10°

9

5°

10

51

Copyright © Usborne Publishing Ltd.

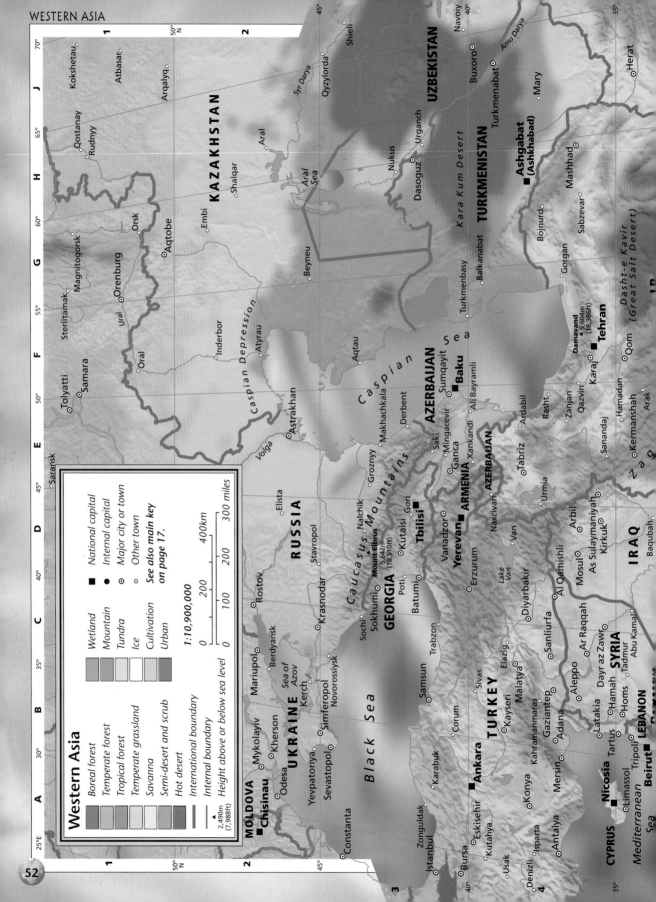

1 **2**

70° 65° 60° 55° 50° 45° 40° 35°

J

Kokshetau
Qostanay
Rudnyy
Atbasar
Shieli
Navoiy
Amu Darya
Arqalyq

UZBEKISTAN

Buxoro
Urganch
Mary
Herat

KAZAKHSTAN

Syr Darya
Qyzylorda

H

Qostanay
Rudnyy
Aral
Nukus
Dasoguz
Turkmenabat
Mashhad

TURKMENISTAN

Ashgabat
(Ashkhabad) ■

Embi
Aral Sea
Shalqar
Aqtobe

G

Magnitogorsk
Sterlitamak
Orsk
Orenburg

Beyneu

Kara Kum Desert

Balkanabat
Turkmenbasy
Bojnurd
Gorgan
Sabzevar

F

Tolyatti
Samara
Oral
Inderbor
Atyrau
Aqtau

Caspian Depression

Caspian Sea

Turkmenbasy

Damavand ▲ 5,604m
(18,386ft)

Dasht-e Kavir
(Great Salt Desert)

AZERBAIJAN
Sumqayit
Baku ■
Ali Bayramli

Rasht
Qazvin
Zanjan
Tehran ■
Karaj
Qom
Hamadan

E

Saransk
Ural

Volga
Astrakhan
Elista

Makhachkala
Derbent

Grozny
Saki
Mingacevir
Ganca
Xankandi

Ardabil
Tabriz
Sanandaj
Kermanshah

D

Stavropol
Rostov

Elista

Nalchik
Mount Elbrus
5,642m
(18,510ft)

RUSSIA

Caucasus Mountains

Tbilisi ■
Gori
Kutaisi
Vanadzor
Yerevan ■
Naxcivan
ARMENIA
Van
Erzurum
Lake Van

Arbil
Mosul
As Sulaymaniyah
Kirkuk
Baqubah

IRAQ

Al Qamishli

C

Krasnodar
Sochi
Sokhumi
Poti

GEORGIA

Batumi
Trabzon

Diyarbakir
Sanliurfa
Ar Raqqah
Dayr az Zawr
Abu Kamal

B

Mariupol
Berdyansk
Sea of Azov
Kerch
Novorossiysk

Samsun
Corum
Sivas
Elazig
Malatya
Kahramanmaras
Gaziantep
Adana
Aleppo
Hamah
Homs
Tadmur

SYRIA

A

MOLDOVA
Chisinau ■

Mykolayiv
Kherson
Odesa
Simferopol
Yevpatoriya
Sevastopol

UKRAINE

Black Sea

Zonguldak
Karabuk
Istanbul
Bursa
Eskisehir
Kutahya
Konya
Mersin
Usak
Isparta
Antalya
Denizli

TURKEY

Ankara ■

Latakia
Tartus
LEBANON
Tripoli
Beirut ■

CYPRUS
Nicosia ■
Limassol

Mediterranean Sea

Constanta

50°N
45°
40°
35°

52

60°   **2**   80°   **1**

A R C

UNITED
KINGDOM
London

Paris

BELGIUM
NETHERLANDS

LUXEMBOURG

FRANCE

GERMANY

Berlin

CZECH
REPUBLIC

AUSTRIA

POLAND

Warsaw

SLOVAKIA

Budapest

HUNGARY

Lviv

ROMANIA

Kiev

MOLDOVA

Chisinau

UKRAINE

Odesa

Kharkiv

Simferopol

Dnipropetrovsk

*Black
Sea*

Ankara

TURKEY

Adana

Aleppo

GEORGIA

Tbilisi

ARMENIA

Yerevan

SYRIA

Mosul

Mount Elbrus
▲
5,642m
(18,510ft)

AZERBAIJAN

Baku

Tabriz

Baghdad

IRAQ

Tehran

Damavand
▲
5,604m
(18,386ft)

Ahvaz

Esfahan

Kuwait City

KUWAIT

SAUDI
ARABIA

Shiraz

Riyadh

Manama

QATAR

Doha

*Bandar-e
Abbas*

Abu Dhabi

*Norwegian
Sea*

Arctic Circle

*North
Sea*

NORWAY

Oslo

DENMARK

SWEDEN

*Baltic
Sea*

Stockholm

FINLAND

Helsinki

LITHUANIA

ESTONIA

LATVIA

Vilnius

Minsk

BELARUS

*Lake
Ladoga*

St. Petersburg

*Lake
Onega*

Cherepovets

Moscow

Ryazan

Nizhniy Novgorod

Voronezh

Volga

Kazan

Perm

Rostov

Volgograd

Krasnodar

Volga

Astrakhan

Oral

Aqtobe

Atyrau

*Caspian
Sea*

Aqtau

*Aral
Sea*

KAZAKHSTAN

Astana

Qaraghandy

Nukus

Dasoguz

UZBEKISTAN

TURKMENISTAN

Turkmenabat

Ashgabat
(Ashkhabad)

Tashkent

Samarqand

Qyzylorda

Shymkent

*Lake
Balkhash*

Balqash

Oskemen

Bishkek

KYRGYZSTAN

Osh

Dushanbe

TAJIKISTAN

Almaty

Aksu

Urumqi

Tien Shan

Herat

Mazar-e Sharif

IRAN

AFGHANISTAN

Kabul

Kandahar

Islamabad

K2
▲
8,611m
(28,251ft)

Srinagar

Indus

Zahedan

Mashhad

PAKISTAN

Lahore

INDIA

Tarim Basin

Taklimakan Desert

Hotan

Altay

Plateau of Tibet

Svalbard
(Norway)

A

B

20°

40°

*Franz Josef
Land*

C

60°

D

80°

Murmansk

North Cape

*Barents
Sea*

*Kola
Peninsula*

*Novaya
Zemlya*

*Kara
Sea*

Arkhangelsk

Vorkuta

Ukhta

Ural Mountains

Ob

Novyy Urengoy

West Siberian

Plain

Surgut

Ob

Yenisey

Yekaterinburg

Chelyabinsk

Orenburg

Omsk

R   U

Tomsk

Krasn

Novosibirsk

Barnaul

Pavlodar

Irtysh

Ne

40°
N

C   60°E   D   80°   E

Persian Gulf (The Gulf)

3

4

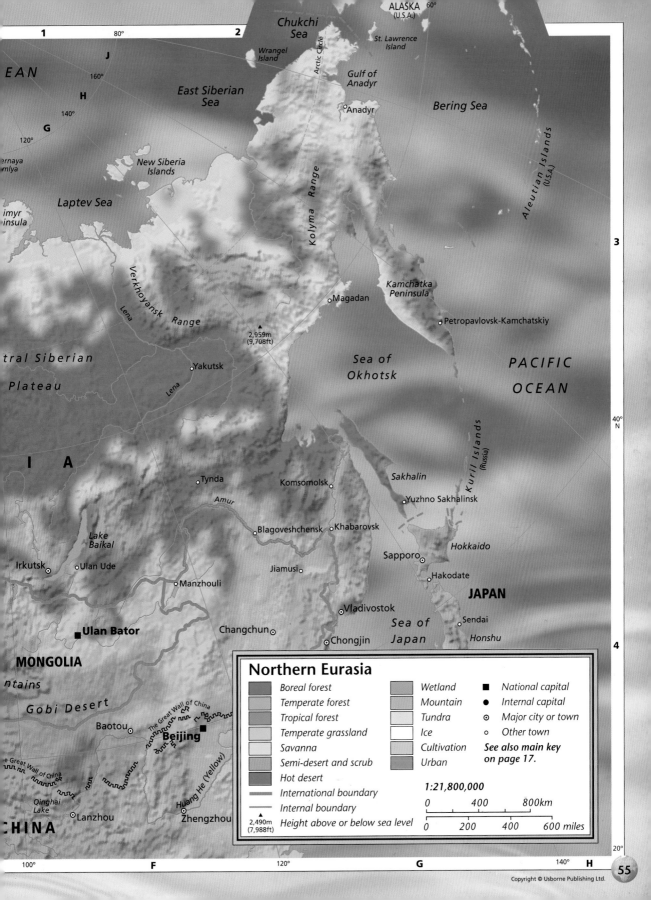

ALASKA (U.S.A.) 60°

Chukchi Sea

J   160°

H   140°

G   120°

East Siberian Sea

Wrangel Island

Arctic Circle

St. Lawrence Island

Gulf of Anadyr

Anadyr

Bering Sea

ᵉrnaya ᵐlya

New Siberia Islands

Laptev Sea

ᶦmyr ᶦnsula

Aleutian Islands (U.S.A.)

3

Kolyma Range

Verkhoyansk Range

Lena

tral Siberian Plateau

Lena

Magadan

▲ 2,959m (9,708ft)

Kamchatka Peninsula

Petropavlovsk-Kamchatskiy

Yakutsk

Sea of Okhotsk

PACIFIC OCEAN

40° N

I   A

Tynda

Amur

Komsomolsk

Kuril Islands (Russia)

Sakhalin

Yuzhno Sakhalinsk

Lake Baikal

Blagoveshchensk

Khabarovsk

Irkutsk

Ulan Ude

Jiamusi

Hokkaido

Sapporo

Manzhouli

Hakodate

Vladivostok

JAPAN

Sendai

Changchun

Sea of Japan

Honshu

Ulan Bator

Chongjin

4

MONGOLIA

ⁿtains

Gobi Desert

The Great Wall of China

Baotou

e Great Wall of China

Beijing

Huang He (Yellow)

Qinghai Lake

Lanzhou

Zhengzhou

CHINA

Northern Eurasia

Boreal forest	Wetland	■ National capital
Temperate forest	Mountain	● Internal capital
Tropical forest	Tundra	⊙ Major city or town
Temperate grassland	Ice	○ Other town
Savanna	Cultivation	**See also main key**
Semi-desert and scrub	Urban	**on page 17.**
Hot desert		

International boundary

Internal boundary

▲ 2,490m (7,988ft) Height above or below sea level

1:21,800,000

0	400	800km

0	200	400	600 miles

20°

EUROPE

Europe is a small continent, packed with over 40 countries and more than 700 million people. It has no deserts, but its geography ranges from high mountain ranges to icy tundra, rocky islands and lush farmland. With dozens of islands and peninsulas, many of Europe's countries are largely surrounded by sea.

The shading on this map is there to help you see clearly the different countries that make up the continent.

Internet links

For links to websites where you can find out more about the countries in Europe, go to
www.usborne-quicklinks.com

Arctic Circle

ARCTIC OCEAN

- Reykjavik
ICELAND

Norwegian Sea

Faroe Islands (Denmark)

SWEDE

Shetland Islands

NORWAY
- Oslo

Orkney Islands

Stockholr

North Sea

DENMARK
Copenhagen ■

IRELAND
Dublin ■

UNITED KINGDOM

The Hague ■ ■ Amsterdam
London ■ **NETHERLANDS** Berlin ■

Brussels ■ **GERMANY**
BELGIUM
LUXEMBOURG **POL**
■ Luxembourg Prague ■
■ Paris **CZECH REPUBLIC**

Rhine

Vienna ■
LIECHTENSTEIN ■ Bratislava
■ Bern ■ Vaduz **AUSTRIA** Buda

Bay of Biscay

FRANCE **SWITZERLAND**

SLOVENIA HUN
Ljubljana ■ Zagr

ATLANTIC

OCEAN

MONACO
CROA
ANDORRA ■
Andorra la Vella **SAN MARINO** **BOSNIA A HERZEGOV**
Sarajev

PORTUGAL
Corsica **ITALY** **MONTEN**
Lisbon ■ ■ Madrid Rome ■ ■ **VATICAN CITY** Podgo
SPAIN

Balearic Islands *Sardinia*

Mediterranean Sea

Sicily

■ **MALTA**
■ Valletta

56

Barents Sea

Arctic Circle

⊙ Murmansk

⊙ Arkhangelsk

FINLAND

R U S S I A

aki

⊙ St. Petersburg

■ Tallinn
ESTONIA

Nizhniy Novgorod ⊙   Kazan ⊙

■ LATVIA

■ Moscow

UANIA
Vilnius

Volga

■ Minsk

BELARUS

saw

■ Kiev

Volgograd ⊙

Dnieper

UKRAINE

KIA

MOLDOVA

■ Chisinau

ROMANIA

ade

■ Bucharest

Black Sea

Danube

tina BULGARIA

vo ■ Sofia

kopje

DONIA

TURKEY

ECE

■ Athens

Crete

Russia and Turkey lie partly in Europe and partly in Asia. This map shows the European parts. You can see full maps of the countries in the Asia section of the atlas, starting on page 42.

Facts

Total land area 10,205,720 sq km (3,940,428 sq miles) (including European Russia)

Total population 731 million (including all of Russia)

Biggest city Paris, France

Biggest country Russia *Total area: 17,075,200 sq km (6,592,735 sq miles) Area of European Russia: 4,294,400 sq km (1,658,068 sq miles)*

Smallest country Vatican City *0.44 sq km (0.17 sq miles)*

Highest mountain Elbrus, Russia *5,642m (18,510ft)*

Longest river Volga *3,692km (2,294 miles)*

Biggest lake Lake Ladoga, Russia *17,700 sq km (6,834 sq miles)*

Highest waterfall Utigard, on the Jostedal Glacier, Norway *818m (2,685ft)*

Biggest desert No deserts in Europe

Biggest island Great Britain *229,870 sq km (88,753 sq miles)*

Main mineral deposits Bauxite, zinc, iron, potash, fluorspar

Main fuel deposits Oil, coal, natural gas, peat, uranium

A dairy cow in Devon, in the south of England

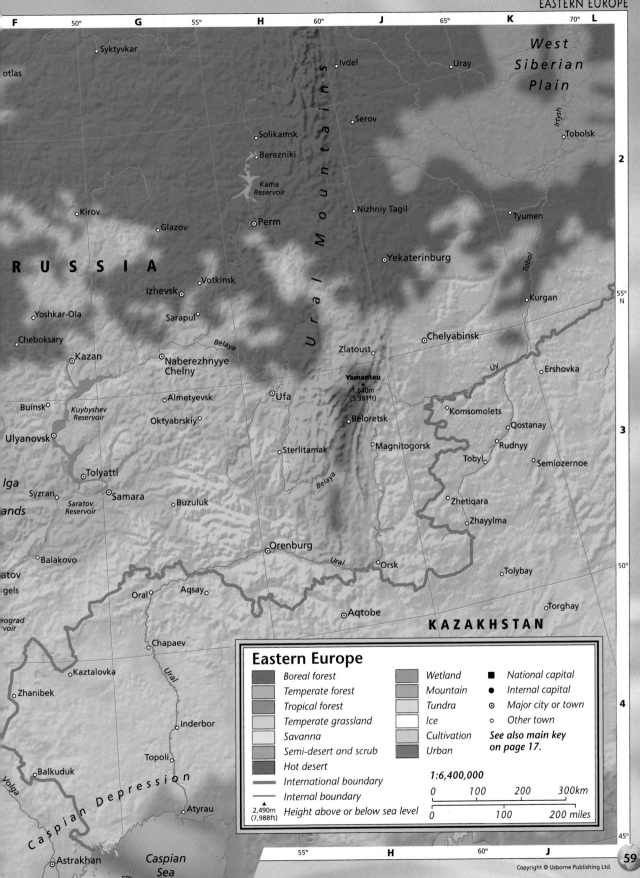

West Siberian Plain

Syktyvkar

otlas

Ivdel

Uray

Irtysh

Serov

Tobolsk

Solikamsk

Berezniki

Kama Reservoir

Kirov

Glazov

Nizhniy Tagil

Tyumen

Perm

R U S S I A

Yekaterinburg

Tobol

Votkinsk

Izhevsk

Kurgan

55° N

Yoshkar-Ola

Sarapul

Belaya

Chelyabinsk

Ershovka

Cheboksary

Zlatoust

Uy

Kazan

Naberezhnyye Chelny

▲ **Yamantau** 1,640m (5,381ft)

Komsomolets

Buinsk

Almetyevsk

Ufa

Qostanay

Kuybyshev Reservoir

Oktyabrskiy

Beloretsk

Rudnyy

lga

Ulyanovsk

Sterlitamak

Magnitogorsk

Tobyl

Semiozernoe

ands

Tolyatti

Belaya

Zhetiqara

Syzran

Samara

Buzuluk

Zhayylma

Saratov Reservoir

Balakovo

Orenburg

Ural

Tolybay

atov

Orsk

50°

gels

Oral

Aqsay

Torghay

ograd voir

Aqtobe

K A Z A K H S T A N

Chapaev

Ural

Kaztalovka

Zhanibek

Inderbor

3

2

4

Topoli

Balkuduk

Volga

Caspian Depression

Atyrau

Astrakhan

Caspian Sea

45°

50°

Eastern Europe

- Boreal forest
- Temperate forest
- Tropical forest
- Temperate grassland
- Savanna
- Semi-desert and scrub
- Hot desert
- International boundary
- Internal boundary
- ▲ 2,490m (7,988ft) Height above or below sea level

- Wetland
- Mountain
- Tundra
- Ice
- Cultivation
- Urban

- ■ National capital
- ● Internal capital
- ⊙ Major city or town
- ○ Other town

See also main key on page 17.

1:6,400,000

0   100   200   300km

0   100   200 miles

Copyright © Usborne Publishing Ltd.

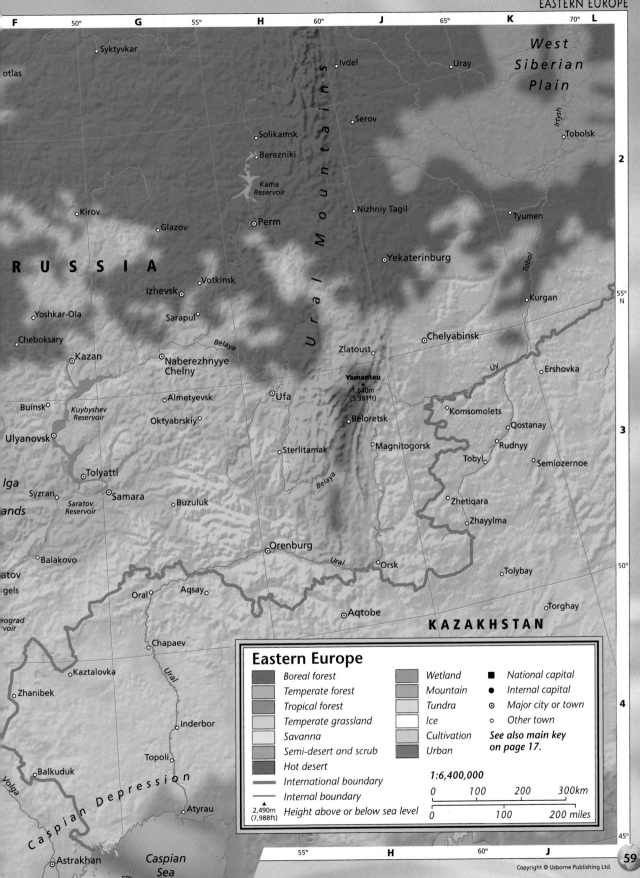

1 68°N 40° M

L

Barents Sea

North Cape

Kola

Peninsula

White
Sea

Lake Vyg

Lake
Onega

Belomorsk

Borovichi

Tikhvin

Kirishi

Volkhov

36° M

L

40°

Severomorsk

Murmansk

Vadso

Kirkenes

Severomorsk

Monchegorsk

3,907ft

Apatity

Kandalaksha

Lake Top

Lake
Kuyto

Kostomuksha

Medvezhyegorsk

Petrozavodsk

Lake
Ladoga

St. Petersburg

Pushkin

Gatchina

Kingisepp

RUSSIA

Narva

32° K

Kirkenes

Utsjoki

Sevettijarvi

Kaamanen

Lake
Inari

Lokan
Reservoir

Sodankyla

Kuusamo

Lake Pya

Lieksa

Pielis Lake

Kuopio

Varkaus

Haukilake

Pihlaja
Lake

Saimaa
Lake

Vyborg

Zelenogorsk

Kouvola

Kotka

Kohtla-
Jarve

Tallinn

28° H

Hammerfest

Alta

Soroya

Tromso

Vadso

Rovaniemi

Lapland

Tornio

Oulu

Raahe

FINLAND

Kiuruvesi

Kajaani

Kuhmo

Jyvaskyla

Mikkeli

Pajanne
Lake

Lappeenranta

Lahti

Helsinki

Espoo

Haapsalu

24° G

Kebnekaise
2,114m
(6,935ft)

Kiruna

Stora
Lule Lake

Boden

Skelleftea

Kokkola

Saarijarvi

Alavus

Tampere

Hameenlinna

Turku

Hiiumaa

20° F

Narvik

Svolvaer

Vestfjorden

Lofoten

Horn Lake

Storavan
Lake

Ume

Umea

Gulf of Bothnia

Vaasa

Kurikka

Pori

Rauma

Aland
Islands

Stockholm

Sodertalje

16° E

Bodo

Moi
Rana

Vesteralen

Ostersund

Indals

Stor
Lake

Sundsvall

Hudiksvall

Gavle

Borlange

Uppsala

Eskilstuna

Orebro

Lake Malar

SWEDEN

12° D

Namsos

Steinkjer

Trondheim

Oppdal

Lillehammer

Karlstad

Klar

Lake
Vaner

8° C

Vikna

Froya

Hitra

Smola

Kristiansund

Honefoss

NORWAY

Oslo

Drammen

Fredrikstad

Larvik

Glama

4° B

Galdhopiggen
2,469m
(8,100ft)

Alesund

Bergen

Odda

Stavanger

Norwegian
Sea

Sula

Sotra

Karmoy

Varhaug

0° A

Arctic Circle

Isafjordhur

4°W

INSET MAP:

Langanes

Seydhisfjordhur

Vatnajokull

Hvannadalshnukur
2,119m
(6,952ft)

Same scale as main map

ICELAND

Siglufjordhur

Reykjavik

Faxafloi

Keflavik

ATLANTIC OCEAN

Arctic Circle

60

Central and Northern Europe

Key

- Boreal forest
- Temperate forest
- Tropical forest
- Temperate grassland
- Savanna
- Semi-desert and scrub
- Hot desert
- Wetland
- Mountain
- Tundra
- Ice
- Cultivation
- Urban

- ■ National capital
- ● Internal capital
- ⊙ Major city or town
- ○ Other town
- ─ International boundary
- ─ Internal boundary
- ▲ 2,490m (7,988ft) Height above or below sea level

See also main key on page 17.

1:6,400,000

0   100   200   300km
0   100   200 miles

DENMARK
Alborg, Varberg, Halmstad, Helsingborg, Viborg, Randers, Arhus, Kolding, Odense, Fyn, Zealand, Lolland, Nykobing, Bornholm (Denmark), Ronne, Malmo, Copenhagen, Esbjerg, Jutland, Flensburg, Kiel, Cuxhaven, North Frisian Islands, Rostock, Lubeck

GERMANY
Berlin, Potsdam, Cottbus, Dresden, Chemnitz, Most

Baltic Sea
North Sea, Kattegat, Oskarshamn, Oland, Kalmar, Karlshamn, Karlskrona, Visby, Gotland, Liepaja, Klaipeda

LATVIA
Riga, Gulf of Riga, Ventspils, Jurmala, Jelgava, Cesis, Aluksne, Opochka, Velikiye Luki, Ludza, Jekabpils, Daugavpils, Panevezys

LITHUANIA
Vilnius, Kaunas, Siauliai, Marijampole, Alytus, Neman

RUSSIA
Kaliningrad, Smolensk, Roslavl, Klintsy, Vitsyebsk, Orsha, Polatsk, Navapolatsk, Western Dvina

BELARUS
Minsk, Maladzyechna, Lida, Hrodna, Baranavichy, Slutsk, Salihorsk, Pinsk, Mazyr, Babruysk, Barysaw, Zhodzina, Mahilyow, Zhlobin, Homyel, Rechytsa, Svyetlahorsk, Dnieper, Pripet, Pripet Marshes

POLAND
Warsaw, Suwalki, Bialystok, Lublin, Radom, Lodz, Wloclawek, Plock, Olsztyn, Gdynia, Gdansk, Gulf of Gdansk, Slupsk, Koszalin, Szczecin, Gorzow Wielkopolski, Zielona Gora, Poznan, Bydgoszcz, Grudziadz, Kalisz, Wroclaw, Legnica, Walbrzych, Opole, Czestochowa, Katowice, Krakow, Kielce, Zamosc, Rzeszow, Tarnow, Rybnik, Oder, Vistula

UKRAINE
Kiev, Chernihiv, Korosten, Zhytomyr, Bila Tserkva, Uman, Vinnytsya, Khmelnytskyy, Kamyanets-Podilskyy, Ternopil, Ivano-Frankivsk, Chernivtsi, Lviv, Shepetivka, Rivne, Lutsk, Kovel, Kievske Reservoir, Dniester, 417m (1,368ft)

MOLDOVA
Chisinau, Tiraspol, Tighina, Balti, Rabnita, Dnieper

ROMANIA
Odesa, Bilhorod-Dnistrovskyy, Galati, Focsani, Brasov, Sibiu, Piatra Neamt, Bacau, Botosani, Suceava, Iasi, Baia Mare, Satu Mare, Cluj-Napoca, Targu Mures, Oradea, Arad, Timisoara, Debrecen, Carpathian Mountains

SLOVAKIA
Kosice, Presov, Miskolc, Zilina, Banska Bystrica, Nitra, Trnava, Bratislava, Gerlachovsky stit 2,655m (8,711ft)

CZECH REPUBLIC
Prague, Liberec, Hradec Kralove, Pilsen, Ceske Budejovice, Brno, Ostrava, Olomouc, Zlin

HUNGARY
Budapest, Kecskemet, Szeged, Szekesfehervar, Szombathely, Zalaegerszeg, Pecs, Subotica, Bekescsaba, Gyor, Lake Balaton, Danube

AUSTRIA
Vienna, St. Polten, Linz, Wels, Graz, Knittelfeld, Klagenfurt, Villach

SLOVENIA
Ljubljana, Maribor, Novo Mesto, Kranj, Trieste, Zagreb

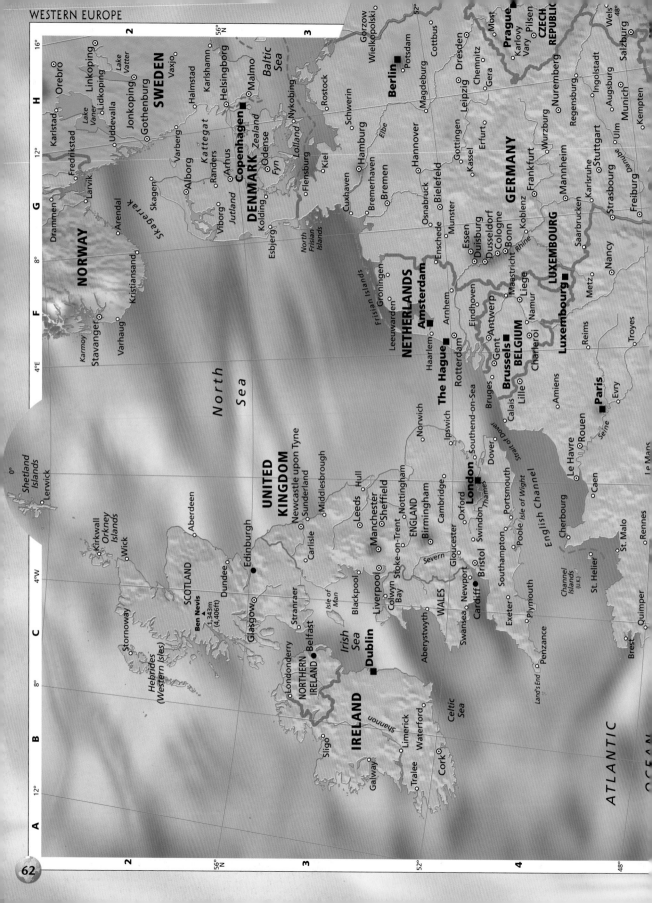

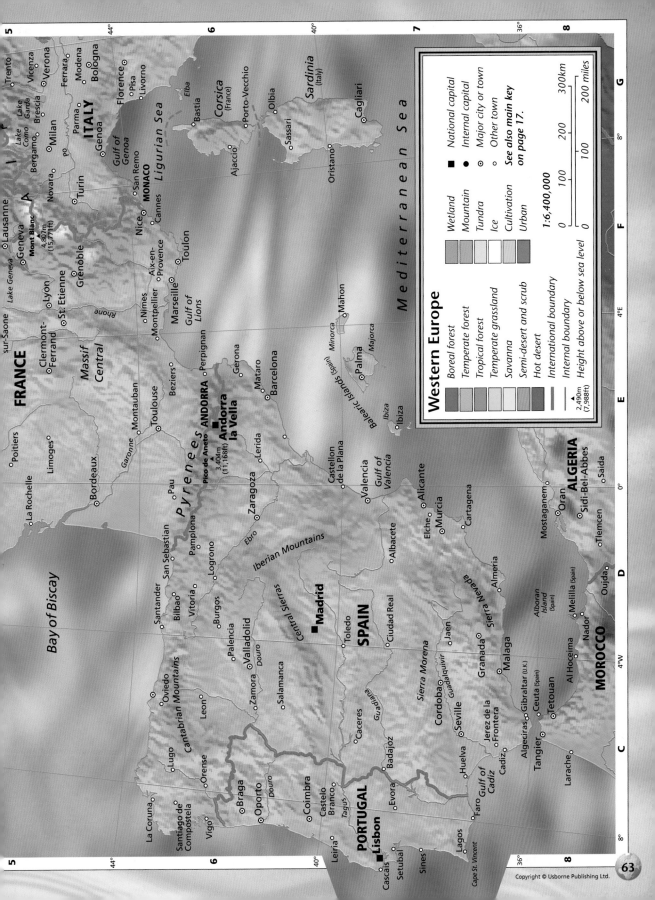

Western Europe

■	National capital	
●	Internal capital	
◉	Major city or town	
○	Other town	

See also main key on page 17.

1:6,400,000

| 0 | 100 | 200 | 300km |
| 0 | 100 | 200 | 200 miles |

Wetland
Mountain
Tundra
Ice
Cultivation
Urban

Boreal forest
Temperate forest
Tropical forest
Temperate grassland
Savanna
Semi-desert and scrub
Hot desert

International boundary
Internal boundary
Height above or below sea level

2,490m
(7,988ft)

ITALY
Trento
Vicenza
Verona
Modena
Bologna
Parma
Ferrara
Lake Como
Lake Garda
Bergamo
Brescia
Milan
Novara
Po
Genoa
Turin
Gulf of Genoa
Florence
Pisa
Livorno
Elba
Corsica (France)
Bastia
Ajaccio
Porto-Vecchio
Olbia
Sassari
Sardinia (Italy)
Oristano
Cagliari
San Remo
MONACO
Nice
Cannes
Ligurian Sea
Mediterranean Sea

Lausanne
Geneva
Mont Blanc
4,807m
(15,771ft)
Lake Geneva
Lyon
St Etienne
Grenoble
Aix-en-Provence
Toulon
Marseille
Gulf of Lions
Montpellier
Nîmes
Rhône
sur-Saône

FRANCE
Poitiers
Limoges
Clermont-Ferrand
Massif Central
La Rochelle
Bordeaux
Garonne
Montauban
Toulouse
Béziers
Perpignan
Pau
Gerona
Mataro
Barcelona
Beziers

ANDORRA
Andorra la Vella
Pico de Aneto
3,404m
(11,168ft)
Pyrenees
Lerida
Zaragoza
Ebro
Pamplona
Logroño
San Sebastian
Vitoria
Burgos
Palencia
Valladolid
Douro
Zamora
Salamanca
León
Lugo
Orense
Braga
Oporto
Douro
Coimbra
Castelo Branco
Leiria
Cascais

Castellon de la Plana
Valencia
Gulf of Valencia
Balearic Islands (Spain)
Minorca
Mahon
Majorca
Palma
Ibiza
Ibiza

PORTUGAL
Lisbon
Évora
Setúbal
Sines
Lagos
Cape St. Vincent
Faro
Gulf of Cadiz
Huelva
Cadiz
Badajoz
Cáceres
Guadiana

SPAIN
Madrid
Toledo
Ciudad Real
Central Sierras
Iberian Mountains
Albacete
Murcia
Elche
Alicante
Cartagena
Almería
Sierra Nevada
Granada
Málaga
Jaén
Córdoba
Guadalquivir
Seville
Sierra Morena
Jerez de la Frontera
Algeciras
Gibraltar (U.K.)
Ceuta (Spain)
Tangier
Larache
Tetouan
Al Hoceima
Nador
Oujda
Melilla (Spain)
Alboran Island (Spain)

MOROCCO
ALGERIA
Oran
Mostaganem
Sidi-Bel-Abbes
Saïda
Tlemcen

Santiago de Compostela
La Coruña
Vigo
Santander
Oviedo
Bilbao
Cantabrian Mountains
Bay of Biscay

Copyright © Usborne Publishing Ltd.

A 0° B 4°E C 8° D 12° E 16°

Cherbourg
Le Havre
Caen
Rouen
Amiens
Charleroi Namur
BELGIUM
Koblenz
Erfurt Gera **Dresden**
Chemnitz Liberec Walb
Wroclaw

Reims
LUXEMBOURG
■**Luxembourg**
Frankfurt
Wurzburg
Most Hradec Kralove
Karlovy Vary ■**Prague**
Pilsen **CZECH REPUBLIC**
Olomou

48°N
■**Paris**
Evry
Metz
Saarbrucken
Mannheim
GERMANY
Nuremberg
Regensburg
Ingolstadt
Ceske Budejovice
Brno

Le Mans
Nancy
Karlsruhe
Stuttgart
Danube
Augsburg
Linz
Wels St. Polten
Vienna

Angers
Orleans
Troyes
Strasbourg
Rhine
Freiburg
Ulm
Munich
Salzburg
Brati

Tours
Nevers
Dijon
Basel
Winterthur
Kempten
Grossglockner
AUSTRIA
Knittelfeld
Szomba

Poitiers
FRANCE
Besancon
Zurich
Lucerne
Innsbruck
3,798m (12,461ft) S
Villach
Graz
Zalaeg

Limoges
Chalon-sur-Saone
Biel
Lausanne
Bern ■
SWITZERLAND
Vaduz ■
LIECHTENSTEIN
Bolzano
A l p
Klagenfurt
Maribor

44°
Clermont-Ferrand
Geneva
Lake Geneva
Lyon
A
Mont Blanc 4,807m (15,771ft)
Grenoble
l
Trento
Bergamo
Lake Como
Lake Garda
Vicenza
Novara
Kranj
Trieste
SLOVENIA ■**Ljubljana**
Novo Mesto
Zagre
CROA

Montauban
Garonne
Massif Central
Rhone
Turin
Po
Milan
Brescia
Verona
Venice
Pula
Rijeka
Karlovac
Sla

Toulouse
Parma
Modena
Bologna
Ferrara
Ravenna
Zadar
Banja Luk
BOSN

Montpellier
Nimes
Aix-en-Provence
Nice
San Remo
MONACO
Genoa
Gulf of Genoa
ITALY
Rimini
Dinaric
AND
HERZEGO

Beziers
Gulf of Lions
Marseille
Cannes
Livorno
Pisa
Florence
SAN MARINO
Ancona
Zadar
Split

■**Andorra la Vella**
Toulon
Ligurian Sea
Perugia
Pescara
Adriatic Sea

Bastia
Elba
Terni
Apennines

Ajaccio
Corsica (France)
VATICAN CITY
Rome ■

Porto-Vecchio

Olbia
Naples
Pompeii
Salerno
Foggia
Ba

Sassari
Sardinia (Italy)
Tyrrhenian Sea
Taranto

40°
Oristano
Cosenza
Catan

Cagliari
Lipari Islands

M e d i t e r r a n e a n   S e a
Trapani
Palermo
Messina

Mount Etna 3,323m (10,902ft)
Sicily
Catania

Annaba
Bizerte
Menzel Bourguiba
Carthage
Agrigento
Ragusa
Syracuse

Guelma
Pantelleria (Italy)

36°
Souk Ahras
Nabeul
Tunis ■
Pelagian Islands (Italy)
MALTA
Valletta ■

TUNISIA
Sousse
Monastir

Tebessa
Kairouan
El Jem

Biskra
Kasserine

Southern Europe

- Boreal forest
- Temperate forest
- Tropical forest
- Temperate grassland
- Savanna
- Semi-desert and scrub
- Hot desert
- Wetland
- Mountain
- Tundra
- Ice
- Cultivation
- Urban

■ National capital
● Internal capital
⊙ Major city or town
○ Other town
▬ International boundary
▲ Internal boundary
2,490m (7,988ft) Height above or below sea level

See also main key on page 17.
1:6,400,000

0 100 200 300km
0 100 200 miles

AFRICA

Africa is the second-biggest
continent and has 53 countries
altogether. More than a quarter
of them are landlocked, with
no access to the sea except
through other countries.
Africa is home to the
world's longest river,
the Nile, and its largest
desert, the Sahara. It
also has vast amounts
of natural resources,
such as gold, copper and
diamonds. Many of them
have not yet begun to be used.

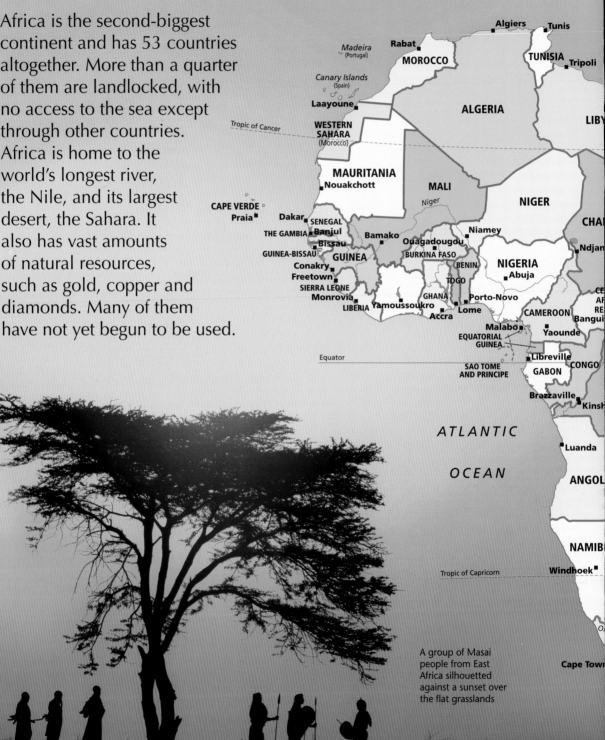

Algiers
Tunis
Madeira
(Portugal)
Rabat
MOROCCO
TUNISIA
Tripoli
Canary Islands
(Spain)
Laayoune
ALGERIA
LIBY
Tropic of Cancer
WESTERN
SAHARA
(Morocco)
MAURITANIA
Nouakchott
MALI
NIGER
CHA
Niger
CAPE VERDE
Praia
Dakar
SENEGAL
Niamey
Ndjam
THE GAMBIA
Banjul
Bamako
Ouagadougou
Bissau
GUINEA-BISSAU
GUINEA
BURKINA FASO
NIGERIA
Conakry
BENIN
Abuja
Freetown
TOGO
CE
AF
RE
SIERRA LEONE
GHANA
Porto-Novo
Monrovia
Yamoussoukro
Lome
CAMEROON
Bangui
LIBERIA
Accra
Malabo
Yaounde
EQUATORIAL
GUINEA
Equator
Libreville
CONGO
SAO TOME
AND PRINCIPE
GABON
Brazzaville
Kinsh

ATLANTIC

OCEAN

Luanda

ANGOL

Tropic of Capricorn
Windhoek
NAMIB

Cape Town

A group of Masai
people from East
Africa silhouetted
against a sunset over
the flat grasslands

Facts

Total land area 30,221,532 sq km (11,668,594 sq miles)

Total population 922 million

Biggest city Cairo, Egypt

Biggest country Sudan *2,505,810 sq km (967,493 sq miles)*

Smallest country Seychelles *455 sq km (176 sq miles)*

Highest mountain Kilimanjaro, Tanzania *5,895m (19,341ft)*

Longest river Nile, running from to Burundi to Egypt *6,671km (4,145 miles)*

Biggest lake Lake Victoria, between Tanzania, Kenya and Uganda *68,800 sq km (26,564 sq miles)*

Highest waterfall Tugela Falls, on the Tugela River, South Africa *610m (2,000ft)*

Biggest desert Sahara, North Africa *9,100,000 sq km (3,500,000 sq miles)*

Biggest island Madagascar *587,040 sq km (226,656 sq miles)*

Main mineral deposits Gold, copper, diamonds, iron ore, manganese, bauxite

Main fuel deposits Coal, uranium, natural gas

The shading on this map is there to help you see clearly the different countries that make up the continent.

Cairo

EGYPT

Tropic of Cancer

Nile

Khartoum

ERITREA
Asmara

SUDAN

DJIBOUTI Djibouti

Addis Ababa

SOMALIA

ETHIOPIA

Mogadishu

UGANDA
Kampala

KENYA

Equator

Kigali

RWANDA
BURUNDI
Bujumbura

Nairobi

Victoria
SEYCHELLES

Dodoma

TANZANIA Dar es Salaam

INDIAN

MALAWI

Moroni
COMOROS

Lilongwe

OCEAN

MBIA
saka

bezi

Harare

ZIMBABWE

MOZAMBIQUE

Antananarivo

MAURITIUS
Port Louis

MADAGASCAR

Reunion
(France)

Tropic of Capricorn

VANA

ne

Pretoria
(Tshwane)

Maputo

Mbabane SWAZILAND
Lobamba

fontein

Maseru

LESOTHO

Internet links

For links to websites where you can find out more about the countries in Africa, go to
www.usborne-quicklinks.com

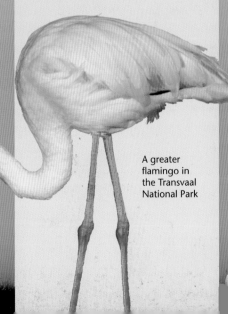

A greater flamingo in the Transvaal National Park

A   0°   B   5°E

Saida
Djelfa
Atlas Mountains
Batna
Tebessa
Biskra
Annaba
Menzel
Bourguiba
Bizerte
Carthage
Tunis
Sicily (Italy)
Catania
Syracuse
GREECE
20°

Kairouan
Sousse
Monastir
El Jem
Sfax
Pantelleria (Italy)
MALTA
Valletta

Gafsa
Tozeur
Kerkenah Islands
Pelagian Islands (Italy)

2

El Oued
Touggourt
Chott el Jerid
Gabes
Gulf of Gabes
Jerba
M e d i t e r r a n e

Ghardaia
Ouargla
Tataouine
TUNISIA
Tripoli
Al Khums
Leptis Magna
Misratah
Cyrene
Al Bayda
Darna

Gharyan
Surt
Gulf of Sidra
Benghazi
Tubr

30°N

Tademait Plateau
Ghadamis
Ajdabiya

Great Eastern Erg

3

ALGERIA

Lib

Illizi
Sabha
LIBYA

25°

Murzuq

Ahaggar Mountains
Ghat

Tropic of Cancer
Mount Tahat
2,918m
(9,573ft)

A

4

Tamanrasset

Djado Plateau
Tibesti Mountains

20°

Emi Koussi
3,415m
(11,204ft)

MALI
S   A   H   A   R   A

5

Agadez
NIGER
Faya-Largeau

Bodele Depression
Ennedi Plateau

15°

Tahoua
CHAD

Dosso
Maradi
Zinder
Mao
Abeche
Mou

Sokoto
S   A   H   E   L
Lake Chad

6

Birnin-Kebbi
Katsina
Kano
Gusau
Ndjamena
Mongo

Kandi
Maiduguri
Am Timan

Zaria
Potiskum
Kainji Reservoir
Kaduna
NIGERIA
Jos
Maroua
Birao

10°

Saki
Minna
Bida
Niger
Kumo
Bongor
CAMEROON
Abuja

7

B   5°E   C   10°   D   15°   E   20°   F

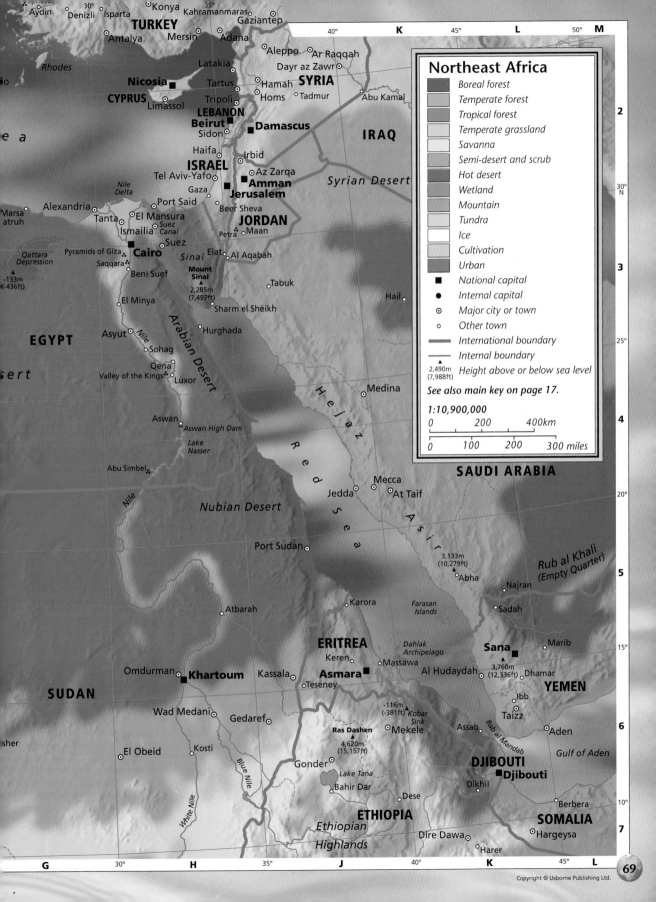

Northeast Africa

	Boreal forest
	Temperate forest
	Tropical forest
	Temperate grassland
	Savanna
	Semi-desert and scrub
	Hot desert
	Wetland
	Mountain
	Tundra
	Ice
	Cultivation
	Urban
■	National capital
●	Internal capital
⊙	Major city or town
○	Other town
———	International boundary
———	Internal boundary
▲ 2,490m (7,988ft)	Height above or below sea level

See also main key on page 17.

1:10,900,000

0 — 200 — 400km

0 — 100 — 200 — 300 miles

TURKEY
Aydin
Denizli
Isparta
Konya
Kahramanmaras
Gaziantep
Antalya
Mersin
Adana
Rhodes
Aleppo
Ar Raqqah
Latakia
Dayr az Zawr
Nicosia
Tartus
Hamah
SYRIA
CYPRUS
Tripoli
Homs
Tadmur
Abu Kamal
Limassol
LEBANON
IRAQ
Beirut
Damascus
Sidon
Haifa
Irbid
Tel Aviv-Yafo
Az Zarqa
ISRAEL
Amman
Gaza
Jerusalem
JORDAN
Syrian Desert
Alexandria
Nile Delta
Port Said
Beer Sheva
Marsa atruh
Tanta
El Mansura
Ismailia
Suez Canal
Maan
Petra
Qattara Depression
Pyramids of Giza
Cairo
Suez
Elat
Al Aqabah
-133m (-436ft)
Saqqara
Beni Suef
Sinai
Mount Sinai
Tabuk
EGYPT
El Minya
2,285m (7,497ft)
Hail
Asyut
Sohag
Nile
Hurghada
Sharm el Sheikh
Qena
Arabian Desert
Valley of the Kings
Luxor
Aswan
Aswan High Dam
Medina
Lake Nasser
Hejaz
Abu Simbel
Nubian Desert
Mecca
At Taif
Nile
Jedda
SAUDI ARABIA
Port Sudan
Red Sea
Asir
Rub al Khali (Empty Quarter)
3,133m (10,279ft)
Abha
Najran
Atbarah
Karora
Sadah
Farasan Islands
Dahlak Archipelago
Marib
ERITREA
Sana
Keren
Massawa
3,760m (12,336ft)
Dhamar
Omdurman
Khartoum
Kassala
Asmara
Al Hudaydah
YEMEN
Teseney
Ibb
SUDAN
Wad Medani
Gedaref
-116m (-381ft)
Kobar Sink
Taizz
Mekele
Assab
Aden
El Obeid
Kosti
Ras Dashen
4,620m (15,157ft)
Bab al Mandab
Gulf of Aden
Gonder
DJIBOUTI
Blue Nile
Lake Tana
Djibouti
Bahir Dar
Dikhil
Berbera
White Nile
Dese
ETHIOPIA
SOMALIA
Ethiopian Highlands
Dire Dawa
Hargeysa
Harer

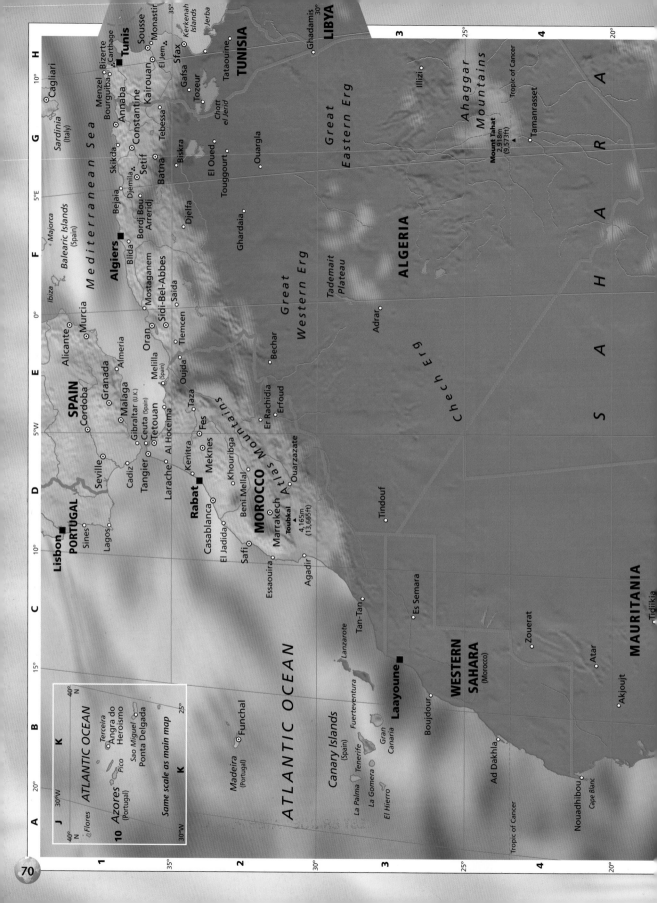

NIGER

Maradi
Tahoua
Gao
Tillaberi
Niamey
Dosso
Gusau
Katsina
Sokoto
Birnin-Kebbi
Zaria
Kaduna
Minna
Bida
Abuja
Zaria
Kainji Reservoir
Niger
Ilorin
NIGERIA
Saki
Ogbomoso
Ibadan
Abeokuta
Owo
Enugu
Onitsha
Benin City
Warri
Port Harcourt
Niger Delta
Lagos
Porto-Novo
Cotonou
Lome
Bight of Benin
Gulf of Guinea
Niger Ocean

Principe
SAO TOME
AND PRINCIPE
Sao Tome
Equator

BENIN
Kandi
Djougou
Natitingou
Parakou
Abomey
TOGO
Sokode
Bassila

BURKINA FASO
Ouagadougou
Fada-Ngourma
Tenkodogo
Bawku
White Volta
Ouahigouya
Dori
Tougan
Koudougou
Bobo Dioulasso
Banfora

Niamey
Tillaberi

Dosso

GHANA
Tamale
Damongo
Wenchi
Lake Volta
Kumasi
Koforidua
Tarkwa
Accra
Cape Coast
Sekondi-Takoradi
Cape Three Points

IVORY COAST
Bondoukou
Bouake
Yamoussoukro
Adzope
Abidjan
Katiola
Bouna
Korhogo
Odienne
Divo
Gagnoa
Daloa
Man
San Pedro
Cape Palmas

GUINEA
Siguiri
Kankan
Kindia
Conakry
Labe
Boke
Kedougou
Dabola

SENEGAL
St. Louis
Louga
Dara
Thies
Dakar
Kaolack
Tambacounda
Kolda
Selibabi
Kayes
Kaedi
Nioro du Sahel
Mopti
Goundam
Atrous
Nionio
Segou
Bamako
Koutiala
Sikasso
Bougouni
Kita
San

THE GAMBIA
Banjul
Ziguinchor
Bignona
GUINEA-BISSAU
Bissau
Bissagos Archipelago

SIERRA LEONE
Freetown
Makeni
Sefadu
Bo
Kenema

LIBERIA
Monrovia
Gueckedou
Nzerekore
1,752m (5,748ft)
Zorzor
Tubmanburg
Harper

ATLANTIC OCEAN

Black Volta
Niger

Northwest Africa

Boreal forest
Temperate forest
Tropical forest
Temperate grassland
Savanna
Semi-desert and scrub
Hot desert
International boundary
Internal boundary
Height above or below sea level
2,490m (7,988ft)

Wetland
Mountain
Tundra
Ice
Cultivation
Urban

1:10,900,000

■ National capital
● Internal capital
⊙ Major city or town
○ Other town

See also main key on page 17.

0   100   200   300 miles
0   200   400km

ATLANTIC OCEAN
CAPE VERDE
Santo Antao
Mindelo
Sao Nicolau
Sal
Boa Vista
Sao Tiago
Maio
Fogo
Praia

Same scale as main map

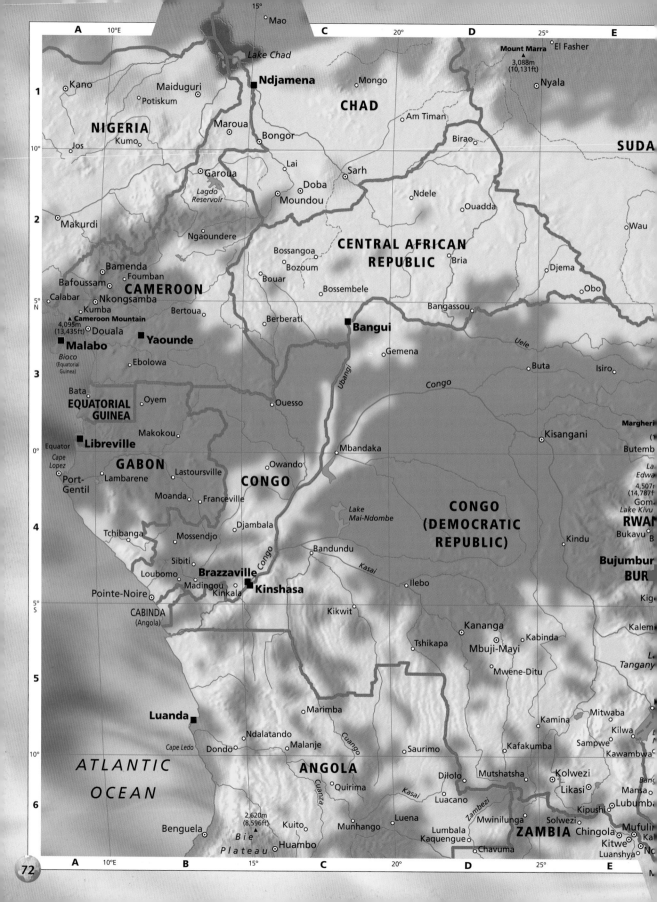

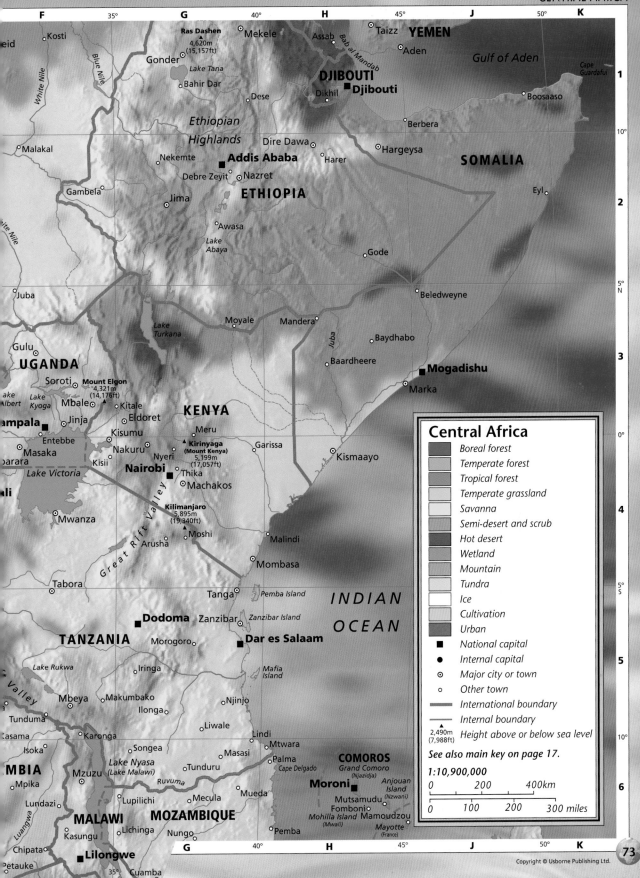

F   35°   G   40°   H   45°   J   50°   K

Kosti

White Nile

Blue Nile

Ras Dashen
4,620m
(15,157ft)

Gonder

Lake Tana

Bahir Dar

Mekele

Assab

Bab al Mandab

Taizz

Aden

YEMEN

Gulf of Aden

Cape
Guardafui

DJIBOUTI

Dikhil   Djibouti

Boosaaso

Dese

Berbera

1

Malakal

Ethiopian
Highlands

Nekemte

Dire Dawa

Harer

Hargeysa

SOMALIA

10°

Addis Ababa

Debre Zeyit   Nazret

Gambela

ETHIOPIA

Eyl

Jima

2

White Nile

Awasa

Lake
Abaya

Gode

5°
N

Juba

Moyale

Mandera

Beledweyne

Gulu

Lake
Turkana

Juba

Baydhabo

UGANDA

Soroti

Mount Elgon
4,321m
(14,176ft)

Baardheere

Mogadishu

3

Lake
Albert

Mbale

Kitale

KENYA

Lake
Kyoga

Jinja

Eldoret

Garissa

Marka

ampala

Entebbe

Kisumu

Nakuru

Meru

Masaka

Kisii

Nyeri

Kirinyaga
(Mount Kenya)
5,199m
(17,057ft)

0°

arara

Lake Victoria

Nairobi

Thika

Kismaayo

li

Mwanza

Machakos

Kilimanjaro
5,895m
(19,340ft)

Moshi

Malindi

4

Great Rift Valley

Arusha

Tabora

Tanga

Pemba Island

INDIAN

5°
S

Dodoma

Zanzibar

Zanzibar Island

OCEAN

TANZANIA

Morogoro

Dar es Salaam

Lake Rukwa

Iringa

Mafia
Island

Mbeya

Makumbako

Njinjo

5

Valley

Ilonga

Tunduma

Liwale

Kasama

Karonga

Songea

Lindi

Mtwara

Isoka

Masasi

Palma   Cape Delgado

COMOROS

Grand Comoro
(Njazidja)

Mpika

Mzuzu

Lake Nyasa
(Lake Malawi)

Tunduru

Moroni

Anjouan
Island
(Nzwani)

6

MBIA

Lundazi

Lupilichi

Mecula

Mueda

Ruvuma

Mutsamudu

Mamoudzou

Lichinga

Nungo

Fomboni

Mohilla Island
(Mwali)

Mayotte
(France)

Kasungu

MALAWI

MOZAMBIQUE

Pemba

Chipata

Lilongwe

G   40°   H   45°   J   50°   K

etauke

Cuamba

35°

Copyright © Usborne Publishing Ltd.

Central Africa

- Boreal forest
- Temperate forest
- Tropical forest
- Temperate grassland
- Savanna
- Semi-desert and scrub
- Hot desert
- Wetland
- Mountain
- Tundra
- Ice
- Cultivation
- Urban
- ■ National capital
- ● Internal capital
- ⊙ Major city or town
- ○ Other town
- ─── International boundary
- ─── Internal boundary
- ▲ 2,490m
  (7,988ft) Height above or below sea level

See also main key on page 17.

1:10,900,000

0   200   400km

0   100   200   300 miles

15°E   20°

Pweto
Mitwaba
Marimba   Kamina   Kilwa   Mbala
1   Mitwaba   Lake
Luanda   Saurimo   Kafakumba   CONGO   Sampwe   Mweru
Ndalatando   Kafakumba   (DEMOCRATIC   Kawambwa
Dondo   Malanje   REPUBLIC)   Lake
Cape Ledo   Dilolo   Mutshatsha   Bangweulu   Ka
10°   Cuanza   Luacano   Kolwezi   Mansa
S   Quirima   Kasai   Likasi   Lubumbashi   Mpika
ANGOLA   Luena   Mwinilunga   Kipushi   Kabunda
2,620m   Kuito   Munhango   Lumbala   Solwezi   Chingola   Mufulira   Ndola
(8,596ft)   Kaquenguec   Kitwe   Ndola
Huambo   Chavuma   Luanshya   Mkushi   Pet
Benguela   *Bie*   Cangombe   Zambezi   **ZAMBIA**   Kabwe
2   Mumbue   *Plateau*   Lumbala   Rufunsa   Cabor
Lucira   Menongue   Nguimbo   Lukulu   Kafue   *Zambezi*   Rese
Cape St. Martha   Matala   Mongu   **Lusaka**   Zumbo
Namibe   Caiundo   Mavinga   Kataba   Ngoma   Karoi
Albino Point   Lubango   Luiana   Lake   Zimba   Chinhoyi   Bindu
15°   Xangongo   *Cunene*   Sesheke   Kariba   Binga   **Harare**
Foz do   Cuangar   Livingstone   Kariba   Kamativi   Kadoma
Cunene   Rundu   Andara   *Caprivi Strip*   Victoria Falls   Binga
3   Opuwo   Ondangwa   *Okavango*   Hwange   **ZIMBABWE**
Etosha   Nokaneng   *Swamp*   Gweru
Okaukuejo   Pan   Tsumeb   Maun   Bulawayo   Zvishava
Kamanjab   Otavi   Tsau   *Lake*   Plumtree   Chiredz
Otjiwarongo   *Ngami*   Makgadikgadi   Mas
20°   Sukses   *Pans*   Francistown
NAMIBIA   Rakops   *(Makarikari)*   Selebi-   Messina
Karibib   Okahandja   Orapa   Phikwe
Swakopmund   Gobabis   **BOTSWANA**   Serowe
Windhoek   Mamuno   Tshwane   Mahalapye
4   Walvis Bay   Leonardville   Kang   Pietersburg
Rehoboth   Molepolole   Warmbad   Gra
Tropic of Capricorn   Tshane   **Gaborone**   Mochudi   **Pretoria**   Ne
Kalkrand   Kanye   Krugersdorp   **(Tshwane)**
Mariental   Gochas   Werda   Benoni   **Mbab**
Terra Firma   Mmabatho   Johannesburg   Springs
25°   Tses   Tshabong   Orkneyo   Standerton   **SWAZILA**
Luderitz   Keetmanshoop   Hotazel   Welkom   Harrismith
Seeheim   Kroonstad   Bethlehem
Grunau   Upington   Kimberley   Tugela Falls   Ladysmith
5   *Orange*   Douglas   Kenhardt   Bloemfontein   **Maseru**
Alexander Bay   Prieska   Mafeteng   **LESOTHO**   Piet
Kenhardt   **SOUTH AFRICA**   *Orange*   Dur
ATLANTIC   De Aar   2,770m
Carnarvon   (9,088ft)   Umtata
30°   Bitterfontein   *Drakensberg*
OCEAN   Beaufort West   Graaff-Reinet   Cradock   Bisho
Great Karoo   *Groot*   **East London**
6   Cape Columbine   Uitenhage   Grahamstown
Paarl   Worcester   Oudtshoorn
Cape Town   Oudtshoorn   Port Elizabeth
Stellenbosch   Cape St. Francis
Cape of Good Hope

Cape Agulhas

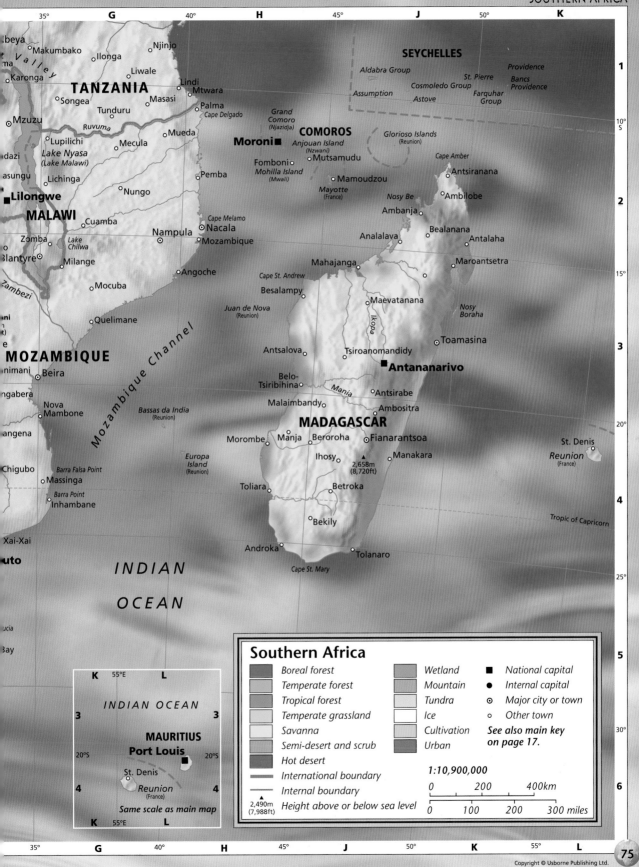

beya
Makumbako
Njinjo
Ilonga
Liwale
Karonga
TANZANIA
Lindi
Mtwara
Songea
Masasi
Tunduru
Palma
Cape Delgado
Mzuzu
Mueda
Ruvuma
Grand
Comoro
(Njazidja)
COMOROS
Moroni
dazi
Lupilichi
Lake Nyasa
(Lake Malawi)
Mecula
Anjouan Island
(Nzwani)
Glorioso Islands
(Reunion)
Fomboni
Mutsamudu
Cape Amber
asungu
Lichinga
Nungo
Mohilla Island
(Mwali)
Antsiranana
Lilongwe
Pemba
Mamoudzou
Ambilobe
MALAWI
Cuamba
Mayotte
(France)
Nosy Be
Ambanja
Zomba
Lake
Chilwa
Nampula
Cape Melamo
Nacala
Analalava
Bealanana
Antalaha
Blantyre
Milange
Mozambique
Mahajanga
Maroantsetra
Zambezi
Angoche
Cape St. Andrew
Besalampy
Maevatanana
Nosy
Boraha
Mocuba
Juan de Nova
(Reunion)
Ikopa
Quelimane
MOZAMBIQUE
Antsalova
Tsiroanomandidy
Toamasina
nimani
Beira
Antananarivo
Mania
ngabera
Belo-
Tsiribihina
Antsirabe
angena
Nova
Mambone
Bassas da India
(Reunion)
Malaimbandy
Ambositra
Chigubo
Europa
Island
(Reunion)
Morombe
Manja
Beroroha
MADAGASCAR
Fianarantsoa
St. Denis
Reunion
(France)
Massinga
Barra Falsa Point
Ihosy
2,658m
(8,720ft)
Manakara
Barra Point
Inhambane
Toliara
Betroka
Xai-Xai
uto
Bekily
INDIAN
Androka
Tolanaro
Cape St. Mary
OCEAN
ucia
Bay

Southern Africa

- Boreal forest
- Temperate forest
- Tropical forest
- Temperate grassland
- Savanna
- Semi-desert and scrub
- Hot desert
- —— International boundary
- —— Internal boundary
- Wetland
- Mountain
- Tundra
- Ice
- Cultivation
- Urban
- ■ National capital
- ● Internal capital
- ⊙ Major city or town
- ○ Other town

See also main key on page 17.

1:10,900,000

2,490m
(7,988ft) Height above or below sea level

0   200   400km
0   100   200   300 miles

MAURITIUS

INDIAN OCEAN

K 55°E L

Port Louis

20°S   20°S

St. Denis
Reunion
(France)

Same scale as main map

K 55°E L

THE ARCTIC

The Arctic is not a continent. It is a region north of the Arctic Circle line of latitude, around the North Pole. The Arctic consists of the Arctic Ocean, islands such as Greenland and the most northerly parts of mainland Europe, North America and Asia. The Arctic region is covered in ice and snow almost all year round.

The large white area in this satellite image is ice covering the Arctic Ocean and Greenland. At the top left of the image is the edge of Russia and at the top right is part of Europe.

These Inuit people are wearing thick, animal-skin coats, boots and gloves to keep warm.

Internet link

For a link to a website where you can discover more about the Arctic, go to **www.usborne-quicklinks.com**

Facts

Size of Arctic Ocean 14,056,000 sq km (5,426,000 sq miles)

Highest point Gunnbjorns Mountain, Greenland *3,700m (12,139ft)*

Lowest point Fram Basin, Arctic Ocean *-4,665m (-15,305ft)*

Lowest recorded temperature -67.8°C (-90°F)

Main mineral deposits Diamonds, gold

Main fuel deposits Oil, natural gas

Seals living in Arctic regions have a thick layer of fat under their skin to keep them warm in the freezing weather.

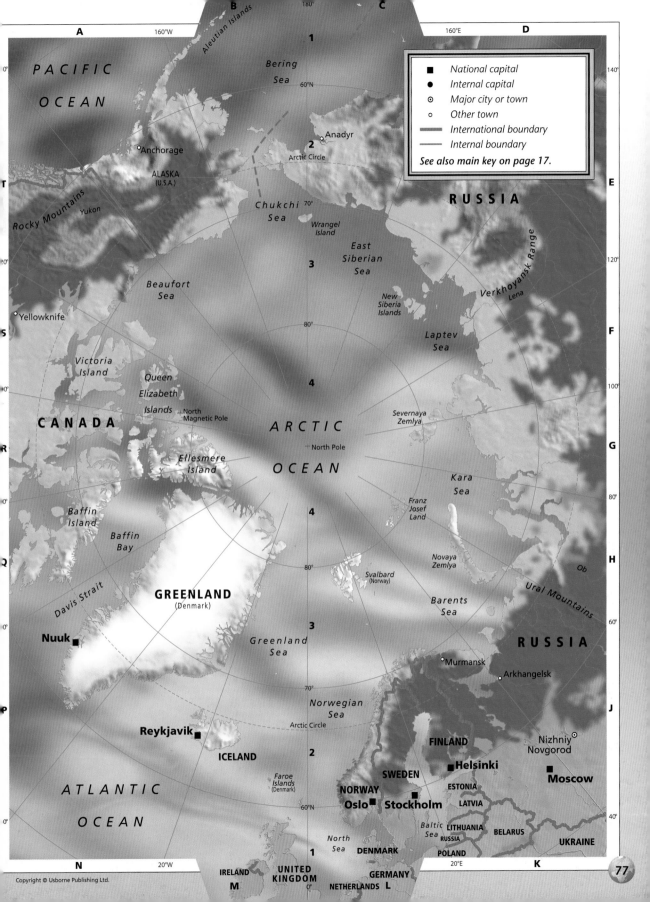

A 160°W B 180 C 160°E D

140°

PACIFIC OCEAN

Aleutian Islands

1

Bering Sea

60°N

2 Anadyr

Arctic Circle

Anchorage

ALASKA
(U.S.A.)

Rocky Mountains

Yukon

Chukchi Sea

70°

Wrangel Island

East Siberian Sea

3

RUSSIA

E

120°

Verkhoyansk Range

Lena

Beaufort Sea

New Siberia Islands

80°

4

Laptev Sea

F

100°

Yellowknife

Victoria Island

Queen Elizabeth Islands

North Magnetic Pole

ARCTIC

Severnaya Zemlya

CANADA

OCEAN

North Pole

Kara Sea

G

80°

Ellesmere Island

Franz Josef Land

Baffin Island

4

Novaya Zemlya

H

60°

Baffin Bay

80°

Svalbard (Norway)

Ob

Ural Mountains

GREENLAND
(Denmark)

Barents Sea

Davis Strait

3

RUSSIA

Nuuk

Greenland Sea

Murmansk

Arkhangelsk

70°

Reykjavik

Norwegian Sea

Arctic Circle

J

ATLANTIC

2

ICELAND

FINLAND

Nizhniy Novgorod

Faroe Islands
(Denmark)

SWEDEN

Helsinki

OCEAN

NORWAY

Oslo Stockholm

ESTONIA

Moscow

60°N

LATVIA

40°

North Sea

Baltic Sea

LITHUANIA

BELARUS

1

DENMARK

RUSSIA

POLAND

UKRAINE

N 20°W K

77

IRELAND M

UNITED KINGDOM

NETHERLANDS L

GERMANY

0°

20°E

KEY

■	National capital
●	Internal capital
☉	Major city or town
○	Other town
—	International boundary
—	Internal boundary

See also main key on page 17.

ANTARCTICA

Antarctica is a huge, frozen continent within the Antarctic Circle. It is almost completely covered by an enormous ice sheet, which is more than 3km (2 miles) deep in some places. Nobody lives permanently in Antarctica, though many scientists visit to study the area. No plants grow in the ice, and the only land animals are tiny mites. But many animals, including penguins, seals, whales and fish, live in the seas around Antarctica.

Facts

Total land area 14,000,000 sq km (5,405,442 sq miles), of which 13,720,000 sq km (5,297,333 sq miles) are covered in ice
Highest point Vinson Massif *5,140m (16,863ft)*
Lowest point Bentley Subglacial Trench *-2,555m (-8,382ft)*
Lowest recorded temperature -89.2°C (-128.6°F)

Main mineral deposits Iron ore, chromium, copper, gold, nickel, platinum

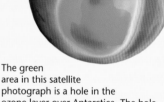

The green area in this satellite photograph is a hole in the ozone layer over Antarctica. The hole is caused by atmospheric pollution.

This ship takes tourists on Antarctic expeditions. Visitors can see animals such as these gentoo penguins, which come onto land to breed.

Internet link

For links to websites where you can find out more about Antarctica, go to **www.usborne-quicklinks.com**

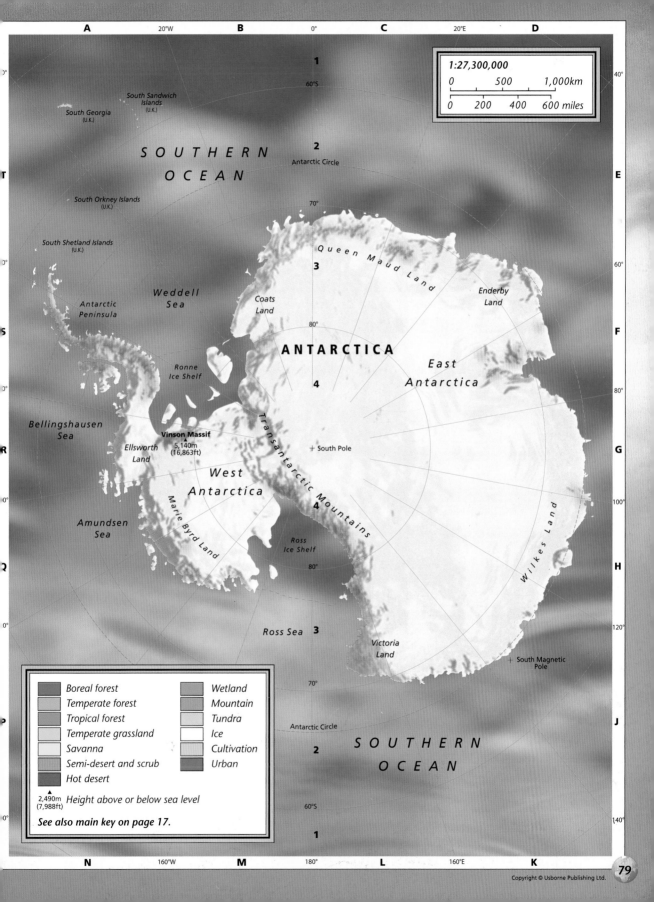

WORLD RECORDS

Here are some of the Earth's longest rivers, highest mountains and other amazing world records. But the world is always changing; mountains wear down, rivers change shape, and new buildings are constructed. Ways of measuring things can also change. That's why you may find slightly different figures in different books.

Highest mountains	
Everest, Nepal/China	8,850m (29,035ft)
K2, Pakistan/China	8,611m (28,251ft)
Kanchenjunga, India/Nepal	8,586m (28,169ft)
Lhotse I, Nepal/China	8,516m (27,940ft)
Makalu I, Nepal/China	8,462m (27,762ft)
Lhotse II, Nepal/China	8,400m (27,560ft)
Dhaulagiri, Nepal	8,167m (26,795ft)
Manaslu I, Nepal	8,156m (26,759ft)
Cho Oyu, Nepal/China	8,201m (26,906ft)
Nanga Parbat, Pakistan	8,126m (26,660ft)

Longest rivers	
Nile, Africa	6,650km (4,132 miles)
Amazon, South America	6,437km (4,000 miles)
Chang Jiang (Yangtze), China	6,380km (3,915 miles)
Mississippi/Missouri, U.S.A.	6,019km (3,741 miles)
Yenisey/Angara, Russia	5,539km (3,445 miles)
Huang He (Yellow), China	5,464km (3,398 miles)
Ob/Irtysh/Black Irtysh, Asia	5,411km (3,362 miles)
Amur/Shilka/Onon, Asia	4,416km (2,744 miles)
Lena, Russia	4,472km (2,734 miles)
Congo, Africa	4,700km (2,922 miles)

Biggest natural lakes	
Caspian Sea	371,000 sq km (143,000 sq mi)
Lake Superior	82,400 sq km (31,820 sq mi)
Lake Victoria	68,800 sq km (26,560 sq mi)
Lake Huron	59,600 sq km (23,010 sq mi)
Lake Michigan	58,000 sq km (22,400 sq mi)
Lake Tanganyika	32,900 sq km (12 702 sq mi)
Lake Baikal	31,494 sq km (12,160 sq mi)
Great Bear Lake	31,153 sq km (12,028 sq mi)
Lake Nyasa	29,600 sq km (11 428 sq mi)
Aral Sea	28,600 sq km (11,042 sq mi)

Deepest ocean
The Mariana Trench, part of the Pacific Ocean, is the deepest part of the sea at 10,911 meters (35,798ft) deep.

Deepest lake
Lake Baikal in Russia is the deepest lake in the world. At its deepest point it is 1,637m (5,370ft) deep.

Biggest islands	
Greenland	2,130,800 sq km (822,706 sq mi)
New Guinea	785,753 sq km (303,381 sq mi)
Borneo	748,168 sq km (288,869 sq mi)
Madagascar	587,713 sq km (226,917 sq mi)
Baffin Island	507,451 sq km (195,928 sq mi)
Sumatra	443,066 sq km (171,069 sq mi)
Honshu	225,800 sq km (87,182 sq mi)
Victoria Island	217,291 sq km (83,897 sq mi)
Great Britain	209,331 sq km (80,823 sq mi)
Ellesmere Island	196,236 sq km (75,767 sq mi)

Tallest inhabited buildings	
Taipei 101, Taipei	509m (1,670ft)
Shanghai WFC, Shanghai	492m (1,614ft)
Petronas Tower, Kuala Lumpur	452m (1,483ft)
Sears Tower, Chicago	442m (1,451ft)
Jin Mao Building, Shanghai	421m (1,381ft)
Two International FC, Hong Kong	415m (1,362ft)
CITIC Plaza, China	391m (1,283ft)
Shun Hing Square, China	384m (1,260ft)
Empire State Building, USA	381m (1,250ft)
Central Plaza, Hong Kong	374m (1,227ft)

Biggest cities/urban areas	
Tokyo-Yokohama, Japan	34.7 million
Jakarta, Indonesia	23.4 million
New York, U.S.A.	21.3 million
Mumbai, India	20.4 million
Manila, Philippines	20.1 million
Delhi, India	19.8 million
Seoul-Incheon, South Korea	19.7 million
Sao Paulo, Brazil	19.5 million
Mexico City, Mexico	18.6 million
Osaka-Kobe-Kyoto, Japan	17.3 million

Famous waterfalls	Height
Angel Falls, Venezuela	979m (3,212ft)
Sutherland Falls, New Zealand	580m (1,904ft)
Mardalfossen, Norway	517m (1,696ft)
Jog Falls, India	253m (830ft)
Victoria Falls, Zimbabwe/Zambia	108m (355ft)
Iguacu Falls, Brazil/Argentina	82m (269ft)
Niagara Falls, Canada/U.S.A.	52m (167ft)

Natural disasters

Natural disasters can be measured in different ways. For example, some earthquakes score highly on the Richter scale, while others cause more destruction. The events listed here are among the most famous and destructive disasters in history.

Earthquakes	Richter scale	Deaths and other effects
San Francisco, U.S.A., 1906	7.9	3,000; deadliest in U.S.; Great Fire
Messina, Italy, 1908	7.5	70-100,000; tsunami killed many
Tokyo-Kanto, Japan, 1923	8.3	142,807; caused Great Tokyo Fire
Quetta, Pakistan, 1935	7.5	30-60,000; Quetta city destroyed
Concepcion, Chile, 1960	8.7	2,000; strongest quake ever
Alaska, U.S.A., 1964	8.6	125; strongest quake ever in U.S.A.
Tangshan, China, 1976	7.9	655,237; deadliest quake of 1900s
Manjil-Rudbar, Iran, 1990	7.7	50,000; landslides; cities destroyed
Kobe, Japan, 1995	6.8	5,500; over $147bn damage
Gujarat, India, 2001	8.0	20,085; strongest quake in India ever

Volcanic eruptions	Disastrous effects
Mount Vesuvius, Italy, AD79	Pompeii flattened; up to 20,000 died
Tambora, Indonesia, 1815	92,000 people starved to death
Krakatoa, Indonesia, 1883	36,500 drowned in resulting tsunami
Mount Pelee, Martinique, 1902	Nearly 30,000 people buried in ash flows
Kelut, Indonesia, 1919	Over 5,000 people drowned in mud
Agung, Indonesia, 1963	1,200 people suffocated in hot ash
Mount St. Helens, U.S.A., 1980	Only 61 died but a large area was destroyed
Ruiz, Colombia, 1985	25,000 people died in giant mud flows
Mt. Pinatubo, Philippines, 1991	800 killed by collapsing roofs and disease
Island of Montserrat, 1995	Volcano left most of the island uninhabitable

Floods	Disastrous effects
Holland, 1228	100,000 drowned by a sea flood
Kaifeng, China, 1642	300,000 died after rebels destroyed a dyke
Johnstown, U.S.A., 1889	2,200 killed in a flood caused by rain
Frejus, France, 1959	More than 500 died after dam burst
Italy, 1963	Vaoint Dam overflowed; 2–3,000 killed
East Pakistan, 1970	Giant wave caused by cyclone killed 250,000
Bangladesh, 1988	1,300 died, 30m homeless in monsoon flood
Southern U.S.A., 1993	$12bn of damage after Mississippi flooded
China, 1998	Chang Jiang overflow left 14m homeless
Indian Ocean, 2004	Devastating tsunami killed 229, 896 people

Storms	Disastrous effects
Caribbean "Great Hurricane", 1780	Biggest ever hurricane killed over 20,000
Hong Kong typhoon, China, 1906	10,000 people died in this giant hurricane
Killer tornado, U.S.A., 1925	Up to 700 people died in Ellington, Missouri
Hurricane Fifi, Honduras, 1974	8,000 people died and 100,000 left homeless
Hurricane Georges, U.S.A., 1998	Caribbean and U.S.A. hit; $5bn of damage
Hurricane Mitch, C. America, 1998	Over 9,000 killed across Central America
Hurricane Katrina, U.S.A., 2005	Over 1,800 killed and $90 bn of damage

Amazing Earth facts

The Earth is 12,103km (7,520 miles) across. Its circumference (the distance around the Equator) is 38,022km (23,627 miles) and it is 149,503,000km (92,897,000 miles) away from the Sun.

To make one complete orbit around the Sun, the Earth has to travel 938,900,000km (583,400,000 miles). To do this in just a year, it has to travel very fast. Because of the atmosphere surrounding the Earth, you can't feel it moving. But you're zooming through space faster than any rocket.

• **Orbit speed** The Earth travels around the Sun at a speed of about 106,000kph (65,868mph).

• **Spinning speed** The Earth spins around an axis, but the speed you're spinning at depends on where you live. Places on the Equator move at 1,600kph (995mph). New York moves at around 1,100kph (684mph). Near the poles, the spinning is not very fast at all.

• **Solar System speed** The whole Solar System, including the Sun, the Earth and its moon, and the other planets and their moons, is moving at 72,400kph (45,000mph) through the galaxy.

• **Galaxy speed** Our galaxy, the Milky Way, whizzes through the universe at 2,172,150kph (1,350,000mph).

Internet links

For links to websites about landscapes, habitats and animals around the world, go to www.usborne-quicklinks.com

TIME ZONES

When it's midday in Rio de Janeiro, it's midnight in Tokyo. This is because we divide the Earth into different time zones. Within each zone, people usually set their clocks to the same time. If you fly between two zones, you change your watch to the time of the new zone.

Dividing up time

There are 25 different time zones. They are separated by one-hour intervals and there is a new time zone roughly every 15 degrees of longitude*. The zones are measured in hours ahead of or behind Greenwich Mean Time, or GMT, which is the time at the Prime Meridian Line*.

Governments can change their countries' time zones. So, for convenience, whole countries usually keep the same local time instead of sticking to the zones exactly. For example, China could be divided into several time zones, but instead the whole country keeps the same time. A few areas, such as India, Iran and parts of Australia, use non-standard half-hour deviations.

Summer time

Some countries adjust their clocks in summer. For example, in the U.K. everybody's clocks go forward one hour. This is known as Daylight Saving Time or Summer Time. It is a way of getting more out of the days by giving people an extra hour of daylight in the evening. It reduces energy use because people don't use as much electricity for lights.

Changing dates

On the opposite side of the world from the Prime Meridian Line is the International Date Line, which runs mostly through the Pacific Ocean and bends to avoid land. Places to the west of it are 24 hours ahead of places to the east. This means that if you travel east across it you lose a day and if you travel west across you gain a day.

This map shows the different times zones. The times at the top of the map tell you the time it is in the different zones when it is noon at the Prime Meridian Line. the numbers in circles tell you how many hours ahead of or behind Greenwich Mean Time an area is.

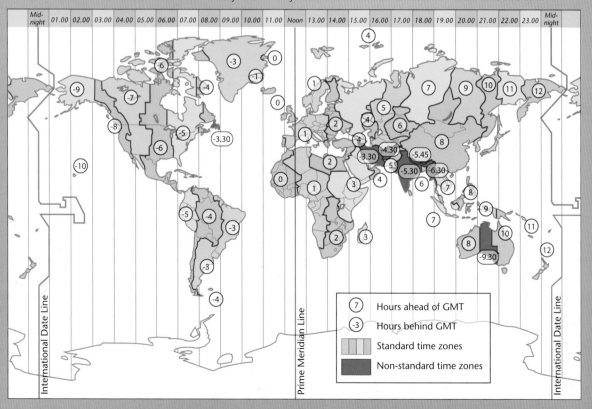

*Longitude, 6; Prime Meridian Line, 6

TYPES OF GOVERNMENTS

Most states have one main leader along with a parliament or assembly of politicians. The main types of governments are listed and explained below. A state can have a combination of more than one of these types of governments. For example, the United States of America is a federal republic.

Anarchy
Anarchy means a situation where there is no government. This can happen after a civil war, when a government has been destroyed and rival groups are battling to take its place.

Capitalist state
In a Capitalist or free-market state, people can own their own businesses and property, and buy services such as healthcare privately. However, most Capitalist governments also provide national health, education and welfare services.

Commonwealth
This word is sometimes used to mean a democratic republic, in which all the state's citizens are seen as having an equal interest in the functioning of the state.

Communist state
Under Communism, the state owns things like factories, farms and businesses, and provides healthcare, welfare and education for its people.

Democracy
In a democracy, the government is elected by the people, using a voting system.

Dictatorship
This is a state run by a single, unelected leader, who may use force to keep control. In a military dictatorship, the army is in power.

Federal government
In a federal system, such as that of the U.S.A., a central government shares power with a number of smaller regional governments.

Monarchy
A monarchy is a state with a king or queen. In some traditional monarchies, the monarch has complete power. A constitutional monarchy, however, also has a separate, usually democratic, government and the monarch's powers are limited.

Regional or local government
A government that controls a smaller area within a state. Some regional governments have very limited powers, and are largely directed by the central government. Others, such as the regional governments in the U.S.A., have much more power and can make their own laws.

Republic
A republic is a state with no monarch. The head of state is usually an elected president.

Revolutionary government
After a revolution, when a government is overthrown by force, the new regime is sometimes called a revolutionary government.

Totalitarian state
This is a state with only one political party, in which individuals are forced to obey the government and may also be prevented from leaving the country.

Transitional government
A government that is changing from one system to another is known as a transitional government. For example, a dictatorship may become a democracy after the dictator dies, but the transition between the systems can take several years.

GAZETTEER OF STATES

Afghanistan

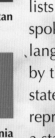

Albania

Algeria

Andorra

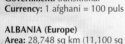

Angola

Antigua and Barbuda

• **Argentina**

This gazetteer lists the world's 194 independent states, along with key facts about each one. In the lists of languages, the language that is most widely spoken is given first, even if it is not the official language. In the lists of religions, the one followed by the most people is also placed first. Every state has a national flag, which is usually used to represent the country abroad. A few states also have a state flag which they prefer to use instead. The state flags appear here with a dot beside them.

AFGHANISTAN (Asia)
Area: 647,500 sq km (250,001 sq miles)
Population: 33,609,937
Capital city: Kabul
Main languages: Dari, Pashto
Main religion: Muslim
Government: transitional
Currency: 1 afghani = 100 puls

ALBANIA (Europe)
Area: 28,748 sq km (11,100 sq miles)
Population: 3,639,453
Capital city: Tirana
Main language: Albanian
Main religions: Muslim, Albanian Orthodox
Government: emerging democracy
Currency: 1 lek = 100 qintars

ALGERIA (Africa)
Area: 2,381,740 sq km (919,595 sq miles)
Population: 34,178,188
Capital city: Algiers
Main languages: Arabic, French, Berber dialects
Main religion: Sunni Muslim
Government: republic
Currency: 1 Algerian dinar = 100 centimes

ANDORRA (Europe)
Area: 468 sq km (181 sq miles)
Population: 83,888
Capital city: Andorra la Vella
Main languages: Catalan, Spanish
Main religion: Roman Catholic
Government: parliamentary democracy
Currency: 1 euro = 100 cents

ANGOLA (Africa)
Area: 1,246,700 sq km (481,354 sq miles)
Population: 12,799,293
Capital city: Luanda
Main languages: Kilongo, Kimbundu, other Bantu languages, Portuguese
Main religions: indigenous, Roman Catholic, Protestant
Government: presidential republic
Currency: 1 kwanza = 100 lwei

ANTIGUA AND BARBUDA (North America)
Area: 443 sq km (171 sq miles)
Population: 85,632
Capital city: Saint John's
Main languages: Caribbean Creole, English
Main religion: Protestant
Government: constitutional monarchy
Currency: 1 East Caribbean dollar = 100 cents

ARGENTINA (South America)
Area: 2,766,890 sq km (1,068,302 sq miles)
Population: 40,913,584
Capital city: Buenos Aires
Main language: Spanish
Main religion: Roman Catholic
Government: republic
Currency: 1 peso = 100 centavos

ARMENIA (Asia)
Area: 29,743 sq km (11,484 sq miles)
Population: 2,967,004
Capital city: Yerevan
Main language: Armenian
Main religion: Armenian Orthodox
Government: republic
Currency: 1 dram = 100 luma

AUSTRALIA (Australasia/Oceania)
Area: 7,741,220 sq km (2,967,909 sq miles)
Population: 21,262,641
Capital city: Canberra
Main language: English
Main religion: Christian
Government: federal democratic monarchy
Currency: 1 Australian dollar = 100 cents

AUSTRIA (Europe)
Area: 83,870 sq km (32,382 sq miles)
Population: 8,210,281
Capital city: Vienna
Main language: German
Main religion: Roman Catholic
Government: federal republic
Currency: 1 euro = 100 cents

Armenia

Australia

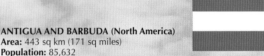

Austria

Azerbaijan

Bahamas, The

Bahrain

Bangladesh

Internet links

For links to websites with flags, maps, quizzes, and facts about every country in the world, go to **www.usborne-quicklinks.com**

Barbados

Belarus

Belgium

Belize

Benin

Bhutan

Bolivia

AZERBAIJAN (Asia)
Area: 86,600 sq km (33,436 sq miles)
Population: 8,238,672
Capital city: Baku
Main language: Azeri
Main religion: Muslim
Government: republic
Currency: 1 manat = 100 gopiks

BAHAMAS, THE (North America)
Area: 13,940 sq km (5,382 sq miles)
Population: 309,156
Capital city: Nassau
Main languages: Bahamian Creole, English
Main religion: Christian
Government: parliamentary democracy
Currency: 1 Bahamian dollar = 100 cents

BAHRAIN (Asia)
Area: 665 sq km (257 miles)
Population: 727,785
Capital city: Manama
Main languages: Arabic, English
Main religion: Muslim
Government: constitutional monarchy
Currency: 1 Bahraini dinar = 1,000 fils

BANGLADESH (Asia)
Area: 144,000 sq km (55,599 sq miles)
Population: 156,050,883
Capital city: Dhaka
Main languages: Bengali, English
Main religions: Muslim, Hindu
Government: parliamentary democracy
Currency: 1 taka = 100 poisha

BARBADOS (North America)
Area: 431 sq km (166 sq miles)
Population: 284,589
Capital city: Bridgetown
Main languages: Bajan, English
Main religion: Christian
Government: parliamentary democracy
Currency: 1 Barbadian dollar = 100 cents

BELARUS (Europe)
Area: 207,600 sq km (80,155 sq miles)
Population: 9,648,533
Capital city: Minsk
Main language: Belarusian
Main religion: Eastern Orthodox
Government: republic
Currency: 1 Belarusian ruble = 100 kopecks

BELGIUM (Europe)
Area: 30,528 sq km (11,787 sq miles)
Population: 10,414,336
Capital city: Brussels
Main languages: Dutch, French, German
Main religions: Roman Catholic, Protestant
Government: constitutional monarchy
Currency: 1 euro = 100 cents

BELIZE (North America)
Area: 22,966 sq km (8,867 sq miles)
Population: 307,899
Capital city: Belmopan
Main languages: Spanish, Belize Creole, English, Garifuna, Maya

Main religions: Roman Catholic, Protestant
Government: parliamentary democracy
Currency: 1 Belizean dollar = 100 cents

BENIN (Africa)
Area: 112,620 sq km (43,483 sq miles)
Population: 8,791,832
Capital city: Porto-Novo
Main languages: Fon, French, Yoruba, Adja
Main religions: indigenous, Christian, Muslim
Government: republic
Currency: 1 CFA* franc = 100 centimes

BHUTAN (Asia)
Area: 47,000 sq km (18,147 sq miles)
Population: 691,141
Capital city: Thimphu
Main languages: Dzongkha, Nepali
Main religions: Buddist, Hindu
Government: constitutional monarchy
Currency: 1 ngultrum = 100 chetrum

BOLIVIA (South America)
Area: 1,098,580 sq km (424,164 sq miles)
Population: 9,775,246
Capital cities: La Paz/Sucre
Main languages: Spanish, Quechua, Aymara
Main religion: Roman Catholic
Government: republic
Currency: 1 boliviano = 100 centavos

BOSNIA AND HERZEGOVINA (Europe)
Area: 51,209 sq km (19,772 sq miles)
Population: 4,613,414
Capital city: Sarajevo
Main languages: Bosnian, Serbian, Croatian
Main religions: Muslim, Orthodox, Roman Catholic
Government: emerging federal republic
Currency: 1 marka = 100 pfenninga

BOTSWANA (Africa)
Area: 600,370 sq km (231,804 sq miles)
Population: 1,990,876
Capital city: Gaborone
Main languages: Setswana, Kalanga, English
Main religions: indigenous, Christian
Government: parliamentary republic
Currency: 1 pula = 100 thebe

BRAZIL (South America)
Area: 8,511,965 sq km (3,286,488 sq miles)
Population: 198,739,269
Capital city: Brasilia
Main language: Portuguese
Main religion: Roman Catholic
Government: federal republic
Currency: 1 real = 100 centavos

BRUNEI (Asia)
Area: 5,770 sq km (2,228 sq miles)
Population: 388,190
Capital city: Bandar Seri Begawan
Main languages: Malay, English, Chinese
Main religions: Muslim, Buddhist
Government: constitutional sultanate (a type of monarchy)
Currency: 1 Bruneian dollar = 100 cents

Bosnia and Herzegovina

Botswana

Brazil

Brunei

Bulgaria

Burkina Faso

Burma (Myanmar)

CFA = Communaute Financiere Africaine

GAZETTEER OF STATES CONTINUED:

Burundi

Cambodia

Cameroon

Canada

Cape Verde

Central African Republic

Chad

BULGARIA (Europe)
Area: 110,910 sq km (42,823 sq miles)
Population: 7,204,687
Capital city: Sofia
Main language: Bulgarian
Main religions: Bulgarian Orthodox, Muslim
Government: parliamentary democracy
Currency: 1 lev = 100 stotinki

BURKINA FASO (Africa)
Area: 274,200 sq km (105,869 sq miles)
Population: 15,746,232
Capital city: Ouagadougou
Main languages: Moore, Jula, French
Main religions: Muslim, indigenous
Government: parliamentary republic
Currency: 1 CFA* franc = 100 centimes

BURMA (MYANMAR) (Asia)
Area: 678,500 sq km (261,970 sq miles)
Population: 48,137,741
Capital city: Rangoon, Naypyidaw
Main language: Burmese
Main religion: Buddhist
Government: military dictatorship
Currency: 1 kyat = 100 pyas

BURUNDI (Africa)
Area: 27,830 sq km (10,745 sq miles)
Population: 8,988,091
Capital city: Bujumbura
Main languages: Kirundi, French, Swahili
Main religions: Christian, indigenous
Government: republic
Currency: 1 Burundi franc = 100 centimes

CAMBODIA (Asia)
Area: 181,040 sq km (69,900 sq miles)
Population: 14,494,293
Capital city: Phnom Penh
Main language: Khmer, French
Main religion: Buddhist
Government: constitutional monarchy
Currency: 1 new riel = 100 sen

CAMEROON (Africa)
Area: 475,440 sq km (183,568 sq miles)
Population: 18,879,301
Capital city: Yaounde
Main languages: Cameroon Pidgin English, Ewondo, Fula, French, English
Main religions: indigenous, Christian, Muslim
Government: republic
Currency: 1 CFA* franc = 100 centimes

CANADA (North America)
Area: 9,984,670 sq km (3,855,103 sq miles)
Population: 33,487,208
Capital city: Ottawa
Main languages: English, French
Main religions: Roman Catholic, Protestant
Government: federal democracy
Currency: 1 Canadian dollar = 100 cents

CAPE VERDE (Africa)
Area: 4,033 sq km (1,557 sq miles)
Population: 429,474
Capital city: Praia
Main languages: Crioulo*, Portuguese

Main religions: Roman Catholic, Protestant
Government: republic
Currency: 1 Cape Verdean escudo = 100 centavos

CENTRAL AFRICAN REPUBLIC (Africa)
Area: 622,984 sq km (240,535 sq miles)
Population: 4,511,488
Capital city: Bangui
Main languages: Sangho, French
Main religions: indigenous, Christian, Muslim
Government: republic
Currency: 1 CFA* franc = 100 centimes

CHAD (Africa)
Area: 1,284,000 sq km (495,755 sq miles)
Population: 10,329,208
Capital city: N'Djamena
Main languages: Arabic, Sara, French
Main religions: Muslim, Christian, indigenous
Government: republic
Currency: 1 CFA* franc = 100 centimes

CHILE (South America)
Area: 756,950 sq km (292,260 sq miles)
Population: 16,601,707
Capital city: Santiago
Main language: Spanish
Main religions: Roman Catholic, Protestant
Government: republic
Currency: 1 Chilean peso = 100 centavos

CHINA (Asia)
Area: 9,596,960 sq km (3,705,407 sq miles)
Population: 1,338,612,968
Capital city: Beijing
Main languages: Mandarin Chinese, Yue, Wu
Main religions: Taoist, Buddhist
Government: communist republic
Currency: 1 yuan = 10 jiao

COLOMBIA (South America)
Area: 1,138,910 sq km (439,736 sq miles)
Population: 45,644,023
Capital city: Bogota
Main language: Spanish
Main religion: Roman Catholic
Government: republic
Currency: 1 Colombian peso = 100 centavos

COMOROS (Africa)
Area: 2,170 sq km (838 sq miles)
Population: 752,438
Capital city: Moroni
Main languages: Comorian*, French, Arabic
Main religion: Sunni Muslim
Government: republic
Currency: 1 Comoran franc = 100 centimes

CONGO (Africa)
Area: 342,000 sq km (132,047 sq miles)
Population: 4,012,809
Capital city: Brazzaville
Main languages: Munukutuba, Lingala, French
Main religions: Christian, animist
Government: republic
Currency: 1 CFA* franc = 100 centimes

Chile

China

Colombia

Comoros

Congo

Congo (Democratic Republic)

Costa Rica

86

*CFA = Communaute Financiere Africaine; Comorian = a blend of Swahili and Arabic; Crioulo = a blend of Portuguese and West African

Croatia

Cuba

Cyprus

Czech Republic

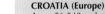

Denmark

Djibouti

Dominica

CONGO (DEMOCRATIC REPUBLIC) (Africa)
Area: 2,345,410 sq km (905,568 sq miles)
Population: 68,692,542
Capital city: Kinshasa
Main languages: Lingala, Swahili, Kikongo, Tshiluba, French, Kingwana
Main religions: Roman Catholic, Protestant, Kimbanguist, Muslim
Government: republic
Currency: 1 Congolese franc = 100 centimes

COSTA RICA (North America)
Area: 51,100 sq km (19,730 sq miles)
Population: 4,253,877
Capital city: San Jose
Main language: Spanish
Main religions: Roman Catholic, Evangelical
Government: democratic republic
Currency: 1 Costa Rican colon = 100 centimos

CROATIA (Europe)
Area: 56,542 sq km (21,831 sq miles)
Population: 4,489,409
Capital city: Zagreb
Main language: Croatian
Main religions: Roman Catholic, Orthodox
Government: republic
Currency: 1 kuna = 100 lipas

CUBA (North America)
Area: 110,860 sq km (42,803 sq miles)
Population: 11,451,652
Capital city: Havana
Main language: Spanish
Main religion: Roman Catholic
Government: communist republic
Currency: 1 Cuban peso = 100 centavos

CYPRUS (Europe)
Area: 9,250 sq km (3,571 sq miles)
Population: 796,740
Capital city: Nicosia
Main languages: Greek, Turkish, English
Main religions: Greek Orthodox, Muslim
Government: republic with a self-proclaimed independent Turkish area
Currency: Greek Cypriot area: 1 euro = 100 cents; Turkish Cypriot area: 1 Turkish lira = 100 kurus

CZECH REPUBLIC (Europe)
Area: 78,866 sq km (30,450 sq miles)
Population: 10,211,904
Capital city: Prague
Main language: Czech
Main religion: Roman Catholic
Government: republic
Currency: 1 koruna = 100 haleru

DENMARK (Europe)
Area: 43,094 sq km (16,639 sq miles)
Population: 5,500,510
Capital city: Copenhagen
Main language: Danish
Main religion: Evangelical Lutheran
Government: constitutional monarchy
Currency: 1 Danish krone = 100 oere

DJIBOUTI (Africa)
Area: 23,000 sq km (8,880 sq miles)
Population: 516,055
Capital city: Djibouti
Main languages: Afar, Somali, Arabic, French
Main religion: Muslim
Government: republic
Currency: 1 Djiboutian franc = 100 centimes

DOMINICA (North America)
Area: 754 sq km (291 sq miles)
Population: 72,660
Capital city: Roseau
Main languages: English, French patois
Main religions: Roman Catholic, Protestant
Government: democratic republic
Currency: 1 East Caribbean dollar = 100 cents

DOMINICAN REPUBLIC (North America)
Area: 48,380 sq km (18,815 sq miles)
Population: 9,650,054
Capital city: Santo Domingo
Main language: Spanish
Main religion: Roman Catholic
Government: democratic republic
Currency: 1 Dominican peso = 100 centavos

EAST TIMOR (TIMOR-LESTE) (Asia)
Area: 15,007 sq km (5,794 sq miles)
Population: 1,131,612
Capital city: Dili
Main languages: Tetun (Tetum), Bahasa Indonesia, Portuguese
Main religions: Roman Catholic, animist
Government: republic
Currency: 1 U.S. dollar = 100 cents

ECUADOR (South America)
Area: 283,560 sq km (109,483 sq miles)
Population: 14,573,101
Capital city: Quito
Main languages: Spanish, Quechua
Main religion: Roman Catholic
Government: republic
Currency: 1 U.S. dollar = 100 cents

EGYPT (Africa)
Area: 1,001,450 sq km (386,662 sq miles)
Population: 83,082,869
Capital city: Cairo
Main language: Arabic
Main religion: Sunni Muslim
Government: republic
Currency: 1 Egyptian pound = 100 piasters

EL SALVADOR (North America)
Area: 21,040 sq km (8,124 sq miles)
Population: 7,185,218
Capital city: San Salvador
Main language: Spanish
Main religion: Roman Catholic
Government: republic
Currency: 1 U.S. dollar = 100 cents

EQUATORIAL GUINEA (Africa)
Area: 28,050 sq km (10,831 sq miles)
Population: 633,441
Capital city: Malabo
Main languages: Fang, Bubi, other Bantu

• **Dominican Republic**

East Timor

• **Ecuador**

Egypt

• **El Salvador**

Equatorial Guinea

Eritrea

CFA = Communaute Financiere Africaine

GAZETTEER OF STATES CONTINUED:

Estonia

languages, Spanish, French, Pidgin English
Main religion: Christian
Government: republic
Currency: 1 CFA* franc = 100 centimes

ERITREA (Africa)
Area: 121,320 sq km (46,842 sq miles)
Population: 5,647,168
Capital city: Asmara
Main languages: Tigrinya, Afar, Arabic
Main religions: Muslim, Coptic Christian,
Roman Catholic, Protestant
Government: republic
Currency: 1 nafka = 100 cents

Ethiopia

ESTONIA (Europe)
Area: 45,226 sq km (17,462 sq miles)
Population: 1,299,371
Capital city: Tallinn
Main languages: Estonian, Russian
Main religions: Evangelical Lutheran,
Russian and Estonian Orthodox, other
Christian
Government: parliamentary democracy
Currency: 1 Estonian kroon = 100 senti

Federated States of Micronesia

ETHIOPIA (Africa)
Area: 1,127,127 sq km (435,186 sq miles)
Population: 85,237,338
Capital city: Addis Ababa
Main languages: Amharic, Tigrinya, Arabic
Main religions: Muslim, Ethiopian
Orthodox, animist
Government: federal republic
Currency: 1 birr = 100 santim

Fiji

FEDERATED STATES OF MICRONESIA
(Australasia/Oceania)
Area: 702 sq km (271 sq miles)
Population: 107,434
Capital city: Palikir
Main languages: Chuuk, Ponapean, English
Main religions: Roman Catholic, Protestant
Government: federal republic
Currency: 1 U.S. dollar = 100 cents

Finland

FIJI (Australasia/Oceania)
Area: 18,270 sq km (7,054 sq miles)
Population: 944,720
Capital city: Suva
Main languages: Fijian, Hindustani, English
Main religions: Christian, Hindu
Government: republic
Currency: 1 Fijian dollar = 100 cents

France

FINLAND (Europe)
Area: 338,145 sq km (130,559 sq miles)
Population: 5,250,275
Capital city: Helsinki
Main language: Finnish, Swedish
Main religion: Evangelical Lutheran
Government: republic
Currency: 1 euro = 100 cents

Gabon

FRANCE (Europe)
Area: 547,030 sq km (211,209 sq miles)
Population: 62,150,775
Capital city: Paris
Main language: French

Main religion: Roman Catholic
Government: republic
Currency: 1 euro = 100 cents

GABON (Africa)
Area: 267,667 sq km (103,347 sq miles)
Population: 1,514,993
Capital city: Libreville
Main languages: Fang, Myene, French
Main religions: Christian, animist
Government: republic
Currency: 1 CFA* franc = 100 centimes

GAMBIA, THE (Africa)
Area: 11,300 sq km (4,363 sq miles)
Population: 1,782,893
Capital city: Banjul
Main languages: Mandinka, Fula, Wolof,
English
Main religion: Muslim
Government: democratic republic
Currency: 1 dalasi = 100 butut

GEORGIA (Asia)
Area: 69,700 sq km (26,911 sq miles)
Population: 4,615,807
Capital city: Tbilisi
Main languages: Georgian, Russian
Main religions: Georgian Orthodox, Muslim,
Russian Orthodox
Government: republic
Currency: 1 lari = 100 tetri

GERMANY (Europe)
Area: 357,021 sq km (137,847 sq miles)
Population: 82,329,758
Capital city: Berlin
Main language: German
Main religions: Protestant, Roman Catholic
Government: federal republic
Currency: 1 euro = 100 cents

GHANA (Africa)
Area: 239,460 sq km (92,456 sq miles)
Population: 23,832,495
Capital city: Accra
Main languages: Twi, Fante, Ga, Hausa,
Dagbani, Ewe, Nzemi, English
Main religions: indigenous, Muslim, Christian
Government: republic
Currency: 1 new cedi = 100 pesewas

GREECE (Europe)
Area: 131,940 sq km (50,942 sq miles)
Population: 10,737,428
Capital city: Athens
Main language: Greek
Main religion: Greek Orthodox
Government: parliamentary republic
Currency: 1 euro = 100 cents

GRENADA (North America)
Area: 344 sq km (133 sq miles)
Population: 90,739
Capital city: Saint George's
Main languages: English, French patois
Main religions: Roman Catholic, Protestant
Government: parliamentary democracy
Currency: 1 East Caribbean dollar = 100 cents

Gambia, The

Georgia

Germany

Ghana

Greece

Grenada

Guatemala

*CFA = Communaute Financiere Africaine

Guinea

Guinea-Bissau

Guyana

Haiti

Honduras

Hungary

Iceland

GUATEMALA (North America)
Area: 108,890 sq km (42,042 sq miles)
Population: 13,276,517
Capital city: Guatemala City
Main languages: Spanish, Amerindian languages including Quiche, Kekchi, Cakchiquel, Mam
Main religions: Roman Catholic, Protestant, indigenous Mayan beliefs
Government: democratic republic
Currency: 1 quetzal = 100 centavos

GUINEA (Africa)
Area: 245,857 sq km (94,925 sq miles)
Population: 10,057,975
Capital city: Conakry
Main languages: Fuuta Jalon, Mallinke, Susu, French
Main religion: Muslim
Government: republic
Currency: 1 Guinean franc = 100 centimes

GUINEA-BISSAU (Africa)
Area: 36,120 sq km (13,946 sq miles)
Population: 1,533,964
Capital city: Bissau
Main languages: Crioulo*, Balante, Pulaar, Mandjak, Mandinka, Portuguese
Main religions: indigenous, Muslim
Government: republic
Currency: 1 CFA* franc = 100 centimes

GUYANA (South America)
Area: 214,970 sq km (83,000 sq miles)
Population: 772,298
Capital city: Georgetown
Main languages: Guyanese Creole, English, Amerindian languages, Caribbean Hindi
Main religions: Christian, Hindu
Government: republic
Currency: 1 Guyanese dollar = 100 cents

HAITI (North America)
Area: 27,750 sq km (10,714 sq miles)
Population: 9,035,536
Capital city: Port-au-Prince
Main languages: Haitian Creole, French
Main religions: Roman Catholic, Protestant, Voodoo
Government: republic
Currency: 1 gourde = 100 centimes

HONDURAS (North America)
Area: 112,090 sq km (43,278 sq miles)
Population: 7,792,854
Capital city: Tegucigalpa
Main language: Spanish
Main religion: Roman Catholic
Government: republic
Currency: 1 lempira = 100 centavos

HUNGARY (Europe)
Area: 93,030 sq km (35,919 sq miles)
Population: 9,905,596
Capital city: Budapest
Main language: Hungarian
Main religions: Roman Catholic, Calvinist
Government: republic
Currency: 1 forint = 100 filler

ICELAND (Europe)
Area: 103,000 sq km (39,769 sq miles)
Population: 306,694
Capital city: Reykjavik
Main language: Icelandic
Main religion: Evangelical Lutheran
Government: constitutional republic
Currency: 1 Icelandic krona = 100 aurar

INDIA (Asia)
Area: 3,287,590 sq km (1,269,345 sq miles)
Population: 1,166,079,217
Capital city: New Delhi
Main languages: Hindi, English, Bengali, Urdu, over 1,600 other languages and dialects
Main religions: Hindu, Muslim
Government: federal republic
Currency: 1 Indian rupee = 100 paise

INDONESIA (Asia)
Area: 1,919,440 sq km (741,100 sq miles)
Population: 240,271,522
Capital city: Jakarta
Main languages: Bahasa Indonesia, English, Dutch, Javanese
Main religion: Muslim
Government: republic
Currency: 1 Indonesian rupiah = 100 sen

IRAN (Asia)
Area: 1,648,000 sq km (636,296 sq miles)
Population: 66,429,284
Capital city: Tehran
Main languages: Farsi and other Persian dialects, Azeri
Main religions: Shi'a Muslim, Sunni Muslim
Government: Islamic republic
Currency: 10 Iranian rials = 1 toman

IRAQ (Asia)
Area: 437,072 sq km (168,754 sq miles)
Population: 28,945,657
Capital city: Baghdad
Main languages: Arabic, Kurdish
Main religion: Muslim
Government: transitional republic
Currency: 1 Iraqi dinar = 1,000 fils

IRELAND (Europe)
Area: 70,280 sq km (27,135 sq miles)
Population: 4,203,200
Capital city: Dublin
Main languages: English, Irish (Gaelic)
Main religion: Roman Catholic
Government: republic
Currency: 1 euro = 100 cents

ISRAEL (Asia)
Area: 20,770 sq km (8,019 sq miles)
Population: 7,233,701
Capital city: Jerusalem
Main languages: Hebrew, Arabic
Main religions: Jewish, Muslim
Government: republic
Currency: 1 Israeli shekel = 100 agorot

ITALY (Europe)
Area: 301,230 sq km (116,306 sq miles)

India

Indonesia

Iran

Iraq

Ireland

Israel

Italy

*CFA = Communaute Financiere Africaine;
Crioulo = a blend of Portuguese and West African

GAZETTEER OF STATES CONTINUED:

Ivory Coast

Population: 58,126,212
Capital city: Rome
Main language: Italian, French, German
Main religion: Roman Catholic
Government: republic
Currency: 1 euro = 100 cents

IVORY COAST (Africa)
Area: 322,460 sq km (124,503 sq miles)
Population: 20,617,068
Capital city: Yamoussoukro
Main languages: Baoule, Dioula, French
Main religions: Christian, Muslim, animist
Government: republic
Currency: 1 CFA* = 100 centimes

Jamaica

JAMAICA (North America)
Area: 10,991 sq km (4,244 sq miles)
Population: 2,825,928
Capital city: Kingston
Main languages: Southwestern Caribbean
Creole, English
Main religion: Protestant
Government: parliamentary democracy
Currency: 1 Jamaican dollar = 100 cents

Japan

JAPAN (Asia)
Area: 377,835 sq km (145,883 sq miles)
Population: 127,078,679
Capital city: Tokyo
Main language: Japanese
Main religions: Shinto, Buddhist
Government: parliamentary monarchy
Currency: 1 yen = 100 sen

Jordan

JORDAN (Asia)
Area: 92,300 sq km (35,637 sq miles)
Population: 6,342,948
Capital city: Amman
Main languages: Arabic, English
Main religion: Sunni Muslim
Government: constitutional monarchy
Currency: 1 Jordanian dinar = 1,000 fils

Kazakhstan

KAZAKHSTAN (Asia)
Area: 2,717,300 sq km (1,049,155 sq miles)
Population: 15,399,437
Capital city: Astana
Main languages: Kazakh, Russian
Main religions: Muslim, Russian Orthodox
Government: republic
Currency: 1 Kazakhstani tenge = 100 tiyn

Kenya

KENYA (Africa)
Area: 582,650 sq km (224,962 sq miles)
Population: 39,002,772
Capital city: Nairobi
Main languages: Swahili, English, Kiswahili,
Bantu languages
Main religions: Christian, indigenous
Government: republic
Currency: 1 Kenyan shilling = 100 cents

Kiribati

KIRIBATI (Australasia/Oceania)
Area: 811 sq km (313 sq miles)
Population: 112,850
Capital city: Bairiki
Main languages: Gilbertese, i-Kiribati, English
Main religions: Roman Catholic, Protestant

Government: republic
Currency: 1 Australian dollar = 100 cents

Kosovo

KOSOVO (Europe)
Area: 10,887 sq km (4 203 sq miles)
Population: 1,804,838
Capital city: Pristina
Main languages: Albanian, Serbian,
Bosnian, Turkish
Main religion: Muslim, Serbian Orthodox,
Roman Catholic
Government: republic
Currency: 1 euro = 100 cents

Kuwait

KUWAIT (Asia)
Area: 17,820 sq km (6,880 sq miles)
Population: 2,691,158
Capital city: Kuwait City
Main languages: Arabic, English
Main religion: Muslim
Government: constitutional monarchy
Currency: 1 Kuwaiti dinar = 1,000 fils

Kyrgyzstan

KYRGYZSTAN (Asia)
Area: 198,500 sq km (76,641 sq miles)
Population: 5,431,747
Capital city: Bishkek
Main languages: Kyrgyz, Russian, Uzbek
Main religions: Muslim, Russian Orthodox
Government: republic
Currency: 1 Kyrgyzstani som = 100 tyiyn

Laos

LAOS (Asia)
Area: 236,800 sq km (91,429 sq miles)
Population: 6,834,942
Capital city: Vientiane
Main languages: Lao, French, English
Main religions: Buddhist, animist
Government: communist republic
Currency: 1 new kip = 100 at

Latvia

LATVIA (Europe)
Area: 64,589 sq km (24,938 sq miles)
Population: 2,231,503
Capital city: Riga
Main languages: Latvian, Russian
Main religions: Lutheran, Roman Catholic,
Russian Orthodox
Government: republic
Currency: 1 Latvian lat = 100 santims

Lebanon

LEBANON (Asia)
Area: 10,400 sq km (4,015 sq miles)
Population: 4,017,095
Capital city: Beirut
Main languages: Arabic, French, English
Main religions: Muslim, Christian
Government: republic
Currency: 1 Lebanese pound = 100 piasters

Lesotho

LESOTHO (Africa)
Area: 30,355 sq km (11,720 sq miles)
Population: 2,130,819
Capital cities: Maseru
Main languages: Sesotho, English, Zulu,
Xhosa
Main religions: Christian, indigenous
Government: constitutional monarchy
Currency: 1 loti = 100 lisente

*CFA = Communaute Financiere Africaine

Liberia

LIBERIA (Africa)
Area: 111,370 sq km (43,000 sq miles)
Population: 3,441,790
Capital city: Monrovia
Main languages: Kpelle, English, Bassa
Main religions: indigenous, Christian, Muslim
Government: republic
Currency: 1 Liberian dollar = 100 cents

LIBYA (Africa)
Area: 1,759,540 sq km (679,362 sq miles)
Population: 6,310,434
Capital city: Tripoli
Main languages: Arabic, Italian, English
Main religion: Sunni Muslim
Government: military rule
Currency: 1 Libyan dinar = 1,000 dirhams

Libya

LIECHTENSTEIN (Europe)
Area: 160 sq km (62 sq miles)
Population: 34,761
Capital city: Vaduz
Main languages: German
Main religion: Roman Catholic
Government: constitutional monarchy
Currency: 1 Swiss franc = 100 centimes

Liechtenstein

LITHUANIA (Europe)
Area: 65,300 sq km (25,212 sq miles)
Population: 3,555,179
Capital city: Vilnius
Main languages: Lithuanian, Polish, Russian
Main religions: Roman Catholic, Lutheran, Russian Orthodox
Government: parliamentary democracy
Currency: 1 Lithuanian litas = 100 centas

Lithuania

LUXEMBOURG (Europe)
Area: 2,586 sq km (998 sq miles)
Population: 491,775
Capital city: Luxembourg
Main languages: Luxemburgish, German, French
Main religion: Roman Catholic
Government: constitutional monarchy
Currency: 1 euro = 100 cents

Luxembourg

MACEDONIA (Europe)
Area: 25,333 sq km (9,781 sq miles)
Population: 2,066,718
Capital city: Skopje
Main languages: Macedonian, Albanian
Main religions: Macedonian Orthodox, Muslim
Government: republic
Currency: 1 Macedonian denar = 100 deni

Macedonia

MADAGASCAR (Africa)
Area: 587,040 sq km (226,657 sq miles)
Population: 20,653,556
Capital city: Antananarivo
Main languages: Malagasy, French, Cotiers
Main religions: indigenous beliefs, Christian
Government: republic
Currency: 1 ariary = 5 irainbilanja

Madagascar

MALAWI (Africa)
Area: 118,480 sq km (45,745 sq miles)
Population: 14,268,711
Capital city: Lilongwe
Main languages: Chichewa, English, Chinyanja
Main religions: Protestant, Roman Catholic, Muslim
Government: republic
Currency: 1 Malawian kwacha = 100 tambala

Malawi

MALAYSIA (Asia)
Area: 329,750 sq km (127,317 sq miles)
Population: 25,715,819
Capital city: Kuala Lumpur
Main languages: Bahasa Melayu, English, Chinese dialects, Tamil
Main religions: Muslim, Buddhist, Daoist
Government: constitutional monarchy
Currency: 1 ringgit = 100 sen

Malaysia

MALDIVES (Asia)
Area: 300 sq km (116 sq miles)
Population: 396,334
Capital city: Male
Main languages: Maldivian, English
Main religion: Sunni Muslim
Government: republic
Currency: 1 rufiyaa = 100 laari

Maldives

MALI (Africa)
Area: 1,240,000 sq km (478,767 sq miles)
Population: 12,666,987
Capital city: Bamako
Main languages: Bambara, Fulani, Songhai, French
Main religion: Muslim
Government: republic
Currency: 1 CFA* franc = 100 centimes

Mali

MALTA (Europe)
Area: 316 sq km (122 sq miles)
Population: 405,165
Capital city: Valletta
Main languages: Maltese, English
Main religion: Roman Catholic
Government: democratic republic
Currency: 1 euro = 100 cents

Malta

MARSHALL ISLANDS (Australasia/Oceania)
Area: 181 sq km (70 sq miles)
Population: 64,522
Capital city: Majuro
Main languages: Marshallese, English
Main religion: Protestant
Government: republic
Currency: 1 U.S. dollar = 100 cents

Marshall Islands

MAURITANIA (Africa)
Area: 1,030,700 sq km (397,955 sq miles)
Population: 3,129,486
Capital city: Nouakchott
Main languages: Arabic, Wolof, French
Main religion: Muslim
Government: miltary rule
Currency: 1 ouguiya = 5 khoums

MAURITIUS (Africa)
Area: 2,040 sq km (788 sq miles)
Population: 1,284,264
Capital city: Port Louis
Main languages: Mauritius Creole French, French, Hindi, Bhojpuri, Urdu, Tamil,

Mauritania

*CFA = Communaute Financiere Africaine

GAZETTEER OF STATES CONTINUED:

Mauritius

English
Main religions: Hindu, Christian, English
Government: parliamentary democracy
Currency: 1 Mauritian rupee = 100 cents

MEXICO (North America)
Nationality: Mexican
Area: 1,972,550 sq km (761,606 sq miles)
Population: 111,211,789
Capital city: Mexico City
Main languages: Spanish, Mayan, Nahuatl
Main religion: Roman Catholic, Protestant
Government: federal republic
Currency: 1 New Mexican peso = 100 centavos

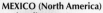

Mexico

MOLDOVA (Europe)
Area: 33,843 sq km (13,067 sq miles)
Population: 4,320,7
Capital city: Chisinau
Main languages: Moldovan, Russian, Gagauz
Main religion: Eastern Orthodox
Government: republic
Currency: 1 Moldovan leu = 100 bani

Moldova

MONACO (Europe)
Area: 1.95 sq km (0.75 sq miles)
Population: 32,965
Capital city: Monaco
Main languages: French, Monegasque, Italian
Main religion: Roman Catholic
Government: constitutional monarchy
Currency: 1 euro = 100 cents

Monaco

MONGOLIA (Asia)
Area: 1,564,116 sq km (603,909 sq miles)
Population: 3,041,142
Capital city: Ulan Bator
Main language: Khalkha Mongol
Main religion: Tibetan Buddist Lamaist
Government: republic
Currency: 1 tugrik = 100 mongos

Mongolia

MONTENEGRO (Europe)
Area: 14,026 sq km (5,415 sq miles)
Population: 672,180
Capital city: Podgorica
Main language: Serbian, Montenegrin
Main religion: Orthodox Christian, Muslim
Government: republic
Currency: 1 euro = 100 cents

Montenegro

MOROCCO (Africa)
Area: 446,550 sq km (172,414 sq miles)
Population: 34,859,364
Capital city: Rabat
Main languages: Arabic, Berber, French
Main religion: Muslim
Government: constitutional monarchy
Currency: 1 Moroccan dirham = 100 centimes

Morocco

MOZAMBIQUE (Africa)
Area: 801,590 sq km (309,496 sq miles)
Population: 21,669,278
Capital city: Maputo
Main languages: Makua, Tsonga, Portuguese, Emskhuwa, Xichangana
Main religions: indigenous, Christian, Muslim
Government: republic
Currency: 1 metical = 100 centavos

NAMIBIA (Africa)
Area: 825,418 sq km (318,696 sq miles)
Population: 2,108,665
Capital city: Windhoek
Main languages: Afrikaans, German, English
Main religions: Christian, indigenous
Government: republic
Currency: 1 Namibian dollar = 100 cents

NAURU (Australasia/Oceania)
Area: 21 sq km (8 sq miles)
Population: 14,019
Capital: Yaren
Main languages: Nauruan, English
Main religion: Christian
Government: republic
Currency: 1 Australian dollar = 100 cents

NEPAL (Asia)
Area: 147,181 sq km (56,827 sq miles)
Population: 28,563,377
Capital city: Kathmandu
Main languages: Nepali, Maithili
Main religions: Hindu, Buddhist
Government: federal republic
Currency: 1 Nepalese rupee = 100 paisa

NETHERLANDS (Europe)
Area: 41,526 sq km (16,033 sq miles)
Population: 16,715,999
Capital cities: Amsterdam, The Hague
Main language: Dutch
Main religion: Protestant, Roman Catholic
Government: constitutional monarchy
Currency: 1 euro = 100 cents

NEW ZEALAND (Australasia/Oceania)
Area: 268,680 sq km (103,738 sq miles)
Population: 4,213,418
Capital city: Wellington
Main languages: English, Maori
Main religion: Christian
Government: parliamentary democracy
Currency: 1 New Zealand dollar = 100 cents

NICARAGUA (North America)
Area: 129,494 sq km (49,998 sq miles)
Population: 5,891,199
Capital city: Managua
Main language: Spanish
Main religion: Roman Catholic, Protestant
Government: republic
Currency: 1 gold cordoba = 100 centavos

NIGER (Africa)
Area: 1,267,000 sq km (489,191 sq miles)
Population: 15,306,252
Capital city: Niamey
Main languages: Hausa, Djerma, French
Main religion: Muslim
Government: republic
Currency: 1 CFA* franc = 100 centimes

NIGERIA (Africa)
Area: 923,768 sq km (356,669 sq miles)
Population: 149,229,090
Capital city: Abuja
Main languages: Hausa, Yoruba, Igbo, English, Fulani

Mozambique

Namibia

Nauru

Nepal

Netherlands

New Zealand

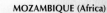

Nicaragua

Niger

Main religions: Muslim, Christian, indigenous
Government: federal republic
Currency: 1 naira = 100 kobo

NORTH KOREA (Asia)
Area: 120,540 sq km (46,541 sq miles)
Population: 22,665,345
Capital city: Pyongyang
Main language: Korean
Main religions: Buddhist, Confucianist
Government: authoritarian socialist
Currency: 1 North Korean won = 100 chon

Nigeria

NORWAY (Europe)
Area: 323,802 sq km (125,021 sq miles)
Population: 4,660,539
Capital city: Oslo
Main language: Norwegian
Main religion: Evangelical Lutheran
Government: constitutional monarchy
Currency: 1 Norwegian krone = 100 oere

North Korea

OMAN (Asia)
Area: 212,460 sq km (82,031 sq miles)
Population: 3,418,085
Capital city: Muscat
Main languages: Arabic, English, Baluchi
Main religion: Muslim
Government: monarchy
Currency: 1 Omani rial = 1,000 baiza

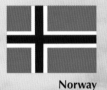

Norway

PAKISTAN (Asia)
Area: 803,940 sq km (310,403 sq miles)
Population: 176,242,949
Capital city: Islamabad
Main languages: Punjabi, Sindhi, Urdu,
English
Main religion: Muslim
Government: federal republic
Currency: 1 Pakistani rupee = 100 paisa

PALAU (Australasia/Oceania)
Area: 458 sq km (177 sq miles)
Population: 20,796
Capital city: Melekeok
Main languages: Palauan, English, Philipino
Main religions: Christian, Modekngei
Government: democratic republic
Currency: 1 U.S. dollar = 100 cents

Oman

PANAMA (North America)
Area: 78,200 sq km (30,193 sq miles)
Population: 3,360,474
Capital city: Panama City
Main languages: Spanish, English
Main religions: Roman Catholic, Protestant
Government: democracy
Currency: 1 balboa = 100 centesimos

Pakistan

PAPUA NEW GUINEA
(Australasia/Oceania)
Area: 462,840 sq km (178,704 sq miles)
Population: 6,057,263
Capital city: Port Moresby
Main languages: Tok Pisin, Hiri Motu,
English
Main religions: Christian, indigenous
Government: parliamentary democracy
Currency: 1 kina = 100 toea

Palau

PARAGUAY (South America)
Area: 406,750 sq km (157,047 sq miles)
Population: 6,995,655
Capital city: Asuncion
Main languages: Guarani, Spanish
Main religion: Roman Catholic
Government: republic
Currency: 1 guarani = 100 centimos

PERU (South America)
Area: 1,285,220 sq km (496,226 sq miles)
Population: 29,546,963
Capital city: Lima
Main languages: Spanish, Quechua, Aymara
Main religion: Roman Catholic
Government: republic
Currency: 1 nuevo sol = 100 centimos

PHILIPPINES (Asia)
Area: 300,000 sq km (115,831 sq miles)
Population: 97,976,603
Capital city: Manila
Main languages: Tagalog, English, Ilocano,
Cebuano
Main religion: Roman Catholic
Government: republic
Currency: 1 Philippine peso = 100 centavos

POLAND (Europe)
Area: 312,679 sq km (120,726 sq miles)
Population: 38,482,919
Capital city: Warsaw
Main language: Polish
Main religion: Roman Catholic
Government: democratic republic
Currency: 1 zloty = 100 groszy

PORTUGAL (Europe)
Area: 92,391 sq km (35,672 sq miles)
Population: 10,707,924
Capital city: Lisbon
Main language: Portuguese
Main religion: Roman Catholic
Government: democratic republic
Currency: 1 euro = 100 cents

QATAR (Asia)
Area: 11,437 sq km (4,416 sq miles)
Population: 833,285
Capital city: Doha
Main languages: Arabic, English
Main religion: Muslim
Government: monarchy
Currency: 1 Qatari riyal = 100 dirhams

ROMANIA (Europe)
Area: 237,500 sq km (91,699 sq miles)
Population: 22,215,421
Capital city: Bucharest
Main languages: Romanian, Hungarian,
German
Main religion: Romanian Orthodox
Government: republic
Currency: 1 leu = 100 bani

RUSSIA (Europe and Asia)
Area: 17,075,200 sq km (6,592,772 sq miles)
Population: 140,041,247
Capital city: Moscow

Panama

Papua
New Guinea

Paraguay

• Peru

Philippines

Poland

Portugal

GAZETTEER OF STATES CONTINUED:

Qatar

Romania

Russia

Rwanda

Saint Kitts and Nevis

Saint Lucia

Saint Vincent and the Grenadines

Main language: Russian
Main religions: Russian Orthodox, Muslim
Government: federal government
Currency: 1 ruble = 100 kopeks

RWANDA (Africa)
Area: 26,338 sq km (10,169 sq miles)
Population: 10,473,282
Capital city: Kigali
Main languages: Kinyarwanda, French, English, Swahili
Main religions: Roman Catholic, Protestant, Adventist
Government: republic
Currency: 1 Rwandan franc = 100 centimes

SAINT KITTS AND NEVIS (North America)
Area: 261 sq km (101 sq miles)
Population: 40,131
Capital city: Basseterre
Main language: English
Main religions: Protestant, Roman Catholic
Government: constitutional monarchy
Currency: 1 East Caribbean dollar = 100 cents

SAINT LUCIA (North America)
Area: 616 sq km (239 sq miles)
Population: 160,267
Capital city: Castries
Main languages: French patois, English
Main religion: Roman Catholic, Protestant
Government: parliamentary democracy
Currency: 1 East Caribbean dollar = 100 cents

SAINT VINCENT AND THE GRENADINES (North America)
Area: 389 sq km (150 sq miles)
Population: 104,574
Capital city: Kingstown
Main languages: English, French patois
Main religions: Protestant, Roman Catholic
Government: parliamentary democracy
Currency: 1 East Caribbean dollar = 100 cents

SAMOA (Australasia/Oceania)
Area: 2,944 sq km (1,137 sq miles)
Population: 217,083
Capital city: Apia
Main languages: Samoan, English
Main religion: Christian
Government: constitutional monarchy
Currency: 1 tala = 100 sene

SAN MARINO (Europe)
Area: 61 sq km (24 sq miles)
Population: 30,324
Capital city: San Marino
Main language: Italian
Main religion: Roman Catholic
Government: republic
Currency: 1 euro = 100 cents

SÃO TOMÉ AND PRINCIPE (Africa)
Area: 1,001 sq km (386 sq miles)
Population: 212,679
Capital city: Sao Tome
Main languages: Crioulo* dialects, Portuguese
Main religion: Christian

Government: republic
Currency: 1 dobra = 100 centimos

SAUDI ARABIA (Asia)
Area: 2,149,690 sq km (830,000 sq miles)
Population: 28,686,633
Capital city: Riyadh
Main language: Arabic
Main religion: Muslim
Government: monarchy
Currency: 1 Saudi riyal = 100 halalah

SENEGAL (Africa)
Area: 196,190 sq km (75,749 sq miles)
Population: 13,711,597
Capital city: Dakar
Main languages: Wolof, French, Pulaar
Main religion: Muslim
Government: democratic republic
Currency: 1 CFA* franc = 100 centimes

SERBIA (Europe)
Area: 77,474 sq km (29,913 sq miles)
Population: 8,354,208
Capital city: Belgrade
Main language: Serbian, Hungarian
Main religion: Serbian Orthodox, Roman Catholic, Muslim
Government: republic
Currency: 1 Serbian dinar = 100 para

SEYCHELLES (Africa)
Area: 455 sq km (176 sq miles)
Population: 87,476
Capital city: Victoria
Main language: Seselwa, English
Main religion: Roman Catholic
Government: republic
Currency: 1 Seychelles rupee = 100 cents

SIERRA LEONE (Africa)
Area: 71,740 sq km (27,699 sq miles)
Population: 6,440,053
Capital city: Freetown
Main languages: Mende, Temne, Krio, English
Main religions: Muslim, indigenous, Christian
Government: republic
Currency: 1 leone = 100 cents

SINGAPORE (Asia)
Area: 693 sq km (267 sq miles)
Population: 4,657,542
Capital city: Singapore
Main languages: Chinese, Malay, English, Tamil
Main religions: Buddhist, Muslim
Government: parliamentary republic
Currency: 1 Singapore dollar = 100 cents

SLOVAKIA (Europe)
Area: 48,845 sq km (18,859 sq miles)
Population: 5,463,046
Capital city: Bratislava
Main languages: Slovak, Hungarian
Main religion: Roman Catholic, Protestant
Government: parliamentary democracy
Currency: 1 euro = 100 cents

Samoa

• San Marino

Sao Tome and Principe

Saudi Arabia

Senegal

• Serbia

Seychelles

*CFA = Communaute Financiere Africaine; Crioulo = a blend of Portuguese and West African

Sierra Leone

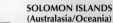
Singapore

Slovakia

Slovenia

Solomon Islands

Somalia

South Africa

SLOVENIA (Europe)
Area: 20,273 sq km (7,827 sq miles)
Population: 2,005,692
Capital city: Ljubljana
Main language: Slovenian
Main religion: Roman Catholic
Government: democratic republic
Currency: 1 euro = 100 cents

SOLOMON ISLANDS
(Australasia/Oceania)
Area: 28,450 sq km (10,985 sq miles)
Population: 595,613
Capital city: Honiara
Main languages: Solomon pidgin, Kwara'ae, To'abaita, English
Main religion: Christian
Government: parliamentary democracy
Currency: 1 Solomon Islands dollar = 100 cents

SOMALIA (Africa)
Area: 637,657 sq km (246,201 sq miles)
Population: 9,832,017
Capital city: Mogadishu
Main languages: Somali, Arabic, Oromo
Main religion: Sunni Muslim
Government: currently has no government
Currency: 1 Somali shilling = 100 cents

SOUTH AFRICA (Africa)
Area: 1,219,912 sq km (471,011 sq miles)
Population: 49,052,489
Capital cities: Pretoria, Cape Town
Main languages: Zulu, Xhosa, Afrikaans, Pedi, English, Tswana, Sotho, Tsonga, Swati, Venda, Ndebele, Isi Zulu, Isi Xhosa
Main religions: Christian, indigenous
Government: republic
Currency: 1 rand = 100 cents

SOUTH KOREA (Asia)
Area: 98,480 sq km (38,023 sq miles)
Population: 48,508,972
Capital city: Seoul
Main language: Korean
Main religions: Christian, Buddhist
Government: republic
Currency: 1 South Korean won = 100 chun

SPAIN (Europe)
Area: 504,750 sq km (194,897 sq miles)
Population: 40,525,002
Capital city: Madrid
Main languages: Castilian Spanish, Catalan
Main religion: Roman Catholic
Government: constitutional monarchy
Currency: 1 euro = 100 cents

SRI LANKA (Asia)
Area: 65,610 sq km (25,332 sq miles)
Population: 21,324,791
Capital cities: Colombo, Sri Jayewardenepura Kotte
Main languages: Sinhala, Tamil, English
Main religions: Buddhist, Hindu, Muslim
Government: republic
Currency: 1 Sri Lankan rupee = 100 cents

SUDAN (Africa)
Area: 2,505,810 sq km (967,499 sq miles)
Population: 40,218,46 41,087,825
Capital city: Khartoum
Main languages: Arabic, English
Main religions: Sunni Muslim, indigenous
Government: Islamic republic
Currency: 1 Sudanese pound = 100 piastres

SURINAME (South America)
Area: 163,270 sq km (63,039 sq miles)
Population: 481,267
Capital city: Paramaribo
Main languages: Sranang Tongo, Dutch, English
Main religions: Hindu, Christian, Muslim
Government: republic
Currency: 1 Surinamese dollar = 100 cents

SWAZILAND (Africa)
Area: 17,363 sq km (6,704 sq miles)
Population: 1,123,913
Capital cities: Mbabane, Lobamba
Main languages: Swati, English
Main religions: Christian, indigenous, Muslim
Government: monarchy
Currency: 1 lilangeni = 100 cents

SWEDEN (Europe)
Area: 449,964 sq km (173,732 sq miles)
Population: 9,059,651
Capital city: Stockholm
Main language: Swedish
Main religion: Lutheran
Government: constitutional monarchy
Currency: 1 Swedish krona = 100 oere

SWITZERLAND (Europe)
Area: 41,290 sq km (15,942 sq miles)
Population: 7,604,467
Capital city: Bern
Main languages: German, French, Italian
Main religions: Roman Catholic, Protestant
Government: federal republic
Currency: 1 Swiss franc, franken or frano = 100 centimes, rappen or centesimi

SYRIA (Asia)
Area: 185,180 sq km (71,498 sq miles)
Population: 20,178,485
Capital city: Damascus
Main languages: Arabic, Kurdish
Main religions: Muslim, Christian
Government: republic under military regime
Currency: 1 Syrian pound = 100 piastres

TAJIKISTAN (Asia)
Area: 143,100 sq km (55,251 sq miles)
Population: 7,349,145
Capital city: Dushanbe
Main languages: Tajik, Russian
Main religion: Sunni Muslim
Government: republic
Currency: 1 somoni = 100 dirams

TANZANIA (Africa)
Area: 945,087 sq km (364,900 sq miles)
Population: 41,048,532
Capital cities: Dar es Salaam, Dodoma
Main languages: Swahili, English, Sukuma

South Korea

Spain

Sri Lanka

Sudan

Suriname

Swaziland

Sweden

GAZETTEER OF STATES CONTINUED:

Switzerland

Main religions: Christian, Muslim, indigenous
Government: republic
Currency: 1 Tanzanian shilling = 100 cents

THAILAND (Asia)
Area: 514,000 sq km (198,457 sq miles)
Population: 65,905,410
Capital city: Bangkok
Main languages: Thai, English, Chaochow
Main religion: Buddhist
Government: constitutional monarchy
Currency: 1 baht = 100 satang

Syria

TOGO (Africa)
Area: 56,785 sq km (21,925 sq miles)
Population: 6,019,877
Capital city: Lome
Main languages: Mina, Ewe, Kabye, French
Main religions: indigenous, Christian, Muslim
Government: republic
Currency: 1 CFA* franc = 100 centimes

TONGA (Australasia/Oceania)
Area: 748 sq km (289 sq miles)
Population: 120,898
Capital city: Nukualofa
Main languages: Tongan, English
Main religion: Christian
Government: constitutional monarchy
Currency: 1 pa'anga = 100 seniti

Tajikistan

TRINIDAD AND TOBAGO (North America)
Area: 5,128 sq km (1,980 sq miles)
Population: 1,229,953
Capital city: Port-of-Spain
Main languages: English, French, Spanish, Hindi
Main religions: Christian, Hindu
Government: parliamentary democracy
Currency: 1 Trinidad and Tobago dollar = 100 cents

Tanzania

TUNISIA (Africa)
Area: 163,610 sq km (63,170 sq miles)
Population: 10,486,339
Capital city: Tunis
Main languages: Arabic, French
Main religion: Muslim
Government: republic
Currency: 1 Tunisian dinar = 1,000 millimes

TURKEY (Europe and Asia)
Area: 780,580 sq km (301,384 sq miles)
Population: 76,805,524
Capital city: Ankara
Main language: Turkish
Main religion: Muslim
Government: democratic republic
Currency: 1 Turkish lira = 100 kurus

Thailand

TURKMENISTAN (Asia)
Area: 488,100 sq km (188,456 sq miles)
Population: 4,884,887
Capital city: Ashgabat (Ashkhabad)
Main languages: Turkmen, Russian
Main religion: Muslim
Government: republic
Currency: 1 Turkmen manat = 100 tenesi

Togo

TUVALU (Australasia/Oceania)
Area: 26 sq km (10 sq miles)
Population: 12,373
Capital city: Funafuti
Main languages: Tuvaluan, English
Main religion: Congregationalist
Government: constitutional monarchy
Currency: 1 Tuvaluan dollar or 1 Australian dollar = 100 cents

UGANDA (Africa)
Area: 236,040 sq km (91,135 sq miles)
Population: 32,369,558
Capital city: Kampala
Main languages: Luganda, English, Swahili
Main religion: Christian, Muslim, indigenous
Government: republic
Currency: 1 Ugandan shilling = 100 cents

UKRAINE (Europe)
Area: 603,700 sq km (233,090 sq miles)
Population: 45,700,395
Capital city: Kiev
Main languages: Ukrainian, Russian
Main religion: Ukrainain Orthodox
Government: republic
Currency: 1 hryvnia = 100 kopiykas

UNITED ARAB EMIRATES (Asia)
Area: 83,600 sq km (32,278 sq miles)
Population: 4,798,491
Capital city: Abu Dhabi
Main languages: Arabic, English
Main religion: Muslim
Government: federation
Currency: 1 Emirati dirham = 100 fils

UNITED KINGDOM (Europe)
Area: 244,820 sq km (94,526 sq miles)
Population: 61,113,205
Capital city: London
Main language: English
Main religions: Anglican, Roman Catholic
Government: constitutional monarchy
Currency: 1 British pound = 100 pence

UNITED STATES OF AMERICA (North America)
Area: 9,826,630 sq km (3,794,083 sq miles)
Population: 307,212,123
Capital city: Washington D.C.
Main language: English
Main religions: Protestant, Roman Catholic
Government: federal republic
Currency: 1 U.S. dollar = 100 cents

URUGUAY (South America)
Area: 176,220 sq km (68,039 sq miles)
Population: 3,494,382
Capital city: Montevideo
Main language: Spanish
Main religion: Roman Catholic
Government: republic
Currency: 1 Uruguayan peso = 100 centesimos

UZBEKISTAN (Asia)
Area: 447,400 sq km (172,742 sq miles)
Population: 27,606,007

Tonga

Trinidad and Tobago

Tunisia

Turkey

Turkmenistan

Tuvalu

Uganda

Ukraine

Capital city: Tashkent
Main languages: Uzbek, Russian
Main religions: Muslim, Eastern Orthodox
Government: republic
Currency: 1 Uzbekistani sum = 100 tyyn

VANUATU (Australasia/Oceania)
Area: 12,200 sq km (4,710 sq miles)
Population: 218,519
Capital city: Port-Vila
Main languages: Bislama, French, English
Main religion: Christian
Government: republic
Currency: 1 vatu = 100 centimes

United Arab Emirates

VATICAN CITY (Europe)
Area: 0.44 sq km (0.17 sq miles)
Population: 826
Capital city: Vatican City
Main languages: Italian, Latin
Main religion: Roman Catholic
Government: led by the Pope
Currency: 1 euro = 100 cents

VENEZUELA (South America)
Area: 912,050 sq km (352,144 sq miles)
Population: 26,814,843
Capital city: Caracas
Main language: Spanish
Main religion: Roman Catholic
Government: federal republic
Currency: 1 bolivar = 100 centimos

United Kingdom

VIETNAM (Asia)
Area: 329,560 sq km (127,244 sq miles)

United States of America

Population: 86,967,524
Capital city: Hanoi
Main languages: Vietnamese, French, English, Khmer, Chinese
Main religion: Buddhist
Government: communist state
Currency: 1 new dong = 100 xu

YEMEN (Asia)
Area: 527,970 sq km (203,850 sq miles)
Population: 23,822,783
Capital city: Sana
Main language: Arabic
Main religion: Muslim
Government: republic
Currency: 1 Yemeni rial = 100 fils

ZAMBIA (Africa)
Area: 752,614 sq km (290,586 sq miles)
Population: 11,862,740
Capital city: Lusaka
Main languages: Bemba, Tonga, Nyanja, English, Kaonda, Lozi, Lunda, Luvale
Main religions: Christian, Muslim, Hindu
Government: republic
Currency: 1 Zambian kwacha = 100 ngwee

ZIMBABWE (Africa)
Area: 390,580 sq km (150,804 sq miles)
Population: 11,392,629
Capital city: Harare
Main languages: Shona, Ndebele, English
Main religions: Christian, indigenous
Government: republic
Currency: 1 Zimbabwean dollar = 100 cents

Vatican City

Venezuela

Vietnam

Yemen

Uruguay

Uzbekistan

Vanuatu

The United Nations

The United Nations (U.N.) is an organization which aims to bring countries together to work for peace and development. Of the world's 194 states, 192 are members of the U.N. Those that don't belong are Kosovo and the Vatican City.

Ban Ki-moon, the Secretary-General of the U.N., shakes hands with Hillary Clinton, the Secretary of State of the U.S.A.

Internet links

For links to websites with flags, facts, maps, quizzes, and more information about the U.N., go to **www.usborne-quicklinks.com**

Zambia

Zimbabwe

MAP INDEX

This is an index of the places and features named on the maps. Each entry consists of the following parts: the name (given in bold type), the country or region within which it is located (given in italics), the page on which the name can be found (given in bold type), and the grid reference (also given in bold type). For some names, there is also a description explaining what kind of place it is – for example a country, internal administrative area (state or province), national capital or internal capital. To find a place on a map, first find the map indicated by the page reference. Then use the grid reference to find the square containing the name or town symbol. See page 7 for help with using the grid.

Brisbane, *Australia, internal capital,* 41 K5
Bristol, *United Kingdom,* 62 D4
Bristol Bay, *U.S.A.,* 24 C3
British Columbia, *Canada, internal admin. area,* 24 G3
Brno, *Czech Republic,* 64 F1
Broken Hill, *Australia,* 40 H6
Brokopondo, *Suriname,* 33 G2
Brooks Range, *U.S.A.,* 24 D2
Brownsville, *U.S.A.,* 26 G5
Bruges, *Belgium,* 62 E4
Brunei, *Asia, country,* 44 D3
Brussels, *Belgium, national capital,* 62 F4
Bryansk, *Russia,* 58 C3
Bucaramanga, *Colombia,* 32 D2
Bucharest, *Romania, national capital,* 65 H2
Budapest, *Hungary, national capital,* 61 F7
Buenaventura, *Colombia,* 32 C3
Buenos Aires, *Argentina, national capital,* 34 G6
Buenos Aires, Lake, *South America,* 35 D9
Buffalo, *U.S.A.,* 27 L2
Buga, *Colombia,* 32 C3
Buinsk, *Russia,* 59 F3
Bujumbura, *Burundi, national capital,* 72 E4
Bukavu, *Democratic Republic of Congo,* 72 E4
Bulawayo, *Zimbabwe,* 74 E4
Bulgan, *Mongolia,* 48 F1
Bulgaria, *Europe, country,* 65 H3
Bunbury, *Australia,* 40 C6
Bundaberg, *Australia,* 41 K4
Buon Me Thuot, *Vietnam,* 46 E5
Buraydah, *Saudi Arabia,* 53 D6
Burgas, *Bulgaria,* 65 H3
Burgos, *Spain,* 63 D6
Burkina Faso, *Africa, country,* 71 E6
Burma, *Asia, country,* 46 C3
Bursa, *Turkey,* 65 J3
Buru, *Indonesia,* 45 G4
Burundi, *Africa, country,* 72 E4
Bushehr, *Iran,* 53 F6
Buta, *Democratic Republic of Congo,* 72 D3
Butare, *Rwanda,* 72 E4
Butembo, *Democratic Republic of Congo,* 72 E3
Buton, *Indonesia,* 45 F4
Butuan, *Philippines,* 47 J6
Buxoro, *Uzbekistan,* 50 A3
Buzau, *Romania,* 65 H2
Buzuluk, *Russia,* 59 G3
Bydgoszcz, *Poland,* 61 F5

C
Cabanatuan, *Philippines,* 47 H4
Cabinda, *Angola, enclave,* 72 B5
Cabonga Reservoir, *Canada,* 27 L1
Cabora Bassa Reservoir, *Mozambique,* 74 F3
Caceres, *Brazil,* 34 G3
Caceres, *Colombia,* 32 C2
Caceres, *Spain,* 63 C7
Cachoeiro de Itapemirim, *Brazil,* 34 K4
Cadiz, *Spain,* 63 C7
Cadiz, Gulf of, *Europe,* 63 C7
Caen, *France,* 62 D4
Cagayan de Oro, *Philippines,* 47 H6
Cagliari, *Italy,* 64 D4
Caicara, *Venezuela,* 32 E2
Cairns, *Australia,* 40 J3
Cairo, *Egypt, national capital,* 69 H3
Caiundo, *Angola,* 74 C3
Cajamarca, *Peru,* 32 C5
Calabar, *Nigeria,* 72 A2
Calais, *France,* 62 E4
Calama, *Chile,* 34 E4
Calamian Group, *Philippines,* 47 G5
Calapan, *Philippines,* 47 H5
Calbayog, *Philippines,* 47 H5
Calcutta, *India,* 51 F6
Calgary, *Canada,* 24 H3

Cali, *Colombia,* 32 C3
Calicut, *India,* 51 D8
California, *U.S.A., internal admin. area,* 26 C3
California, Gulf of, *Mexico,* 28 B2
Camaguey, *Cuba,* 29 J3
Cambodia, *Asia, country,* 46 E5
Cambridge, *United Kingdom,* 62 E3
Cameroon, *Africa, country,* 72 B2
Cameroon Mountain, *Cameroon,* 72 A3
Cameta, *Brazil,* 33 J4
Camiri, *Bolivia,* 34 F4
Campeche, *Mexico,* 28 F4
Campeche, Bay of, *Mexico,* 28 F3
Campina Grande, *Brazil,* 33 L5
Campinas, *Brazil,* 34 J4
Campo Grande, *Brazil,* 34 H4
Campos, *Brazil,* 34 K4
Canada, *North America, country,* 24 J3
Canadian, *U.S.A.,* 26 F3
Canakkale, *Turkey,* 65 H3
Canary Islands, *Atlantic Ocean,* 70 B3
Canaveral, Cape, *U.S.A.,* 27 K5
Canberra, *Australia, national capital,* 41 J7
Cancun, *Mexico,* 29 G3
Cangombe, *Angola,* 74 D2
Cannes, *France,* 63 F6
Can Tho, *Vietnam,* 46 E5
Cantabrian Mountains, *Spain,* 63 C6
Canton, *China,* 49 H6
Cape Coast, *Ghana,* 71 E7
Cape Town, *South Africa, national capital,* 74 C6
Cape Verde, *Atlantic Ocean, country,* 71 L11
Cape York Peninsula, *Australia,* 40 H2
Cap-Haitien, *Haiti,* 29 K4
Caprivi Strip, *Namibia,* 74 D3
Caracas, *Venezuela, national capital,* 32 E1
Cardiff, *United Kingdom, internal capital,* 62 D4
Caribbean Sea, *North/South America,* 29 J4
Carlisle, *United Kingdom,* 62 D3
Carnarvon, *Australia,* 40 B4
Carnarvon, *South Africa,* 74 D6
Carnot, Cape, *Australia,* 40 G7
Caroline Islands, *Federated States of Micronesia,* 38 B4
Carpathian Mountains, *Europe,* 61 H7
Carpentaria, Gulf of, *Australia,* 40 G2
Carson City, *U.S.A., internal capital,* 26 C3
Cartagena, *Colombia,* 32 C1
Cartagena, *Spain,* 63 D7
Carthage, *Tunisia,* 68 D1
Cartwright, *Canada,* 25 P3
Caruaru, *Brazil,* 33 L5
Casablanca, *Morocco,* 70 D2
Cascade Range, *U.S.A.,* 26 B2
Cascais, *Portugal,* 63 B7
Cascavel, *Brazil,* 34 H4
Casper, *U.S.A.,* 26 E2
Caspian Depression, *Asia,* 52 F2
Caspian Sea, *Asia,* 59 G4
Castellon de la Plana, *Spain,* 63 D7
Castelo Branco, *Portugal,* 63 C7
Castries, *St. Lucia, national capital,* 28 M5
Catamarca, *Argentina,* 34 E5
Catania, *Italy,* 64 F4
Catanzaro, *Italy,* 64 F4
Cat Island, *The Bahamas,* 27 L6
Caucasus Mountains, *Asia/Europe,* 52 D3
Caxias do Sul, *Brazil,* 34 H5
Cayenne, *French Guiana, national capital,* 33 H3
Cayman Islands, *North America,* 29 H4
Cebu, *Philippines,* 47 H5
Cedar Lake, *Canada,* 24 J3
Cedar Rapids, *U.S.A.,* 27 H2
Cedros Island, *Mexico,* 28 A2
Ceduna, *Australia,* 40 F6
Celaya, *Mexico,* 28 D3
Celebes, *Indonesia,* 45 F4

Celebes Sea, *Asia,* 47 H7
Celtic Sea, *Europe,* 62 C4
Central African Republic, *Africa, country,* 72 C2
Central Cordillera, *Peru,* 32 C5
Central Russian Uplands, *Russia,* 58 D3
Central Siberian Plateau, *Russia,* 55 F2
Central Sierras, *Spain,* 63 D6
Ceram, *Indonesia,* 45 G4
Ceram Sea, *Indonesia,* 45 G4
Cerro de Pasco, *Peru,* 32 C6
Cesis, *Latvia,* 61 H4
Ceske Budejovice, *Czech Republic,* 64 E1
Ceuta, *Africa,* 63 C8
Chacabuco, *Argentina,* 34 F6
Chad, *Africa, country,* 68 E5
Chad, Lake, *Africa,* 68 D6
Chala, *Peru,* 32 D7
Chalan Kanoa, *Northern Marianas,* 38 B3
Chalkida, *Greece,* 65 G4
Challapata, *Bolivia,* 34 E3
Chalon-sur-Saone, *France,* 63 F5
Chanaral, *Chile,* 34 D5
Chandigarh, *India,* 50 D4
Chandrapur, *India,* 51 D7
Changchun, *China,* 49 L2
Changde, *China,* 48 H5
Changhua, *China,* 49 K6
Chang Jiang, *China,* 49 J4
Changsha, *China,* 49 H5
Changzhi, *China,* 49 H3
Chania, *Greece,* 65 G5
Channel Islands, *Europe,* 62 D4
Channel Islands, *U.S.A.,* 26 C4
Chapaev, *Kazakhstan,* 59 G3
Charagua, *Bolivia,* 34 F3
Charleroi, *Belgium,* 62 F4
Charleston, *South Carolina, U.S.A.,* 27 L4
Charleston, *West Virginia, U.S.A., internal capital,* 27 K3
Charlotte, *U.S.A.,* 27 K3
Charlottesville, *U.S.A.,* 27 L3
Charlottetown, *Canada, internal capital,* 25 N4
Chatham Islands, *New Zealand,* 41 R8
Chattanooga, *U.S.A.,* 27 J3
Chavuma, *Zambia,* 74 D2
Cheboksary, *Russia,* 59 F2
Chech Erg, *Africa,* 70 E3
Cheju, *South Korea,* 49 L4
Chelyabinsk, *Russia,* 59 J2
Chemnitz, *Germany,* 62 H4
Chengdu, *China,* 48 F4
Chennai, *India,* 51 E8
Chenzhou, *China,* 49 H5
Cherbourg, *France,* 62 D4
Cherepovets, *Russia,* 58 D2
Cherkasy, *Ukraine,* 58 C4
Chernihiv, *Ukraine,* 58 C3
Chernivtsi, *Ukraine,* 61 H6
Chesterfield Islands, *New Caledonia,* 41 M3
Cheyenne, *U.S.A., internal capital,* 26 F2
Chiang Mai, *Thailand,* 46 C4
Chicago, *U.S.A.,* 27 J2
Chiclayo, *Peru,* 32 C5
Chico, *U.S.A.,* 26 B3
Chicoutimi, *Canada,* 25 M4
Chidley, Cape, *Canada,* 25 N2
Chifeng, *China,* 49 J2
Chigubo, *Mozambique,* 75 F4
Chihli, Gulf of, *China,* 49 J3
Chihuahua, *Mexico,* 28 C2
Chile, *South America, country,* 34 D6
Chillan, *Chile,* 35 D7
Chiloe Island, *Chile,* 35 C8
Chilung, *China,* 49 K5
Chilwa, Lake, *Africa,* 75 G3
Chimanimani, *Zimbabwe,* 75 F3
Chimbote, *Peru,* 32 C5
China, *Asia, country,* 48 E3
Chincha Alta, *Peru,* 32 C6
Chingola, *Zambia,* 74 E2
Chinhoyi, *Zimbabwe,* 74 F3
Chios, *Greece,* 65 H4
Chipata, *Zambia,* 75 F2

Chiredzi, *Zimbabwe,* 74 F4
Chisinau, *Moldova, national capital,* 61 J2
Chittagong, *Bangladesh,* 51 G6
Chongjin, *North Korea,* 49 L2
Chongju, *South Korea,* 49 L3
Chongqing, *China,* 48 G5
Chonos Archipelago, *Chile,* 35 C8
Chott el Jerid, *Tunisia,* 68 C2
Christchurch, *New Zealand,* 41 P8
Christmas Island, *Asia,* 44 C6
Chukchi Sea, *Arctic Ocean,* 77 B2
Chulucanas, *Peru,* 32 B5
Chumphon, *Thailand,* 46 C5
Churchill, *Canada,* 25 K3
Churchill Falls, *Canada,* 25 N3
Cienfuegos, *Cuba,* 29 H3
Cilacap, *Indonesia,* 44 C5
Cincinnati, *U.S.A.,* 27 K3
Ciudad Bolivar, *Venezuela,* 32 F2
Ciudad del Carmen, *Mexico,* 28 F4
Ciudad del Este, *Paraguay,* 34 H5
Ciudad Guayana, *Venezuela,* 32 F2
Ciudad Juarez, *Mexico,* 28 C1
Ciudad Obregon, *Mexico,* 28 C2
Ciudad Real, *Spain,* 63 D7
Ciudad Victoria, *Mexico,* 28 E3
Clark Hill Lake, *U.S.A.,* 27 K4
Clermont-Ferrand, *France,* 63 E5
Cleveland, *U.S.A.,* 27 K2
Cluj-Napoca, *Romania,* 65 G2
Coast Mountains, *Canada,* 24 F3
Coast Ranges, *U.S.A.,* 26 B2
Coats Land, *Antarctica,* 79 A3
Coatzacoalcos, *Mexico,* 28 F4
Cobija, *Bolivia,* 34 E2
Cochabamba, *Bolivia,* 34 E3
Cochin, *India,* 51 D9
Cocos Island, *Costa Rica,* 29 G6
Cod, Cape, *U.S.A.,* 27 N2
Coeur d'Alene, *U.S.A.,* 26 C1
Coiba Island, *Panama,* 29 H6
Coihaique, *Chile,* 35 D9
Coimbatore, *India,* 51 D8
Coimbra, *Portugal,* 63 B6
Colima, *Mexico,* 28 D4
Cologne, *Germany,* 62 F4
Colombia, *South America, country,* 32 D3
Colombo, *Sri Lanka, national capital,* 51 D9
Colon, *Panama,* 29 J6
Colorado, *Argentina,* 35 F7
Colorado, *U.S.A.,* 26 D4
Colorado, *U.S.A., internal admin. area,* 26 E3
Colorado Plateau, *U.S.A.,* 26 D3
Colorado Springs, *U.S.A.,* 26 F3
Columbia, *U.S.A.,* 26 C1
Columbia, *U.S.A., internal capital,* 27 K4
Columbine, Cape, *South Africa,* 74 C6
Columbus, *U.S.A., internal capital,* 27 K3
Colwyn Bay, *United Kingdom,* 62 D3
Communism Peak, *Tajikistan,* 50 C3
Como, Lake, *Italy,* 64 D2
Comodoro Rivadavia, *Argentina,* 35 E9
Comoros, *Africa, country,* 75 H2
Conakry, *Guinea, national capital,* 71 C7
Concepcion, *Bolivia,* 34 F3
Concepcion, *Chile,* 35 D7
Concepcion, *Paraguay,* 34 G4
Concord, *U.S.A., internal capital,* 27 M2
Concordia, *Argentina,* 34 G6
Congo, *Africa,* 72 C4
Congo, *Africa, country,* 72 C4
Congo, Democratic Republic of, *Africa, country,* 72 D4
Connecticut, *U.S.A., internal admin. area,* 27 M2
Con Son, *Vietnam,* 46 E6
Constanta, *Romania,* 65 J2
Constantine, *Algeria,* 70 G1
Cook Islands, *Oceania,* 38 G7
Cook, Mount, *New Zealand,* 41 P8
Cook Strait, *New Zealand,* 41 P8
Copenhagen, *Denmark, national capital,* 61 E5
Copiapo, *Chile,* 34 D5

Himalayas, *Asia*, 50 E4
Hindu Kush, *Asia*, 50 B3
Hinton, *Canada*, 24 H3
Hiroshima, *Japan*, 49 M4
Hispaniola, *North America*, 29 K4
Hitra, *Norway*, 60 D3
Hobart, *Australia, internal capital*, 40 J8
Ho Chi Minh City, *Vietnam*, 46 E5
Hohhot, *China*, 48 H2
Hokkaido, *Japan*, 49 P2
Holguin, *Cuba*, 29 J3
Homs, *Syria*, 52 C5
Homyel, *Belarus*, 61 J5
Honduras, *North America, country*, 29 G4
Honduras, Gulf of, *North America*, 29 G4
Honefoss, *Norway*, 60 D3
Hong Kong, *China*, 49 H6
Honiara, *Solomon Islands, national capital*, 38 D5
Honolulu, *U.S.A., internal capital*, 27 P7
Honshu, *Japan*, 49 N3
Horlivka, *Ukraine*, 58 D4
Hormuz, Strait of, *Asia*, 53 G6
Horn, Cape, *Chile*, 35 D11
Horn Lake, *Sweden*, 60 F2
Hotan, *China*, 50 D4
Hotazel, *South Africa*, 74 D5
Houston, *U.S.A.*, 27 G5
Hradec Kralove, *Czech Republic*, 64 E1
Hrodna, *Belarus*, 61 G5
Huacrachuco, *Peru*, 32 C5
Huaihua, *China*, 48 H6
Huambo, *Angola*, 74 C2
Huancayo, *Peru*, 32 C6
Huang He, *China*, 49 H3
Huanuco, *Peru*, 32 C5
Huascaran, Mount, *Peru*, 32 C5
Hubli, *India*, 51 D7
Hudiksvall, *Sweden*, 60 F3
Hudson Bay, *Canada*, 25 L3
Hudson Strait, *Canada*, 25 M2
Hue, *Vietnam*, 46 E4
Huelva, *Spain*, 63 C7
Hull, *United Kingdom*, 62 D3
Hulun Lake, *China*, 49 J1
Hungary, *Europe, country*, 61 F7
Huntsville, *Canada*, 25 M4
Huntsville, *U.S.A.*, 27 J4
Huron, Lake, *U.S.A.*, 27 K2
Hurghada, *Egypt*, 69 H3
Hvannadalshnukur, *Iceland*, 60 P2
Hwange, *Zimbabwe*, 74 E3
Hyderabad, *India*, 51 D7
Hyderabad, *Pakistan*, 50 B5
Hyesan, *North Korea*, 49 L2

i

Iasi, *Romania*, 65 H2
Ibadan, *Nigeria*, 71 F7
Ibague, *Colombia*, 32 C3
Ibarra, *Ecuador*, 32 C3
Ibb, *Yemen*, 53 D9
Iberian Mountains, *Spain*, 63 D6
Ibiza, *Spain*, 63 E7
Ica, *Peru*, 32 C6
Iceland, *Europe, country*, 60 P2
Idaho, *U.S.A., internal admin. area*, 26 C2
Idaho Falls, *U.S.A.*, 26 D2
Ierapetra, *Greece*, 65 H5
Iguacu Falls, *South America*, 34 H5
Ihosy, *Madagascar*, 75 J4
Ikopa, *Madagascar*, 75 J3
Ilagan, *Philippines*, 47 H4
Ilebo, *Democratic Republic of Congo*, 72 D4
Ilheus, *Brazil*, 34 L2
Iliamna Lake, *U.S.A.*, 24 D2
Iligan, *Philippines*, 47 H6
Illapel, *Chile*, 34 D6
Illimani, Mount, *Bolivia*, 34 E3
Illinois, *U.S.A., internal admin. area*, 27 J2
Illizi, *Algeria*, 70 G3
Ilmen, Lake, *Russia*, 60 J4
Iloilo, *Philippines*, 47 H5
Ilonga, *Tanzania*, 73 G5
Ilorin, *Nigeria*, 71 F7

Imperatriz, *Brazil*, 33 J5
Imphal, *India*, 51 G6
Inari, Lake, *Finland*, 60 H1
Inchon, *South Korea*, 49 L3
Indals, *Sweden*, 60 E3
Inderbor, *Kazakhstan*, 59 G4
India, *Asia, country*, 51 D6
Indiana, *U.S.A., internal admin. area*, 27 J2
Indianapolis, *U.S.A., internal capital*, 27 J3
Indian Ocean, 21
Indonesia, *Asia, country*, 44 C5
Indore, *India*, 51 D6
Indus, *Asia*, 50 B5
Ingolstadt, *Germany*, 62 G4
Inhambane, *Mozambique*, 75 G4
Inner Mongolia, *China*, 49 H2
Innsbruck, *Austria*, 64 D2
Inukjuak, *Canada*, 25 M3
Inuvik, *Canada*, 24 F2
Invercargill, *New Zealand*, 41 N9
Inyangani, *Zimbabwe*, 75 F3
Ioannina, *Greece*, 65 G4
Ionian Sea, *Europe*, 65 F4
Iowa, *U.S.A., internal admin. area*, 27 H2
Ipiales, *Colombia*, 32 C3
Ipoh, *Malaysia*, 44 B3
Ipswich, *United Kingdom*, 62 E3
Iqaluit, *Canada, internal capital*, 25 N2
Iquique, *Chile*, 34 D4
Iquitos, *Peru*, 32 D4
Irakleio, *Greece*, 65 H5
Iran, *Asia, country*, 52 F5
Iranshahr, *Iran*, 53 H6
Iraq, *Asia, country*, 52 D5
Irbid, *Jordan*, 52 C5
Ireland, *Europe, country*, 62 B3
Iringa, *Tanzania*, 73 G5
Irish Sea, *Europe*, 62 C3
Irkutsk, *Russia*, 55 F3
Irrawaddy, *Burma*, 46 C4
Irrawaddy, Mouths of the, *Burma*, 46 B4
Irtysh, *Asia*, 54 D3
Isabela, *Ecuador*, 32 N10
Isafjordhur, *Iceland*, 60 N2
Isiro, *Democratic Republic of Congo*, 72 E3
Islamabad, *Pakistan, national capital*, 50 C4
Isle of Man, *Europe*, 62 C3
Isle of Wight, *United Kingdom*, 62 D4
Ismailia, *Egypt*, 69 H2
Isoka, *Zambia*, 75 F2
Isparta, *Turkey*, 65 J4
Israel, *Asia, country*, 53 B5
Issyk, Lake, *Kyrgyzstan*, 50 D2
Istanbul, *Turkey*, 65 J3
Itaituba, *Brazil*, 33 G4
Itajai, *Brazil*, 34 J5
Italy, *Europe, country*, 64 D2
Itapetininga, *Brazil*, 34 J4
Ivano-Frankivsk, *Ukraine*, 61 H6
Ivanovo, *Russia*, 58 E2
Ivdel, *Russia*, 59 J1
Ivory Coast, *Africa, country*, 71 D7
Ivujivik, *Canada*, 25 M2
Izhevsk, *Russia*, 59 G2
Izmir, *Turkey*, 65 H4

j

Jabalpur, *India*, 51 D6
Jackson, *Mississippi, U.S.A., internal capital*, 27 H4
Jackson, *Tennessee, U.S.A.*, 27 J3
Jacksonville, *U.S.A.*, 27 K4
Jaen, *Spain*, 63 D7
Jaffna, *Sri Lanka*, 51 E9
Jaipur, *India*, 50 D5
Jakarta, *Indonesia, national capital*, 44 C5
Jalalabad, *Afghanistan*, 50 C4
Jalal-Abad, *Kyrgyzstan*, 50 C2
Jamaica, *North America, country*, 29 J4
Jambi, *Indonesia*, 44 B4
James Bay, *Canada*, 25 L3
Jamestown, *U.S.A.*, 27 L2

Jammu, *India*, 50 C4
Jammu and Kashmir, *Asia*, 50 D4
Jamnagar, *India*, 51 C6
Jamshedpur, *India*, 51 F6
Japan, *Asia, country*, 49 N3
Japan, Sea of, *Asia*, 49 M2
Japura, *Brazil*, 32 E4
Jatai, *Brazil*, 34 H3
Java, *Indonesia*, 44 C5
Java Sea, *Indonesia*, 44 C5
Jayapura, *Indonesia*, 45 K4
Jedda, *Saudi Arabia*, 53 C7
Jefferson City, *U.S.A., internal capital*, 27 H3
Jekabpils, *Latvia*, 61 H4
Jelgava, *Latvia*, 61 G4
Jember, *Indonesia*, 44 D5
Jerba, *Tunisia*, 68 D2
Jerez de la Frontera, *Spain*, 63 C7
Jerusalem, *Israel, national capital*, 53 C5
Jhansi, *India*, 50 D5
Jiamusi, *China*, 49 M1
Jilin, *China*, 49 L2
Jima, *Ethiopia*, 73 G2
Jinhua, *China*, 49 J5
Jining, *China*, 49 J3
Jinja, *Uganda*, 73 F3
Jinzhou, *China*, 49 K2
Jixi, *China*, 49 M1
Jizzax, *Uzbekistan*, 50 B2
Joao Pessoa, *Brazil*, 33 M5
Jodhpur, *India*, 50 C5
Johannesburg, *South Africa*, 74 E5
Johnston Atoll, *Oceania*, 38 G3
Johor Bahru, *Malaysia*, 44 B3
Jolo, *Philippines*, 47 H6
Jonesboro, *U.S.A.*, 27 H3
Jonkoping, *Sweden*, 61 E4
Jordan, *Asia, country*, 53 C5
Jorhat, *India*, 50 G5
Jos, *Nigeria*, 72 A2
Juan de Nova, *Africa*, 75 H3
Juazeiro, *Brazil*, 33 K5
Juazeiro do Norte, *Brazil*, 33 L5
Juba, *Africa*, 73 G3
Juba, *Sudan*, 73 F3
Juchitan, *Mexico*, 28 E4
Juiz de Fora, *Brazil*, 34 K4
Juliaca, *Peru*, 32 D7
Juneau, *U.S.A., internal capital*, 24 F3
Jurmala, *Latvia*, 61 G4
Jurua, *Brazil*, 32 E5
Jutland, *Europe*, 61 D4
Jyvaskyla, *Finland*, 60 H3

k

K2, *Asia*, 50 D3
Kaamanen, *Finland*, 60 H1
Kabinda, *Democratic Republic of Congo*, 72 D5
Kabul, *Afghanistan, national capital*, 50 B4
Kabunda, *Democratic Republic of Congo*, 72 E6
Kabwe, *Zambia*, 74 E2
Kadoma, *Zimbabwe*, 74 E3
Kaduna, *Nigeria*, 71 G6
Kaedi, *Mauritania*, 71 C5
Kafakumba, *Democratic Republic of Congo*, 72 D5
Kafue, *Zambia*, 74 E3
Kagoshima, *Japan*, 49 M4
Kahramanmaras, *Turkey*, 52 C4
Kahului, *U.S.A.*, 27 P7
Kainji Reservoir, *Nigeria*, 71 F6
Kairouan, *Tunisia*, 68 D1
Kajaani, *Finland*, 60 H2
Kakhovske Reservoir, *Ukraine*, 58 C4
Kalahari Desert, *Africa*, 74 D4
Kalamata, *Greece*, 65 G4
Kalemie, *Democratic Republic of Congo*, 72 E5
Kalgoorlie, *Australia*, 40 D6
Kaliningrad, *Russia*, 61 G5
Kalisz, *Poland*, 61 F6
Kalkrand, *Namibia*, 74 C4

Kalmar, *Sweden*, 61 F4
Kaluga, *Russia*, 58 D3
Kamanjab, *Namibia*, 74 B3
Kama Reservoir, *Russia*, 59 H2
Kamativi, *Zimbabwe*, 74 E3
Kamchatka Peninsula, *Russia*, 55 H3
Kamenka, *Russia*, 58 E3
Kamina, *Democratic Republic of Congo*, 72 E5
Kamloops, *Canada*, 24 G3
Kampala, *Uganda, national capital*, 73 F3
Kampong Cham, *Cambodia*, 46 E5
Kampong Chhnang, *Cambodia*, 46 D5
Kampong Saom, *Cambodia*, 46 D5
Kamyanets-Podilskyy, *Ukraine*, 61 H6
Kamyshin, *Russia*, 58 F3
Kananga, *Democratic Republic of Congo*, 72 D5
Kanazawa, *Japan*, 49 N3
Kandahar, *Afghanistan*, 50 B4
Kandalaksha, *Russia*, 60 K2
Kandi, *Benin*, 71 F6
Kandy, *Sri Lanka*, 51 E9
Kang, *Botswana*, 74 D4
Kangaroo Island, *Australia*, 40 G7
Kanggye, *North Korea*, 49 L2
Kankan, *Guinea*, 71 D6
Kano, *Nigeria*, 68 C6
Kanpur, *India*, 50 E5
Kansas, *U.S.A., internal admin. area*, 26 G3
Kansas City, *U.S.A.*, 27 H3
Kanye, *Botswana*, 74 E4
Kaohsiung, *China*, 49 K6
Kaolack, *Senegal*, 71 B6
Kara-Balta, *Kyrgyzstan*, 50 C2
Karabuk, *Turkey*, 65 K3
Karachi, *Pakistan*, 51 B6
Karaj, *Iran*, 52 F4
Karakol, *Kyrgyzstan*, 50 D2
Karakorum Range, *Asia*, 50 D3
Kara Kum Desert, *Turkmenistan*, 52 G3
Karaman, *Turkey*, 65 K4
Karamay, *China*, 50 E1
Kara Sea, *Russia*, 54 D2
Kariba, *Zimbabwe*, 74 E3
Kariba, Lake, *Africa*, 74 E3
Karibib, *Namibia*, 74 C4
Karimata Strait, *Indonesia*, 44 C4
Karlovac, *Croatia*, 64 E2
Karlovy Vary, *Czech Republic*, 64 E1
Karlshamn, *Sweden*, 61 E4
Karlsruhe, *Germany*, 62 G4
Karlstad, *Sweden*, 60 E4
Karmoy, *Norway*, 60 C4
Karonga, *Malawi*, 75 F1
Karora, *Eritrea*, 69 J5
Karpathos, *Greece*, 65 H5
Karratha, *Australia*, 40 C4
Kasai, *Africa*, 72 C4
Kasama, *Zambia*, 74 F2
Kashi, *China*, 50 D3
Kassala, *Sudan*, 69 J5
Kassel, *Germany*, 62 G4
Kasungu, *Malawi*, 75 F2
Kataba, *Zambia*, 74 E3
Kathmandu, *Nepal, national capital*, 50 F5
Katiola, *Ivory Coast*, 71 D7
Katowice, *Poland*, 61 F6
Katsina, *Nigeria*, 71 G6
Kattegat, *Europe*, 61 D4
Kauai, *U.S.A.*, 27 P7
Kaukau Veld, *Africa*, 74 C4
Kaunas, *Lithuania*, 61 G5
Kavala, *Greece*, 65 H3
Kawambwa, *Zambia*, 74 E1
Kayes, *Mali*, 71 C6
Kayseri, *Turkey*, 52 C4
Kazakhstan, *Asia, country*, 54 C3
Kazan, *Russia*, 59 F2
Kaztalovka, *Kazakhstan*, 59 F4
Kebnekaise, *Sweden*, 60 F2
Kecskemet, *Hungary*, 61 F7
Kedougou, *Senegal*, 71 C6
Keetmanshoop, *Namibia*, 74 C5

Minneapolis, *U.S.A.*, **27 H2**
Minnesota, *U.S.A., internal admin. area,* **27 G1**
Minorca, *Spain,* **63 E6**
Minot, *U.S.A.,* **26 F1**
Minsk, *Belarus, national capital,* **61 H5**
Miri, *Malaysia,* **44 D3**
Mirim Lake, *Brazil,* **34 H6**
Miskolc, *Hungary,* **61 G6**
Misool, *Indonesia,* **45 H4**
Misratah, *Libya,* **68 E2**
Mississippi, *U.S.A.* **27 H4**
Mississippi, *U.S.A., internal admin. area,* **27 H4**
Mississippi Delta, *U.S.A.,* **27 J5**
Missoula, *U.S.A.,* **26 D1**
Missouri, *U.S.A.,* **26 G2**
Missouri, *U.S.A., internal admin. area,* **27 H3**
Mistassini, Lake, *Canada,* **25 M3**
Mitwaba, *Democratic Republic of Congo,* **72 E5**
Mkushi, *Zambia,* **74 E2**
Mmabatho, *South Africa,* **74 E5**
Moanda, *Gabon,* **72 B4**
Mobile, *U.S.A.,* **27 J4**
Mochudi, *Botswana,* **74 E4**
Mocuba, *Mozambique,* **75 G3**
Modena, *Italy,* **64 D2**
Mogadishu, *Somalia, national capital,* **73 J3**
Mogao Caves, *China,* **48 E2**
Mohilla Island, *Comoros,* **75 H2**
Mo i Rana, *Norway,* **60 E2**
Mojave Desert, *U.S.A.,* **26 C4**
Moldova, *Europe, country,* **65 J2**
Moldoveanu, Mount, *Romania,* **58 C4**
Molepolole, *Botswana,* **74 E4**
Mollendo, *Peru,* **32 D7**
Molokai, *U.S.A.,* **27 P7**
Molopo, *Africa,* **74 D5**
Molucca Sea, *Indonesia,* **45 F4**
Mombasa, *Kenya,* **73 G4**
Monaco, *Europe, country,* **63 F6**
Monastir, *Tunisia,* **68 D1**
Monchegorsk, *Russia,* **60 K2**
Monclova, *Mexico,* **28 D2**
Moncton, *Canada,* **25 N4**
Mongo, *Chad,* **68 E6**
Mongolia, *Asia, country,* **48 F1**
Mongu, *Zambia,* **74 D3**
Monrovia, *Liberia, national capital,* **71 C7**
Montalvo, *Ecuador,* **32 C4**
Montana, *U.S.A., internal admin. area,* **26 E1**
Montauban, *France,* **63 E5**
Montego Bay, *Jamaica,* **29 J4**
Montenegro, *Europe,* **65 F3**
Monterrey, *Mexico,* **28 D2**
Montes Claros, *Brazil,* **34 K3**
Montevideo, *Uruguay, national capital,* **34 G6**
Montgomery, *U.S.A., internal capital,* **27 J4**
Montpelier, *U.S.A., internal capital,* **27 M2**
Montpellier, *France,* **63 E6**
Montreal, *Canada,* **25 M4**
Montserrat, *North America,* **28 M4**
Monywa, *Burma,* **46 C3**
Moose Jaw, *Canada,* **24 J3**
Mopti, *Mali,* **71 E6**
Moree, *Australia,* **41 J5**
Morelia, *Mexico,* **28 D4**
Morocco, *Africa, country,* **70 D2**
Morogoro, *Tanzania,* **73 G5**
Morombe, *Madagascar,* **75 H4**
Moroni, *Comoros, national capital,* **75 H2**
Morotai, *Indonesia,* **45 G3**
Morpara, *Brazil,* **34 K2**
Moscow, *Russia, national capital,* **58 D2**
Moshi, *Tanzania,* **73 G4**
Mosquitos, Gulf of, *North America,* **29 H5**
Mossendjo, *Congo,* **72 B4**
Mossoro, *Brazil,* **33 L5**
Most, *Czech Republic,* **64 E1**

Mostaganem, *Algeria,* **70 F1**
Mostar, *Bosnia and Herzegovina,* **64 F3**
Mosul, *Iraq,* **52 D4**
Moulmein, *Burma,* **46 C4**
Moundou, *Chad,* **72 C2**
Mount Gambier, *Australia,* **40 H7**
Mount Hagen, *Papua New Guinea,* **45 K5**
Mount Isa, *Australia,* **40 G4**
Mount Li, *China,* **48 G4**
Moyobamba, *Peru,* **32 C5**
Mozambique, *Africa, country,* **75 F3**
Mozambique, *Mozambique,* **75 H3**
Mozambique Channel, *Africa,* **75 G4**
Mpika, *Zambia,* **74 F2**
Mtwara, *Tanzania,* **73 H6**
Mudanjiang, *China,* **49 L2**
Mueda, *Mozambique,* **75 G2**
Mufulira, *Zambia,* **74 E2**
Multan, *Pakistan,* **50 C4**
Mumbai, *India,* **51 C7**
Mumbue, *Angola,* **74 C2**
Munhango, *Angola,* **74 C2**
Munich, *Germany,* **62 E4**
Munster, *Germany,* **62 F4**
Murcia, *Spain,* **63 D7**
Murmansk, *Russia,* **60 K1**
Murom, *Russia,* **58 E2**
Murray, *Australia,* **40 G6**
Murzuq, *Libya,* **68 D3**
Muscat, *Oman, national capital,* **53 G7**
Mutare, *Zimbabwe,* **75 F3**
Mutoko, *Zimbabwe,* **74 F3**
Mutsamudu, *Comoros,* **75 H2**
Mutshatsha, *Democratic Republic of Congo,* **72 D6**
Mwali, *Comoros,* **75 H2**
Mwanza, *Tanzania,* **73 F4**
Mwene-Ditu, *Democratic Republic of Congo,* **72 D5**
Mweru, Lake, *Africa,* **74 E1**
Mwinilunga, *Zambia,* **74 D2**
Myanmar, *Asia, country,* **46 C3**
Myitkyina, *Burma,* **46 C2**
Mykolayiv, *Ukraine,* **58 C4**
Mysore, *India,* **51 D8**
Mzuzu, *Malawi,* **75 F2**

n

Naberezhnyye Chelny, *Russia,* **59 G2**
Nabeul, *Tunisia,* **64 D4**
Nacala, *Mozambique,* **75 H2**
Nador, *Morocco,* **63 D8**
Naga, *Philippines,* **47 H5**
Nagasaki, *Japan,* **49 L4**
Nagoya, *Japan,* **49 N3**
Nagpur, *India,* **51 D6**
Nain, *Canada,* **25 N3**
Nairobi, *Kenya, national capital,* **73 G4**
Najran, *Saudi Arabia,* **53 D8**
Nakhodka, *Russia,* **49 M2**
Nakhon Ratchasima, *Thailand,* **46 D5**
Nakhon Sawan, *Thailand,* **46 D4**
Nakhon Si Thammarat, *Thailand,* **46 D6**
Nakuru, *Kenya,* **73 G4**
Nalchik, *Russia,* **52 D3**
Namangan, *Uzbekistan,* **50 C2**
Namib Desert, *Africa,* **74 B3**
Namibe, *Angola,* **74 B3**
Namibia, *Africa, country,* **74 C4**
Nam Lake, *China,* **50 G4**
Nampo, *North Korea,* **49 L3**
Nampula, *Mozambique,* **75 G3**
Namsos, *Norway,* **60 D2**
Namur, *Belgium,* **62 F4**
Nanaimo, *Canada,* **24 G4**
Nanchang, *China,* **49 J5**
Nancy, *France,* **62 F4**
Nanded, *India,* **51 D7**
Nanjing, *China,* **49 J4**
Nanning, *China,* **48 G6**
Nanping, *China,* **49 J5**
Nantes, *France,* **62 D4**
Napier, *New Zealand,* **41 Q7**
Naples, *Italy,* **64 E3**
Narmada, *India,* **51 C6**

Narva, *Estonia,* **60 J4**
Narvik, *Norway,* **60 F1**
Nashik, *India,* **51 C6**
Nashville, *U.S.A., internal capital,* **27 J3**
Nasi Lake, *Finland,* **60 G3**
Nassau, *The Bahamas, national capital,* **27 L5**
Nasser, Lake, *Egypt,* **69 H4**
Natal, *Brazil,* **33 L5**
Natitingou, *Benin,* **71 F6**
Natuna Islands, *Indonesia,* **44 C3**
Nauru, *Oceania, country,* **38 D5**
Navapolatsk, *Belarus,* **61 J5**
Navoiy, *Uzbekistan,* **50 B2**
Nawabshah, *Pakistan,* **50 B5**
Naxcivan, *Azerbaijan,* **52 E4**
Naypyidaw, *Burma, national capital,* **46 C4**
Nazca, *Peru,* **32 D6**
Nazret, *Ethiopia,* **73 G2**
Ndalatando, *Angola,* **74 B1**
Ndele, *Central African Republic,* **72 D2**
Ndjamena, *Chad, national capital,* **68 E6**
Ndola, *Zambia,* **74 E2**
Near Islands, *U.S.A.,* **25 A3**
Nebraska, *U.S.A., internal admin. area,* **26 F2**
Necochea, *Argentina,* **35 G7**
Negombo, *Sri Lanka,* **51 D9**
Negro, *Brazil,* **32 F4**
Negro, Cape, *Peru,* **32 B5**
Negros, *Philippines,* **47 H6**
Neiva, *Colombia,* **32 C3**
Nekemte, *Ethiopia,* **73 G2**
Nellore, *India,* **51 E8**
Nelson, *New Zealand,* **41 P8**
Nelspruit, *South Africa,* **74 F5**
Nema, *Mauritania,* **71 D5**
Neman, *Europe,* **61 G5**
Nepal, *Asia, country,* **50 F5**
Netherlands, *Europe, country,* **62 F3**
Netherlands Antilles, *North America, dependency,* **29 L5**
Nettiling Lake, *Canada,* **25 M2**
Neuquen, *Argentina,* **35 E7**
Nevada, *U.S.A., internal admin. area,* **26 C3**
Nevers, *France,* **63 E5**
New Amsterdam, *Guyana,* **33 G2**
Newark, *U.S.A.,* **27 M2**
New Britain, *Papua New Guinea,* **45 M5**
New Brunswick, *Canada, internal admin. area,* **25 N4**
Newcastle, *Australia,* **41 K6**
Newcastle upon Tyne, *United Kingdom,* **62 D3**
New Delhi, *India, national capital,* **50 D5**
Newfoundland, *Canada,* **25 P4**
Newfoundland, *Canada, internal admin. area,* **25 N3**
New Guinea, *Asia/Oceania,* **45 J4**
New Hampshire, *U.S.A., internal admin. area,* **27 M2**
New Ireland, *Papua New Guinea,* **45 M4**
New Jersey, *U.S.A., internal admin. area,* **27 M3**
New Mexico, *U.S.A., internal admin. area,* **26 E4**
New Orleans, *U.S.A.,* **27 J5**
New Plymouth, *New Zealand,* **41 P7**
Newport, *United Kingdom,* **62 D4**
New Siberia Islands, *Russia,* **55 H2**
New South Wales, *Australia, internal admin. area,* **40 H6**
New York, *U.S.A.,* **27 M2**
New York, *U.S.A., internal admin. area,* **27 M2**
New Zealand, *Australasia, country,* **41 Q8**
Ngami, Lake, *Botswana,* **74 D4**
Ngaoundere, *Cameroon,* **72 B2**
Ngoma, *Zambia,* **74 E3**
Nha Trang, *Vietnam,* **46 E5**
Niagara Falls, *North America,* **25 M4**
Niamey, *Niger, national capital,* **71 F6**
Nias, *Indonesia,* **44 A3**

Nicaragua, *North America, country,* **29 G5**
Nicaragua, Lake, *Nicaragua,* **29 H5**
Nice, *France,* **63 F6**
Nicobar Islands, *India,* **51 G9**
Nicosia, *Cyprus, national capital,* **65 K5**
Nieuw Nickerie, *Suriname,* **33 G2**
Niger, *Africa,* **71 G7**
Niger, *Africa, country,* **68 D5**
Niger Delta, *Nigeria,* **71 G8**
Nigeria, *Africa, country,* **71 F7**
Niigata, *Japan,* **49 N3**
Nikopol, *Ukraine,* **58 C4**
Niksic, *Montenegro,* **65 F3**
Nile, *Africa,* **69 H3**
Nile Delta, *Egypt,* **69 H2**
Nimes, *France,* **63 F6**
Ningbo, *China,* **49 K5**
Niono, *Mali,* **71 D6**
Nioro du Sahel, *Mali,* **71 D5**
Nipigon, Lake, *Canada,* **25 L4**
Nis, *Serbia,* **65 G3**
Nitra, *Slovakia,* **61 F6**
Niue, *Oceania,* **38 G6**
Nizhniy Novgorod, *Russia,* **58 E2**
Nizhniy Tagil, *Russia,* **59 H2**
Njazidja, *Comoros,* **75 H2**
Njinjo, *Tanzania,* **73 G5**
Nkongsamba, *Cameroon,* **72 A3**
Nogales, *Mexico,* **28 B1**
Nokaneng, *Botswana,* **74 D3**
Norfolk Island, *Australia,* **41 N5**
Norilsk, *Russia,* **54 E2**
Norrkoping, *Sweden,* **60 F4**
North America, **20**
North Bay, *Canada,* **25 M4**
North Cape, *New Zealand,* **41 P6**
North Cape, *Norway,* **60 J1**
North Carolina, *U.S.A., internal admin. area,* **27 K3**
North Dakota, *U.S.A., internal admin. area,* **26 F1**
Northern Ireland, *United Kingdom, internal admin. area,* **62 C3**
Northern Mariana Islands, *Oceania,* **38 B3**
Northern Territory, *Australia, internal admin. area,* **40 F3**
North European Plain, *Russia,* **58 C2**
North Frisian Islands, *Europe,* **62 F3**
North Island, *New Zealand,* **41 Q7**
North Korea, *Asia, country,* **49 L2**
North Sea, *Europe,* **62 E2**
North West Cape, *Australia,* **40 B4**
Northwest Territories, *Canada, internal admin. area,* **24 G2**
Norway, *Europe, country,* **60 D3**
Norwegian Sea, *Europe,* **60 C2**
Norwich, *United Kingdom,* **62 E3**
Nosy Be, *Madagascar,* **75 J2**
Nosy Boraha, *Madagascar,* **75 J3**
Nottingham, *United Kingdom,* **62 D3**
Nouadhibou, *Mauritania,* **70 B4**
Nouakchott, *Mauritania, national capital,* **70 B5**
Noumea, *New Caledonia,* **41 N4**
Nova Iguacu, *Brazil,* **34 K4**
Nova Mambone, *Mozambique,* **75 G4**
Novara, *Italy,* **64 D2**
Nova Scotia, *Canada, internal admin. area,* **25 N4**
Novaya Zemlya, *Russia,* **54 C2**
Novgorod, *Russia,* **60 J4**
Novi Sad, *Serbia,* **65 F2**
Novo Mesto, *Slovenia,* **64 E2**
Novocherkassk, *Russia,* **58 E4**
Novorossiysk, *Russia,* **52 C3**
Novosibirsk, *Russia,* **54 E3**
Novyy Urengoy, *Russia,* **54 D2**
Nubian Desert, *Africa,* **69 H4**
Nueva Loja, *Ecuador,* **32 C3**
Nukualofa, *Tonga, national capital,* **38 F7**
Nukus, *Uzbekistan,* **52 G3**
Nullarbor Plain, *Australia,* **40 E6**
Nunavut, *Canada, internal admin. area,* **25 K2**
Nungo, *Mozambique,* **75 G2**
Nunivak Island, *U.S.A.,* **24 C3**

Nuqui, *Colombia,* 32 C2
Nuremberg, *Germany,* 62 G4
Nyala, *Sudan,* 68 F6
Nyasa, Lake, *Africa,* 73 F6
Nyeri, *Kenya,* 73 G4
Nykobing, *Denmark,* 61 D5
Nzerekore, *Guinea,* 71 D7
Nzwani, *Comoros,* 75 H2

O

Oahu, *U.S.A.,* 27 P7
Oaxaca, *Mexico,* 28 E4
Ob, *Russia,* 54 D2
Obi, *Indonesia,* 45 G4
Obninsk, *Russia,* 58 D2
Obo, *Central African Republic,* 72 E2
Odda, *Norway,* 60 C3
Odemis, *Turkey,* 65 J4
Odense, *Denmark,* 61 D5
Oder, *Europe,* 61 E5
Odesa, *Ukraine,* 58 C4
Odienne, *Ivory Coast,* 71 D7
Ogbomoso, *Nigeria,* 71 F7
Ogden, *U.S.A.,* 26 D2
Ohio, *U.S.A.,* 27 J3
Ohio, *U.S.A., internal admin. area,* 27 K2
Ojinaga, *Mexico,* 28 D2
Ojos del Salado, Mount, *South America,* 34 E5
Oka, *Russia,* 58 E2
Okahandja, *Namibia,* 74 C4
Okaukuejo, *Namibia,* 74 C3
Okavango, *Africa,* 74 D3
Okavango Swamp, *Botswana,* 74 D3
Okayama, *Japan,* 49 M4
Okeechobee, Lake, *U.S.A.,* 27 K5
Okhotsk, Sea of, *Asia,* 55 H3
Okinawa, *Japan,* 49 L5
Oklahoma, *U.S.A., internal admin. area,* 26 G4
Oklahoma City, *U.S.A., internal capital,* 26 G3
Oktyabrskiy, *Russia,* 59 G3
Oland, *Sweden,* 61 F4
Olavarria, *Argentina,* 35 F7
Olbia, *Italy,* 64 D3
Oleksandriya, *Ukraine,* 58 C4
Ollague, *Chile,* 34 E4
Olomouc, *Czech Republic,* 64 F1
Olongapo, *Philippines,* 47 H5
Olsztyn, *Poland,* 61 G5
Olympia, *U.S.A., internal capital,* 26 B1
Olympus, Mount, *Greece,* 65 G3
Omaha, *U.S.A.,* 27 G2
Oman, *Asia, country,* 53 G7
Oman, Gulf of, *Asia,* 53 G7
Omdurman, *Sudan,* 69 H5
Omsk, *Russia,* 54 D3
Ondangwa, *Namibia,* 74 C3
Onega, Lake, *Russia,* 60 K3
Onitsha, *Nigeria,* 71 G7
Ontario, *Canada, internal admin. area,* 25 L3
Ontario, Lake, *U.S.A.,* 27 L2
Opochka, *Russia,* 61 J4
Opole, *Poland,* 61 F6
Oporto, *Portugal,* 63 B6
Oppdal, *Norway,* 60 D3
Opuwo, *Namibia,* 74 B3
Oradea, *Romania,* 65 G2
Oral, *Kazakhstan,* 59 G3
Oran, *Algeria,* 70 E1
Orange, *Africa,* 74 C5
Orange, Cape, *Brazil,* 33 H3
Orapa, *Botswana,* 74 E4
Orebro, *Sweden,* 60 E4
Oregon, *U.S.A., internal admin. area,* 26 B2
Orel, *Russia,* 58 D3
Orenburg, *Russia,* 59 H3
Orense, *Spain,* 63 C6
Orinoco, *Venezuela,* 32 F2
Orinoco Delta, *Venezuela,* 32 F2
Oristano, *Italy,* 64 D4
Orizaba, *Mexico,* 28 E4

Orkney, *South Africa,* 74 E5
Orkney Islands, *United Kingdom,* 62 D2
Orlando, *U.S.A.,* 27 K5
Orleans, *France,* 62 E5
Orsha, *Belarus,* 61 J5
Orsk, *Russia,* 59 H3
Oruro, *Bolivia,* 34 E3
Osaka, *Japan,* 49 N4
Osh, *Kyrgyzstan,* 50 C2
Osijek, *Croatia,* 65 F2
Oskarshamn, *Sweden,* 61 F4
Oslo, *Norway, national capital,* 60 D4
Osnabruck, *Germany,* 62 G3
Osorno, *Chile,* 35 D8
Ostersund, *Sweden,* 60 E3
Ostrava, *Czech Republic,* 65 F1
Otavi, *Namibia,* 74 C3
Otjiwarongo, *Namibia,* 74 C4
Ottawa, *Canada, national capital,* 25 M4
Ouadda, *Central African Republic,* 72 D2
Ouagadougou, *Burkina Faso, national capital,* 71 E6
Ouahigouya, *Burkina Faso,* 71 E6
Ouargla, *Algeria,* 70 G2
Ouarzazate, *Morocco,* 70 D2
Oudtshoorn, *South Africa,* 74 D6
Ouesso, *Congo,* 72 C3
Oujda, *Morocco,* 70 E2
Oulu, *Finland,* 60 H2
Oulu Lake, *Finland,* 60 H2
Ovalle, *Chile,* 34 D6
Oviedo, *Spain,* 63 C6
Owando, *Congo,* 72 C4
Owen Sound, *Canada,* 25 L4
Owo, *Nigeria,* 71 G7
Oxford, *United Kingdom,* 62 D4
Oyem, *Gabon,* 72 B3
Ozark Plateau, *U.S.A.,* 27 H3

P

Paarl, *South Africa,* 74 C6
Pacasmayo, *Peru,* 32 C5
Pacific Ocean, 20
Padang, *Indonesia,* 44 B4
Pafuri, *Mozambique,* 74 F4
Pagadian, *Philippines,* 47 H6
Paijanne Lake, *Finland,* 60 H3
Pakistan, *Asia, country,* 50 B5
Pakxe, *Laos,* 46 E4
Palangkaraya, *Indonesia,* 44 D4
Palau, *Oceania, country,* 38 A4
Palawan, *Philippines,* 47 G6
Palembang, *Indonesia,* 44 B4
Palencia, *Spain,* 63 C6
Palermo, *Italy,* 64 E4
Palikir, *Federated States of Micronesia, national capital,* 38 C4
Palk Strait, *Asia,* 51 D9
Palma, *Mozambique,* 75 H2
Palma, *Spain,* 63 E7
Palmas, Cape, *Africa,* 71 D8
Palmyra Atoll, *Oceania,* 38 G4
Palopo, *Indonesia,* 45 F4
Palu, *Indonesia,* 45 E4
Pampas, *Argentina,* 35 F7
Pamplona, *Colombia,* 32 D2
Pamplona, *Spain,* 63 D6
Panama, *North America, country,* 29 H6
Panama Canal, *Panama,* 29 J6
Panama City, *Panama, national capital,* 29 J6
Panama, Gulf of, *North America,* 29 J6
Panay, *Philippines,* 47 H5
Panevezys, *Lithuania,* 61 H5
Pangkalpinang, *Indonesia,* 44 C4
Panjgur, *Pakistan,* 50 A5
Pantelleria, *Italy,* 64 E4
Panzhihua, *China,* 48 F5
Papeete, *French Polynesia,* 39 J6
Paphos, *Cyprus,* 65 K5
Papua, Gulf of, *Papua New Guinea,* 45 K5
Papua New Guinea, *Oceania, country,* 45 L5
Paracel Islands, *Asia,* 47 F4
Paraguaipoa, *Venezuela,* 32 D1

Paraguay, *South America,* 34 G4
Paraguay, *South America, country,* 34 F4
Parakou, *Benin,* 71 F7
Paramaribo, *Suriname, national capital,* 33 G2
Parana, *South America,* 34 G6
Paranagua, *Brazil,* 34 J5
Parepare, *Indonesia,* 45 E4
Paris, *France, national capital,* 62 E4
Parma, *Italy,* 64 D2
Parnaiba, *Brazil,* 33 K4
Parnu, *Estonia,* 60 H4
Parry Islands, *Canada,* 24 J1
Pasadena, *U.S.A.,* 26 C4
Passo Fundo, *Brazil,* 34 H5
Pasto, *Colombia,* 32 C3
Patagonia, *Argentina,* 35 E9
Pathein, *Burma,* 46 B4
Patna, *India,* 50 F5
Patos de Minas, *Brazil,* 34 J3
Patos Lagoon, *Brazil,* 34 H6
Patra, *Greece,* 65 G4
Pattaya, *Thailand,* 46 D5
Pau, *France,* 63 D6
Pavlodar, *Kazakhstan,* 54 D3
Paysandu, *Uruguay,* 34 G6
Peace River, *Canada,* 24 H3
Pecos, *U.S.A.,* 26 F4
Pecs, *Hungary,* 61 F7
Pedro Juan Caballero, *Paraguay,* 34 G4
Pegu, *Burma,* 46 C4
Peipus, Lake, *Europe,* 60 H4
Peiraias, *Greece,* 65 G4
Pekanbaru, *Indonesia,* 44 B3
Pelagian Islands, *Italy,* 64 E5
Peleng, *Indonesia,* 45 F4
Pelotas, *Brazil,* 34 H6
Pematangsiantar, *Indonesia,* 44 A3
Pemba, *Mozambique,* 75 H2
Pemba Island, *Tanzania,* 73 G5
Penang, *Malaysia,* 44 B3
Penas, Gulf of, *Chile,* 35 C9
Pennsylvania, *U.S.A., internal admin. area,* 27 L2
Pensacola, *U.S.A.,* 27 J4
Penza, *Russia,* 58 F3
Penzance, *United Kingdom,* 62 C4
Peoria, *U.S.A.,* 27 J2
Pereira, *Colombia,* 32 C3
Perm, *Russia,* 59 H2
Perpignan, *France,* 63 E6
Persepolis, *Iran,* 53 F6
Persian Gulf, *Asia,* 53 F6
Perth, *Australia, internal capital,* 40 C6
Peru, *South America, country,* 32 C5
Perugia, *Italy,* 64 E3
Pescara, *Italy,* 64 E3
Peshawar, *Pakistan,* 50 C4
Petauke, *Zambia,* 74 F2
Petra, *Jordan,* 53 C5
Petrolina, *Brazil,* 33 K5
Petropavlovsk-Kamchatskiy, *Russia,* 55 H3
Petrozavodsk, *Russia,* 60 K3
Philadelphia, *U.S.A.,* 27 L3
Philippines, *Asia, country,* 47 J5
Philippine Sea, *Asia,* 47 H5
Phitsanulok, *Thailand,* 46 D4
Phnom Penh, *Cambodia, national capital,* 46 D5
Phoenix, *U.S.A., internal capital,* 26 D4
Phongsali, *Laos,* 46 D3
Piatra Neamt, *Romania,* 65 H2
Pica, *Chile,* 34 E4
Pielis Lake, *Finland,* 60 J3
Pierre, *U.S.A., internal capital,* 26 F2
Pietermaritzburg, *South Africa,* 74 F5
Pietersburg, *South Africa,* 74 E4
Pihlaja Lake, *Finland,* 60 J3
Pik Pobedy, *Asia,* 50 E2
Pilcomayo, *South America,* 34 F4
Pilsen, *Czech Republic,* 64 E1
Pinar del Rio, *Cuba,* 29 H3
Pindus Mountains, *Greece,* 65 G4
Pingdingshan, *China,* 49 H4
Pinsk, *Belarus,* 61 H5

Pisa, *Italy,* 64 D3
Pitcairn Islands, *Oceania,* 39 L7
Pitesti, *Romania,* 65 H2
Pittsburgh, *U.S.A.,* 27 L2
Piura, *Peru,* 32 B5
Platte, *U.S.A.,* 26 F2
Pleven, *Bulgaria,* 65 H3
Plock, *Poland,* 61 F5
Ploiesti, *Romania,* 65 H2
Plovdiv, *Bulgaria,* 65 H3
Plumtree, *Zimbabwe,* 74 E4
Plymouth, *United Kingdom,* 62 C4
Po, *Italy,* 64 D2
Pocos de Caldas, *Brazil,* 34 J4
Podgorica, *Montenegro, national capital,* 65 F3
Podolsk, *Russia,* 58 D2
Pointe-Noire, *Congo,* 72 B4
Poitiers, *France,* 63 E5
Pokhara, *Nepal,* 50 E4
Poland, *Europe, country,* 61 F6
Polatsk, *Belarus,* 61 J5
Poltava, *Ukraine,* 58 C4
Polynesia, *Oceania,* 38 G5
Pompeii, *Italy,* 64 E3
Ponta Delgada, *Azores,* 70 K10
Ponta Pora, *Brazil,* 34 G4
Pontianak, *Indonesia,* 44 C3
Poole, *United Kingdom,* 62 D4
Poopo, Lake, *Bolivia,* 34 E3
Popayan, *Colombia,* 32 C3
Porbandar, *India,* 51 B6
Pori, *Finland,* 60 G3
Porlamar, *Venezuela,* 28 M5
Port-au-Prince, *Haiti, national capital,* 29 K4
Port Blair, *India,* 51 G8
Port Elizabeth, *South Africa,* 74 E6
Port-Gentil, *Gabon,* 72 A4
Port Harcourt, *Nigeria,* 71 G8
Port Hardy, *Canada,* 24 G3
Port Hedland, *Australia,* 40 C4
Portland, *Australia,* 40 H7
Portland, *Maine, U.S.A.,* 27 M2
Portland, *Oregon, U.S.A.,* 26 B1
Port Louis, *Mauritius, national capital,* 75 L4
Port Macquarie, *Australia,* 41 K6
Port McNeill, *Canada,* 24 G3
Port Moresby, *Papua New Guinea, national capital,* 45 L5
Porto Alegre, *Brazil,* 34 H5
Port-of-Spain, *Trinidad and Tobago, national capital,* 28 M5
Porto-Novo, *Benin, national capital,* 71 F7
Porto-Vecchio, *France,* 63 G6
Porto Velho, *Brazil,* 32 F5
Port Said, *Egypt,* 69 H2
Portsmouth, *United Kingdom,* 62 D4
Port Sudan, *Sudan,* 69 J5
Portugal, *Europe, country,* 63 B7
Port-Vila, *Vanuatu, national capital,* 41 N3
Porvenir, *Chile,* 35 D10
Posadas, *Argentina,* 34 G5
Poti, *Georgia,* 52 D3
Potiskum, *Nigeria,* 68 D6
Potosi, *Bolivia,* 34 E3
Potsdam, *Germany,* 62 H3
Poyang Lake, *China,* 49 J5
Poznan, *Poland,* 61 F5
Prachuap Khiri Khan, *Thailand,* 46 C5
Prague, *Czech Republic, national capital,* 64 E1
Praia, *Cape Verde, national capital,* 71 M12
Presidente Prudente, *Brazil,* 34 H4
Presov, *Slovakia,* 61 G6
Pretoria, *South Africa, national capital,* 74 E5
Preveza, *Greece,* 65 G4
Prieska, *South Africa,* 74 D5
Prilep, *Macedonia,* 65 G3
Prince Albert, *Canada,* 24 J3
Prince Edward Island, *Canada, internal admin. area,* 25 N4
Prince George, *Canada,* 24 G3

Prince of Wales Island, *Canada,* 25 K1
Prince Rupert, *Canada,* 24 F3
Principe, *Sao Tome and Principe,* 71 G8
Pripet, *Europe,* 61 J6
Pripet Marshes, *Europe,* 61 H5
Pristina, *Kosovo, national capital,* 65 G3
Providence, *Seychelles,* 75 K1
Providence, *U.S.A., internal capital,*
    27 M2
Providence, Cape, *New Zealand,* 41 N9
Provo, *U.S.A.,* 26 D2
Prudhoe Bay, *U.S.A.,* 24 E1
Pskov, *Russia,* 61 J4
Pskov, Lake, *Europe,* 60 J4
Pucallpa, *Peru,* 32 D5
Puebla, *Mexico,* 28 E4
Pueblo, *U.S.A.,* 26 F3
Puerto Ayora, *Ecuador,* 32 N10
Puerto Cabezas, *Nicaragua,* 29 H5
Puerto Inirida, *Colombia,* 32 E3
Puerto Leguizamo, *Colombia,* 32 D4
Puerto Maldonado, *Peru,* 32 E6
Puerto Montt, *Chile,* 35 D8
Puerto Natales, *Chile,* 35 D10
Puerto Paez, *Venezuela,* 32 E2
Puerto Princesa, *Philippines,* 47 G6
Puerto Rico, *North America,* 28 L4
Puerto Suarez, *Bolivia,* 34 G3
Puerto Vallarta, *Mexico,* 28 C3
Pula, *Croatia,* 64 E2
Pulog, Mount, *Philippines,* 47 H4
Puncak Jaya, *Indonesia,* 45 J4
Pune, *India,* 51 C7
Puno, *Peru,* 32 D7
Punta Arenas, *Chile,* 35 D10
Puntarenas, *Costa Rica,* 29 H5
Purus, *Brazil,* 32 E5
Pusan, *South Korea,* 49 L3
Pushkin, *Russia,* 60 J4
Puula Lake, *Finland,* 60 H3
Pweto, *Democratic Republic of Congo,*
    72 E5
Pya, Lake, *Russia,* 60 J2
Pye, *Burma,* 46 C4
Pyinmana, *Burma,* 46 C4
Pyongyang, *North Korea, national capital,*
    49 L3
Pyramids of Giza, *Egypt,* 69 H3
Pyrenees, *Europe,* 63 D6
Pyrgos, *Greece,* 65 G4

q
Qaidam Basin, *China,* 50 G3
Qaraghandy, *Kazakhstan,* 54 D3
Qatar, *Asia, country,* 53 F6
Qattara Depression, *Egypt,* 69 G3
Qazvin, *Iran,* 52 E4
Qena, *Egypt,* 69 H3
Qingdao, *China,* 49 K3
Qinghai Lake, *China,* 48 F3
Qinhuangdao, *China,* 49 J3
Qiqihar, *China,* 49 K1
Qom, *Iran,* 52 F5
Qostanay, *Kazakhstan,* 59 J3
Quanzhou, *China,* 49 J6
Quebec, *Canada, internal admin. area,*
    25 M3
Quebec, *Canada, internal capital,* 25 M4
Queen Charlotte Islands, *Canada,* 24 F3
Queen Elizabeth Islands, *Canada,* 24 H1
Queen Maud Land, *Antarctica,* 79 C3
Queensland, *Australia, internal admin. area,*
    40 H4
Quelimane, *Mozambique,* 75 G3
Quellon, *Chile,* 35 D8
Quetta, *Pakistan,* 50 B4
Quevedo, *Ecuador,* 32 C4
Quezaltenango, *Guatemala,* 28 F4
Quezon City, *Philippines,* 47 H5
Quibdo, *Colombia,* 32 C2
Quillabamba, *Peru,* 32 D6
Quimper, *France,* 62 C5
Quincy, *U.S.A.,* 27 H3
Qui Nhon, *Vietnam,* 46 E5
Quirima, *Angola,* 74 C2

r
Raahe, *Finland,* 60 H2
Rabat, *Morocco, national capital,* 70 D2
Rabaul, *Papua New Guinea,* 45 M4
Rabnita, *Moldova,* 65 J2
Radisson, *Canada,* 25 M3
Radom, *Poland,* 61 G6
Ragusa, *Italy,* 64 E4
Rahimyar Khan, *Pakistan,* 50 C5
Rainier, Mount, *U.S.A.,* 26 B1
Raipur, *India,* 51 E6
Rajahmundry, *India,* 51 E7
Rajkot, *India,* 51 C6
Rajshahi, *Bangladesh,* 51 F6
Rakops, *Botswana,* 74 D4
Raleigh, *U.S.A., internal capital,* 27 L3
Ralik Islands, *Marshall Islands,* 38 D3
Ramnicu Valcea, *Romania,* 65 H2
Rancagua, *Chile,* 34 D6
Ranchi, *India,* 51 F6
Randers, *Denmark,* 61 D4
Rangoon, *Burma, national capital,* 46 C4
Rangpur, *Bangladesh,* 50 F5
Rapid City, *U.S.A.,* 26 F2
Ras Dashen, *Ethiopia,* 73 G1
Rasht, *Iran,* 52 E4
Ratak Islands, *Marshall Islands,* 38 E3
Rat Islands, *U.S.A.,* 25 A3
Rauma, *Finland,* 60 G3
Ravenna, *Italy,* 64 E2
Rawalpindi, *Pakistan,* — [see note]
Rawson, *Argentina,* 35 E8
Rechytsa, *Belarus,* 61 J5
Recife, *Brazil,* 33 M5
Reconquista, *Argentina,* 34 G5
Red, *Asia,* 48 F6
Red, *U.S.A.,* 27 G4
Red Deer, *Canada,* 24 H3
Red Sea, *Africa/Asia,* 69 J4
Redding, *U.S.A.,* 26 B2
Regensburg, *Germany,* 62 H4
Regina, *Canada, internal capital,* 24 J3
Regina, *French Guiana,* 33 H3
Rehoboth, *Namibia,* 74 C4
Reims, *France,* 62 F4
Reindeer Lake, *Canada,* 24 J3
Rennell Island, *Solomon Islands,* 41 M2
Rennes, *France,* 62 D4
Reno, *U.S.A.,* 26 C3
Reunion, *Indian Ocean,* 75 L4
Revelstoke, *Canada,* 24 H3
Revillagigedo Islands, *Mexico,* 28 B4
Reykjavik, *Iceland, national capital,* 60 N2
Rhine, *Europe,* 62 F4
Rhode Island, *U.S.A., internal admin. area,*
    27 M2
Rhodes, *Greece,* 65 J4
Rhone, *Europe,* 63 F5
Riau Islands, *Indonesia,* 44 B3
Ribeirao Preto, *Brazil,* 34 J4
Riberalta, *Bolivia,* 34 E2
Richards Bay, *South Africa,* 74 F5
Richmond, *U.S.A., internal capital,* 27 L3
Riga, *Latvia, national capital,* 61 H4
Riga, Gulf of, *Europe,* 61 G4
Rijeka, *Croatia,* 64 E2
Rimini, *Italy,* 64 E2
Rio Branco, *Brazil,* 32 E5
Rio Cuarto, *Argentina,* 34 F6
Rio de Janeiro, *Brazil,* 34 K4
Rio Gallegos, *Argentina,* 35 E10
Rio Grande, *Argentina,* 35 E10
Rio Grande, *Brazil,* 34 H6
Rio Grande, *U.S.A.,* 26 F5
Riohacha, *Colombia,* 32 D1
Rivas, *Nicaragua,* 29 G5
Rivera, *Uruguay,* 34 G6
Riverside, *U.S.A.,* 26 C4
Rivne, *Ukraine,* 61 H6
Riyadh, *Saudi Arabia, national capital,*
    53 E7
Roanoke, *U.S.A.,* 27 L3
Robson, Mount, *Canada,* 24 H3

Rochester, *U.S.A.,* 27 L2
Rockford, *U.S.A.,* 27 J2
Rockhampton, *Australia,* 41 K4
Rocky Mountains, *U.S.A.,* 26 D1
Romania, *Europe, country,* 65 G2
Rome, *Italy, national capital,* 64 E3
Rondonopolis, *Brazil,* 34 H3
Ronne, *Denmark,* 61 E5
Ronne Ice Shelf, *Antarctica,* 79 S3
Roraima, Mount, *South America,* 32 F2
Rosario, *Argentina,* 34 F6
Roseau, *Dominica, national capital,*
    28 M4
Roslavl, *Russia,* 61 K5
Ross Ice Shelf, *Antarctica,* 79 M4
Rosso, *Mauritania,* 71 B5
Ross Sea, *Antarctica,* 79 M3
Rostock, *Germany,* 62 H3
Rostov, *Russia,* 58 D4
Roti, *Indonesia,* 45 F6
Rotorua, *Australia,* 41 Q7
Rotterdam, *Netherlands,* 62 F4
Rouen, *France,* 62 E4
Rovaniemi, *Finland,* 60 H2
Roxas, *Philippines,* 47 H5
Rub al Khali, *Asia,* 53 E8
Rudnyy, *Kazakhstan,* 59 J3
Rufino, *Argentina,* 34 F6
Rufunsa, *Zambia,* 74 E3
Rukwa, Lake, *Tanzania,* 73 F5
Rundu, *Namibia,* 74 C3
Rurrenabaque, *Bolivia,* 34 E2
Ruse, *Bulgaria,* 65 H3
Russia, *Asia/Europe, country,* 54 E3
Ruvuma, *Africa,* 73 G6
Rwanda, *Africa, country,* 72 E4
Ryazan, *Russia,* 58 D3
Rybinsk, *Russia,* 58 D2
Rybinsk Reservoir, *Russia,* 58 D2
Rybnik, *Poland,* 61 F6
Ryukyu Islands, *Japan,* 49 L5
Rzeszow, *Poland,* 61 G6
Rzhev, *Russia,* 58 C2

s
Saarbrucken, *Germany,* 62 F4
Saarijarvi, *Finland,* 60 H3
Sabha, *Libya,* 68 D3
Sabzevar, *Iran,* 52 G4
Sacramento, *U.S.A., internal capital,*
    26 B3
Sadah, *Yemen,* 53 E8
Safi, *Morocco,* 70 D2
Sahara, *Africa,* 68 C5
Saharanpur, *India,* 50 D5
Sahel, *Africa,* 68 C5
Sahiwal, *Pakistan,* 50 C4
Saida, *Algeria,* 70 F2
Saigon, *Vietnam,* 46 E5
Saimaa Lake, *Finland,* 60 H3
St. Andrew, Cape, *Madagascar,* 75 H3
St. Denis, *Reunion,* 75 L4
St. Etienne, *France,* 63 F5
St. Francis, Cape, *South Africa,* 74 D6
St. George, *U.S.A.,* 26 D3
St. George's, *Grenada, national capital,*
    28 M5
St. Helier, *Channel Islands,* 62 D4
Saint John, *Canada,* 25 N4
St. John's, *Antigua and Barbuda, national
    capital,* 28 M4
St. John's, *Canada, internal capital,* 25 P4
St. Kitts and Nevis, *North America,*
    country, 28 M4
St. Lawrence, *Canada,* 25 M4
St. Lawrence, Gulf of, *Canada,* 25 N4
St. Lawrence Island, *U.S.A.,* 24 B2
St. Louis, *Senegal,* 71 B5
St. Louis, *U.S.A.,* 27 H3
St. Lucia, *North America, country,* 28 M5
St. Lucia, Cape, *South Africa,* 75 F5
St. Malo, *France,* 62 D4
St. Martha, Cape, *Angola,* 74 B2
St. Martin, *North America,* 28 M4
St. Mary, Cape, *Madagascar,* 75 J5
St. Paul, *U.S.A., internal capital,* 27 H1

St. Petersburg, *Russia,* 60 J4
St. Petersburg, *U.S.A.,* 27 K5
St. Pierre, *Seychelles,* 75 J1
St. Pierre and Miquelon, *North America,*
    25 P4
St. Polten, *Austria,* 64 E1
St. Vincent and the Grenadines,
    North America, country, 28 M5
St. Vincent, Cape, *Portugal,* 63 B7
Sakhalin, *Russia,* 55 H3
Saki, *Azerbaijan,* 52 E3
Saki, *Nigeria,* 71 F7
Sakishima Islands, *Japan,* 49 K6
Sal, *Cape Verde,* 71 M11
Salado, *Argentina,* 34 F5
Salalah, *Oman,* 53 F8
Salamanca, *Spain,* 63 C6
Salem, *India,* 51 D8
Salem, *U.S.A., internal capital,* 26 B1
Salerno, *Italy,* 64 E3
Salihorsk, *Belarus,* 61 H5
Salinas, *U.S.A.,* 26 B3
Salta, *Argentina,* 34 E4
Saltillo, *Mexico,* 28 D2
Salt Lake City, *U.S.A., internal capital,*
    26 D2
Salto, *Uruguay,* 34 G6
Salton Sea, *U.S.A.,* 26 C4
Salvador, *Brazil,* 33 L6
Salween, *Asia,* 46 C4
Salzburg, *Austria,* 64 E2
Samar, *Philippines,* 47 J5
Samara, *Russia,* 59 G3
Samarinda, *Indonesia,* 44 E4
Samarqand, *Uzbekistan,* 50 B3
Sambalpur, *India,* 51 E6
Samoa, *Oceania, country,* 38 F6
Sampwe, *Democratic Republic of Congo,*
    72 E5
Sam Rayburn Reservoir, *U.S.A.,* 27 H4
Samsun, *Turkey,* 52 C3
San, *Mali,* 71 E6
Sana, *Yemen, national capital,* 53 D8
Sanandaj, *Iran,* 52 E4
San Andres Island, *Colombia,* 29 H5
San Antonio, *U.S.A.,* 26 G5
San Antonio, Cape, *Argentina,* 35 G7
San Antonio Oeste, *Argentina,* 35 F8
San Cristobal, *Ecuador,* 32 P10
San Cristobal, *Venezuela,* 32 D2
Sandakan, *Malaysia,* 45 E2
San Diego, *U.S.A.,* 26 C4
Sandoway, *Burma,* 46 B4
San Fernando, *Chile,* 34 D6
San Fernando de Apure, *Venezuela,*
    32 E2
San Francisco, *Argentina,* 34 F6
San Francisco, *U.S.A.,* 26 B3
San Francisco, Cape, *Ecuador,* 32 B3
Sangihe Islands, *Indonesia,* 45 G3
San Jorge, Gulf of, *Argentina,* 35 E9
San Jose, *Costa Rica, national capital,*
    29 H6
San Jose, *U.S.A.,* 26 B3
San Jose de Chiquitos, *Bolivia,* 34 F3
San Jose del Guaviare, *Colombia,* 32 D3
San Juan, *Argentina,* 34 E6
San Juan, *Puerto Rico,* 28 L4
San Julian, *Argentina,* 35 E9
Sanliurfa, *Turkey,* 52 C4
San Lucas, Cape, *Mexico,* 28 B3
San Luis, *Argentina,* 34 E6
San Luis Obispo, *U.S.A.,* 26 B3
San Luis Potosi, *Mexico,* 28 D3
San Marino, *Europe, country,* 64 E3
San Matias, Gulf of, *Argentina,* 35 F8
San Miguel de Tucuman, *Argentina,* 34 E5
San Nicolas de los Arroyos, *Argentina,*
    34 F6
San Pedro, *Ivory Coast,* 71 D8
San Pedro de Atacama, *Chile,* 34 E4
San Rafael, *Argentina,* 34 E6
San Remo, *Italy,* 64 C3
San Salvador, *Ecuador,* 32 N10
San Salvador, *El Salvador, national capital,*
    28 G5

San Salvador de Jujuy, *Argentina, 34 E4*
San Sebastian, *Spain, 63 D6*
Santa Clara, *Cuba, 29 H3*
Santa Cruz, *Bolivia, 34 F3*
Santa Cruz, *Ecuador, 32 N10*
Santa Cruz Islands, *Solomon Islands, 41 N2*
Santa Elena, *Venezuela, 32 F3*
Santa Fe, *Argentina, 34 F6*
Santa Fe, *U.S.A., internal capital, 26 E3*
Santa Maria, *Brazil, 34 H5*
Santa Marta, *Colombia, 32 D1*
Santander, *Spain, 63 D6*
Santarem, *Brazil, 33 H4*
Santa Rosa, *Argentina, 35 F7*
Santiago, *Chile, national capital, 34 D6*
Santiago, *Dominican Republic, 29 K4*
Santiago, *Panama, 29 H6*
Santiago de Compostela, *Spain, 63 B6*
Santiago de Cuba, *Cuba, 29 J3*
Santiago del Estero, *Argentina, 34 F5*
Santo Antao, *Cape Verde, 71 L11*
Santo Domingo, *Dominican Republic, national capital, 29 L4*
Santo Domingo de los Colorados, *Ecuador, 32 C4*
San Valentin, Mount, *Chile, 35 D9*
Sanya, *China, 48 G7*
Sao Francisco, *Brazil, 33 L5*
Sao Jose do Rio Preto, *Brazil, 34 J4*
Sao Luis, *Brazil, 33 K4*
Sao Miguel, *Azores, 70 K10*
Sao Nicolau, *Cape Verde, 71 M11*
Sao Paulo, *Brazil, 34 J4*
Sao Roque, Cape, *Brazil, 33 L4*
Sao Tiago, *Cape Verde, 71 M11*
Sao Tome, *Sao Tome and Principe, national capital, 71 G8*
Sao Tome and Principe, *Africa, country, 71 G8*
Sapporo, *Japan, 49 P2*
Saqqara, *Egypt, 69 H3*
Sarajevo, *Bosnia and Herzegovina, national capital, 65 F3*
Saransk, *Russia, 58 F3*
Sarapul, *Russia, 59 G2*
Saratov, *Russia, 59 F3*
Saratov Reservoir, *Russia, 59 F3*
Sardinia, *Italy, 64 D3*
Sargodha, *Pakistan, 50 C4*
Sarh, *Chad, 72 C2*
Sarremaa, *Estonia, 60 G4*
Saskatchewan, *Canada, internal admin. area, 24 J3*
Saskatoon, *Canada, 24 J3*
Sassari, *Italy, 64 D3*
Satu Mare, *Romania, 65 G2*
Saudi Arabia, *Asia, country, 53 E7*
Sault Ste. Marie, *Canada, 25 L4*
Saurimo, *Angola, 74 D1*
Savannah, *U.S.A., 27 K4*
Savannakhet, *Laos, 46 D4*
Sawu, *Indonesia, 45 F6*
Sawu Sea, *Indonesia, 45 F5*
Schwerin, *Germany, 62 G3*
Scotland, *United Kingdom, internal admin. area, 62 C2*
Seattle, *U.S.A., 26 B1*
Seeheim, *Namibia, 74 C5*
Sefadu, *Sierra Leone, 71 C7*
Seg, Lake, *Russia, 60 K3*
Segou, *Mali, 71 D6*
Seine, *France, 62 F4*
Sekondi-Takoradi, *Ghana, 71 E8*
Selebi-Phikwe, *Botswana, 74 E4*
Selibabi, *Mauritania, 71 C5*
Selvas, *Brazil, 32 E5*
Semarang, *Indonesia, 44 D5*
Semenov, *Russia, 58 E2*
Semiozernoe, *Kazakhstan, 59 J3*
Sendai, *Japan, 49 P3*
Senegal, *Africa, 71 C5*
Senegal, *Africa, country, 71 B6*
Seoul, *South Korea, national capital, 49 L3*
Serang, *Indonesia, 44 C5*

Serbia, *Europe, country, 65 G2*
Seremban, *Malaysia, 44 B3*
Sergiyev Posad, *Russia, 58 D2*
Serov, *Russia, 59 J2*
Serowe, *Botswana, 74 E4*
Serpukhov, *Russia, 58 D3*
Serres, *Greece, 65 G3*
Sesheke, *Zambia, 74 D3*
Setif, *Algeria, 70 G1*
Setubal, *Portugal, 63 B7*
Sevastopol, *Ukraine, 65 K2*
Severn, *United Kingdom, 62 D3*
Severnaya Zemlya, *Russia, 55 F2*
Severomorsk, *Russia, 60 K1*
Sevettijarvi, *Finland, 60 J1*
Seville, *Spain, 63 C7*
Seward, *U.S.A., 24 E2*
Seward Peninsula, *U.S.A., 24 C2*
Seychelles, *Indian Ocean, country, 75 J1*
Seydhisfjordhur, *Iceland, 60 Q2*
Sfax, *Tunisia, 68 D2*
Shalqar, *Kazakhstan, 52 G2*
Shanghai, *China, 49 K4*
Shannon, *Ireland, 62 C3*
Shantou, *China, 49 J6*
Shaoguan, *China, 49 H6*
Sharjah, *United Arab Emirates, 53 G6*
Sharm el Sheikh, *Egypt, 69 H3*
Shasta, Mount, *U.S.A., 26 B2*
Sheffield, *United Kingdom, 62 D3*
Shenyang, *China, 49 K2*
Shepetivka, *Ukraine, 61 H6*
Shetland Islands, *United Kingdom, 62 D1*
Shieli, *Kazakhstan, 52 J3*
Shihezi, *China, 50 F2*
Shijiazhuang, *China, 49 H3*
Shikoku, *Japan, 49 M4*
Shillong, *India, 50 G5*
Shiraz, *Iran, 53 F6*
Shishaldin Volcano, *U.S.A., 25 C3*
Shiyan, *China, 48 H4*
Shizuoka, *Japan, 49 N3*
Shkoder, *Albania, 65 F3*
Shreveport, *U.S.A., 27 H4*
Shumen, *Bulgaria, 65 H3*
Shymkent, *Kazakhstan, 50 B2*
Sialkot, *Pakistan, 50 C4*
Siauliai, *Lithuania, 61 G5*
Sibiti, *Congo, 72 B4*
Sibiu, *Romania, 65 H2*
Sibolga, *Indonesia, 44 A3*
Sibu, *Malaysia, 44 D3*
Sicily, *Italy, 64 E4*
Sicuani, *Peru, 32 D6*
Sidi-Bel-Abbes, *Algeria, 70 E1*
Sidon, *Lebanon, 52 C5*
Sidra, Gulf of, *Africa, 68 E2*
Sierra Leone, *Africa, country, 71 C7*
Sierra Morena, *Spain, 63 D7*
Sierra Nevada, *Spain, 63 D7*
Sierra Nevada, *U.S.A., 26 B3*
Siglufjordhur, *Iceland, 60 P2*
Siguiri, *Guinea, 71 D6*
Sikasso, *Mali, 71 D6*
Sikhote Alin Range, *Russia, 49 N1*
Siling Lake, *China, 50 F4*
Simao, *China, 48 F6*
Simeulue, *Indonesia, 44 A3*
Simferopol, *Ukraine, 65 K2*
Simpson Desert, *Australia, 40 G4*
Sinai, *Egypt, 69 H3*
Sinai, Mount, *Egypt, 69 H3*
Sincelejo, *Colombia, 32 C2*
Sines, *Portugal, 63 B7*
Singapore, *Asia, country, 44 B3*
Singapore, *Singapore, national capital, 44 B3*
Sinnamary, *French Guiana, 33 H2*
Sinuiju, *North Korea, 49 K2*
Sioux City, *U.S.A., 27 G2*
Sioux Falls, *U.S.A., 27 G2*
Sirjan, *Iran, 53 G6*
Sittwe, *Burma, 46 B3*
Sivas, *Turkey, 52 C4*
Skagen, *Denmark, 61 D4*
Skagerrak, *Europe, 61 C4*

Skelleftea, *Sweden, 60 G2*
Skikda, *Algeria, 70 G1*
Skopje, *Macedonia, national capital, 65 G3*
Skyros, *Greece, 65 H4*
Slavonski Brod, *Croatia, 64 F2*
Sligo, *Ireland, 62 B3*
Sliven, *Bulgaria, 65 H3*
Slovakia, *Europe, country, 61 F6*
Slovenia, *Europe, country, 64 E2*
Slovyansk, *Ukraine, 58 D4*
Slupsk, *Poland, 61 F5*
Slutsk, *Belarus, 61 H5*
Smallwood Reservoir, *Canada, 25 N3*
Smola, *Norway, 60 C3*
Smolensk, *Russia, 61 J5*
Sobradinho Reservoir, *Brazil, 33 K6*
Sobral, *Brazil, 33 K4*
Sochi, *Russia, 52 C3*
Society Islands, *French Polynesia, 39 J6*
Socotra, *Yemen, 53 F9*
Sodankyla, *Finland, 60 H2*
Sodertalje, *Sweden, 60 F4*
Sofia, *Bulgaria, national capital, 65 G3*
Sohag, *Egypt, 69 H3*
Sokhumi, *Georgia, 52 D3*
Sokode, *Togo, 71 F7*
Sokoto, *Nigeria, 71 G6*
Solapur, *India, 51 D7*
Solikamsk, *Russia, 59 H2*
Solomon Islands, *Oceania, country, 38 D5*
Solomon Sea, *Papua New Guinea, 45 M5*
Solwezi, *Zambia, 74 E2*
Somalia, *Africa, country, 73 J2*
Somerset Island, *Canada, 25 K1*
Songea, *Tanzania, 73 G6*
Songo, *Mozambique, 75 F3*
Son La, *Vietnam, 46 D3*
Sorong, *Indonesia, 45 H4*
Soroti, *Uganda, 73 F3*
Soroya, *Norway, 60 G1*
Sotra, *Norway, 60 C3*
Souk Ahras, *Algeria, 64 C4*
Sousse, *Tunisia, 68 D1*
South Africa, *Africa, country, 74 D6*
South America, *20*
Southampton, *United Kingdom, 62 D4*
Southampton Island, *Canada, 25 L2*
South Australia, *Australia, internal admin. area, 40 F5*
South Bend, *U.S.A., 27 J2*
South Carolina, *U.S.A., internal admin. area, 27 K4*
South China Sea, *Asia, 47 F5*
South Dakota, *U.S.A., internal admin. area, 26 F2*
South East Cape, *Australia, 40 J8*
Southend-on-Sea, *United Kingdom, 62 E4*
Southern Ocean, *20*
Southern Sierra Madre, *Mexico, 28 D4*
South Georgia, *Atlantic Ocean, 35 L10*
South Island, *New Zealand, 41 N8*
South Korea, *Asia, country, 49 L3*
South Orkney Islands, *Atlantic Ocean, 35 J12*
South Sandwich Islands, *Atlantic Ocean, 35 N10*
South Shetland Islands, *Atlantic Ocean, 35 G12*
South West Cape, *New Zealand, 41 N9*
Spain, *Europe, country, 63 D7*
Split, *Croatia, 64 F3*
Spokane, *U.S.A., 26 C1*
Spratly Islands, *Asia, 47 F5*
Springfield, *Illinois, U.S.A., internal capital, 27 J3*
Springfield, *Massachusetts, U.S.A., 27 M2*
Springfield, *Missouri, U.S.A., 27 H3*
Springs, *South Africa, 74 E5*
Sri Jayewardenepura Kotte, *Sri Lanka, national capital, 51 E9*
Sri Lanka, *Asia, country, 51 E9*
Srinagar, *India, 50 C4*
Standerton, *South Africa, 74 E5*
Stanley, *Falkland Islands, 35 G10*
Stara Zagora, *Bulgaria, 65 H3*

Staryy Oskol, *Russia, 58 D3*
Stavanger, *Norway, 60 C4*
Stavropol, *Russia, 52 D2*
Steinkjer, *Norway, 60 D2*
Stellenbosch, *South Africa, 74 C6*
Sterlitamak, *Russia, 59 H3*
Stewart Island, *New Zealand, 41 N9*
Stockholm, *Sweden, national capital, 60 F4*
Stoeng Treng, *Cambodia, 46 E5*
Stoke-on-Trent, *United Kingdom, 62 D3*
Stora Lule Lake, *Sweden, 60 F2*
Storavan Lake, *Sweden, 60 F2*
Stor Lake, *Sweden, 60 E3*
Stornoway, *United Kingdom, 62 C2*
Stranraer, *United Kingdom, 62 C3*
Strasbourg, *France, 62 F4*
Sturt Stony Desert, *Australia, 40 G5*
Stuttgart, *Germany, 62 G4*
Subotica, *Serbia, 65 F2*
Suceava, *Romania, 65 H2*
Sucre, *Bolivia, national capital, 34 E3*
Sudan, *Africa, country, 69 G5*
Sudbury, *Canada, 25 L4*
Suez, *Egypt, 69 H3*
Suez Canal, *Egypt, 69 H2*
Suhar, *Oman, 53 G7*
Sukkur, *Pakistan, 50 B5*
Sukses, *Namibia, 74 C4*
Sula, *Norway, 60 C3*
Sula Islands, *Indonesia, 45 G4*
Sullana, *Peru, 32 B4*
Sulu Archipelago, *Philippines, 47 H6*
Sulu Sea, *Asia, 47 G6*
Sumatra, *Indonesia, 44 B3*
Sumba, *Indonesia, 45 E5*
Sumbawa, *Indonesia, 44 E5*
Sumqayit, *Azerbaijan, 52 E3*
Sumy, *Ukraine, 58 C3*
Sunderland, *United Kingdom, 62 D3*
Sundsvall, *Sweden, 60 F3*
Superior, Lake, *U.S.A., 27 J1*
Sur, *Oman, 53 G7*
Surabaya, *Indonesia, 44 D5*
Surakarta, *Indonesia, 44 D5*
Surat, *India, 51 C6*
Surgut, *Russia, 54 D2*
Surigao, *Philippines, 47 J6*
Suriname, *South America, country, 33 G3*
Surt, *Libya, 68 E2*
Sutherland Falls, *New Zealand, 41 N8*
Suva, *Fiji, national capital, 41 Q3*
Suwalki, *Poland, 61 G5*
Suwon, *South Korea, 49 L3*
Svalbard, *Norway, 54 A2*
Svolvaer, *Norway, 60 E1*
Svyetlahorsk, *Belarus, 61 J5*
Swakopmund, *Namibia, 74 B4*
Swan Islands, *Honduras, 29 H4*
Swansea, *United Kingdom, 62 D4*
Swaziland, *Africa, country, 74 F5*
Sweden, *Europe, country, 60 E3*
Swift Current, *Canada, 24 J3*
Swindon, *United Kingdom, 62 D4*
Switzerland, *Europe, country, 64 C2*
Sydney, *Australia, internal capital, 41 K6*
Sydney, *Canada, 25 N4*
Syktyvkar, *Russia, 59 G1*
Sylhet, *Bangladesh, 51 G6*
Syracuse, *Italy, 64 E4*
Syracuse, *U.S.A., 27 L2*
Syr Darya, *Asia, 52 H2*
Syria, *Asia, country, 52 C4*
Syrian Desert, *Asia, 53 C5*
Syzran, *Russia, 59 F3*
Szczecin, *Poland, 61 E5*
Szeged, *Hungary, 61 G7*
Szekesfehervar, *Hungary, 61 F7*
Szombathely, *Hungary, 61 F7*

t

Tabora, *Tanzania, 73 F5*
Tabriz, *Iran, 52 E4*
Tabuk, *Saudi Arabia, 53 C6*
Tacloban, *Philippines, 47 J5*
Tacna, *Peru, 32 D7*

Tacoma, *U.S.A.*, **26 B1**
Tacuarembo, *Uruguay*, **34 G6**
Tademait Plateau, *Algeria*, **70 F3**
Tadmur, *Syria*, **52 C5**
Taegu, *South Korea*, **49 L3**
Taejon, *South Korea*, **49 L3**
Tagus, *Europe*, **63 B7**
Tahat, Mount, *Algeria*, **70 G4**
Tahiti, *French Polynesia*, **39 J6**
Tahoua, *Niger*, **68 C6**
Taian, *China*, **49 J3**
Taichung, *China*, **49 K6**
Tai Lake, *China*, **49 J4**
Taimyr Peninsula, *Russia*, **55 F2**
Tainan, *China*, **49 K6**
Taipei, *China*, **49 K5**
Taiping, *Malaysia*, **44 B3**
Taiwan, *China*, **49 K6**
Taiwan Strait, *Asia*, **49 J6**
Taiyuan, *China*, **48 H3**
Taizz, *Yemen*, **53 D9**
Tajikistan, *Asia, country*, **50 B3**
Taj Mahal, *India*, **50 D5**
Tajumulco, *Guatemala*, **28 F4**
Talara, *Peru*, **32 B4**
Talaud Islands, *Indonesia*, **45 G3**
Talca, *Chile*, **35 D7**
Taldyqorghan, *Kazakhstan*, **50 D1**
Tallahassee, *U.S.A., internal capital*, **27 K4**
Tallinn, *Estonia, national capital*, **60 H4**
Taltal, *Chile*, **34 D5**
Tamale, *Ghana*, **71 E7**
Tamanrasset, *Algeria*, **70 G4**
Tambacounda, *Senegal*, **71 C6**
Tambov, *Russia*, **58 E3**
Tampa, *U.S.A.*, **27 K5**
Tampere, *Finland*, **60 G3**
Tampico, *Mexico*, **28 E3**
Tana, Lake, *Ethiopia*, **73 G1**
Tandil, *Argentina*, **35 G7**
Tanga, *Tanzania*, **73 G5**
Tanganyika, Lake, *Africa*, **72 E5**
Tangier, *Morocco*, **70 D1**
Tangshan, *China*, **49 J3**
Tanimbar Islands, *Indonesia*, **45 H5**
Tanjungkarang-Telukbetung, *Indonesia*, **44 C5**
Tanjungredeb, *Indonesia*, **44 E3**
Tanta, *Egypt*, **69 H2**
Tan-Tan, *Morocco*, **70 C3**
Tanzania, *Africa, country*, **73 F5**
Tapachula, *Mexico*, **28 F5**
Tapajos, *Brazil*, **33 G5**
Tarakan, *Indonesia*, **44 E3**
Taranto, *Italy*, **64 F3**
Taraz, *Kazakhstan*, **50 C2**
Targu Mures, *Romania*, **65 H2**
Tarija, *Bolivia*, **34 F4**
Tarim Basin, *China*, **50 E3**
Tarkwa, *Ghana*, **71 E7**
Tarnow, *Poland*, **61 G6**
Tarragona, *Spain*, **63 E6**
Tartagal, *Argentina*, **34 F4**
Tartu, *Estonia*, **60 H4**
Tartus, *Syria*, **52 C5**
Tashkent, *Uzbekistan, national capital*, **50 B2**
Tasmania, *Australia, internal admin. area*, **41 J8**
Tasman Sea, *Australasia*, **41 L7**
Tataouine, *Tunisia*, **68 D2**
Tatvan, *Turkey*, **52 D3** — ...

Taungya, *Burma*, **46 C3**
Taupo, *New Zealand*, **41 Q7**
Taurus Mountains, *Turkey*, **65 J4**
Tavoy, *Burma*, **46 C5**
Tawau, *Malaysia*, **45 E3**
Taytay, *Philippines*, **47 G5**
Taza, *Morocco*, **70 E2**
Tbilisi, *Georgia, national capital*, **52 D3**
Tchibanga, *Gabon*, **72 B4**
Tebessa, *Algeria*, **70 G1**
Tegal, *Indonesia*, **44 C5**
Tegucigalpa, *Honduras, national capital*, **29 G5**
Tehran, *Iran, national capital*, **52 F4**

Tehuacan, *Mexico*, **28 E4**
Tehuantepec, Gulf of, *Mexico*, **28 E4**
Tehuantepec, Isthmus of, *Mexico*, **28 E4**
Tekirdag, *Turkey*, **65 H3**
Tel Aviv-Yafo, *Israel*, **53 B5**
Teller, *U.S.A.*, **24 C2**
Temuco, *Chile*, **35 D7**
Ten Degree Channel, *India*, **51 G9**
Tenerife, *Canary Islands*, **70 B3**
Tenkodogo, *Burkina Faso*, **71 E6**
Tennessee, *U.S.A.*, **27 J3**
Tennessee, *U.S.A., internal admin. area*, **27 J3**
Teofilo Otoni, *Brazil*, **34 K3**
Teotihuacan, *Mexico*, **28 E4**
Terceira, *Azores*, **70 K10**
Teresina, *Brazil*, **33 K4**
Ternate, *Indonesia*, **45 G3**
Terni, *Italy*, **64 E3**
Ternopil, *Ukraine*, **61 H6**
Terracotta Army, *China*, **48 G4**
Terra Firma, *South Africa*, **74 D5**
Teseney, *Eritrea*, **69 J5**
Tete, *Mozambique*, **75 F3**
Tetouan, *Morocco*, **70 D1**
Tetovo, *Macedonia*, **65 G3**
Texarkana, *U.S.A.*, **27 H4**
Texas, *U.S.A., internal admin. area*, **26 G4**
Thailand, *Asia, country*, **46 D4**
Thailand, Gulf of, *Asia*, **46 D6**
Thai Nguyen, *Vietnam*, **46 E3**
Thames, *United Kingdom*, **62 D4**
Thanh Hoa, *Vietnam*, **46 E4**
Thar Desert, *Asia*, **50 B5**
Thasos, *Greece*, **65 H3**
Thaton, *Burma*, **46 C4**
Thessaloniki, *Greece*, **65 G3**
Thies, *Senegal*, **71 B6**
Thika, *Kenya*, **73 G4**
Thimphu, *Bhutan, national capital*, **50 F5**
Thompson, *Canada*, **25 K3**
Three Points, Cape, *Africa*, **71 E8**
Thunder Bay, *Canada*, **25 L4**
Tianjin, *China*, **49 J3**
Tibesti Mountains, *Africa*, **68 E4**
Tibet, *China*, **50 F4**
Tibet, Plateau of, *China*, **50 F4**
Tidjikja, *Mauritania*, **70 C5**
Tien Shan, *Asia*, **50 D2**
Tierra del Fuego, *South America*, **35 E10**
Tighina, *Moldova*, **65 J2**
Tigris, *Asia*, **53 E5**
Tijuana, *Mexico*, **28 A1**
Tikal, *Guatemala*, **28 G4**
Tikhvin, *Russia*, **60 K4**
Tillaberi, *Niger*, **71 F6**
Timbuktu, *Mali*, **71 E5**
Timisoara, *Romania*, **65 G2**
Timor, *Asia*, **45 F5**
Timor Leste, *see East Timor*
Timor Sea, *Asia/Australasia*, **45 G6**
Tindouf, *Algeria*, **70 D3**
Tirana, *Albania, national capital*, **65 F3**
Tiraspol, *Moldova*, **65 J2**
Tiruchchirappalli, *India*, **51 D8**
Titicaca, Lake, *South America*, **32 E7**
Tlemcen, *Algeria*, **70 E2**
Toamasina, *Madagascar*, **75 J3**
Tobago, *Trinidad and Tobabo*, **28 M5**
Tobol, *Asia*, **59 K2**
Tobolsk, *Russia*, **59 K2**
Tobyl, *Kazakhstan*, **59 J3**
Tocantins, *Brazil*, **33 J4**
Togo, *Africa, country*, **71 F7**
Tokelau, *Oceania*, **38 F5**
Tokyo, *Japan, national capital*, **49 N3**
Tolanaro, *Madagascar*, **75 J5**
Toledo, *Spain*, **63 D7**
Toledo, *U.S.A.*, **27 K2**
Toledo Bend Reservoir, *U.S.A.*, **27 H4**
Toliara, *Madagascar*, **75 H4**
Tolyatti, *Russia*, **59 F3**
Tolybay, *Kazakhstan*, **59 J3**

Tomakomai, *Japan*, **49 P2**
Tombouctou, *Mali*, **71 E5**
Tomsk, *Russia*, **54 E3**
Tonga, *Oceania, country*, **38 F6**
Tongliao, *China*, **49 K2**
Tonkin, Gulf of, *Asia*, **46 E4**
Tonle Sap, *Cambodia*, **46 D5**
Toowoomba, *Australia*, **41 K5**
Topeka, *U.S.A., internal capital*, **27 G3**
Top, Lake, *Russia*, **60 K2**
Topoli, *Kazakhstan*, **59 G4**
Torghay, *Kazakhstan*, **59 J4**
Tornio, *Finland*, **60 H2**
Toronto, *Canada, internal capital*, **25 M4**
Torrens, Lake, *Australia*, **40 G6**
Torreon, *Mexico*, **28 D2**
Torres Strait, *Australasia*, **40 H2**
Tortuga Island, *Venezuela*, **32 E1**
Toubkal, *Morocco*, **70 D2**
Tougan, *Burkina Faso*, **71 E6**
Touggourt, *Algeria*, **70 G2**
Toulon, *France*, **63 F6**
Toulouse, *France*, **63 E6**
Tours, *France*, **62 E5**
Townsville, *Australia*, **40 J3**
Toyama, *Japan*, **49 N3**
Tozeur, *Tunisia*, **68 C2**
Trabzon, *Turkey*, **52 C3**
Tralee, *Ireland*, **62 B3**
Transantarctic Mountains, *Antarctica*, **79 S4**
Transylvanian Alps, *Romania*, **65 G2**
Trapani, *Italy*, **64 E4**
Trento, *Italy*, **64 D2**
Trenton, *U.S.A., internal capital*, **27 M2**
Tres Arroyos, *Argentina*, **35 F7**
Tres Marias Reservoir, *Brazil*, **34 J3**
Tres Puntas, Cape, *Argentina*, **35 E9**
Trieste, *Italy*, **64 E2**
Trincomalee, *Sri Lanka*, **51 E9**
Trinidad, *Bolivia*, **34 F2**
Trinidad, *Trinidad and Tobago*, **28 M5**
Trinidad and Tobago, *North America, country*, **28 M5**
Tripoli, *Lebanon*, **52 C5**
Tripoli, *Libya, national capital*, **68 D2**
Trivandrum, *India*, **51 D9**
Trnava, *Slovakia*, **61 F6**
Trois-Rivieres, *Canada*, **25 M4**
Tromso, *Norway*, **60 F1**
Trondheim, *Norway*, **60 D3**
Troyes, *France*, **62 F4**
Trujillo, *Peru*, **32 C5**
Tsau, *Botswana*, **74 D4**
Tses, *Namibia*, **74 C5**
Tshabong, *Botswana*, **74 D5**
Tshane, *Botswana*, **74 D4**
Tshikapa, *Democratic Republic of Congo*, **72 D5**
Tshwane, *Botswana*, **74 D4**
Tsimlyansk Reservoir, *Russia*, **58 E4**
Tsiroanomandidy, *Madagascar*, **75 J3**
Tsumeb, *Namibia*, **74 C3**
Tuamotu Archipelago, *French Polynesia*, **39 K6**
Tubmanburg, *Liberia*, **71 C7**
Tubruq, *Libya*, **68 F2**
Tubuai Islands, *French Polynesia*, **39 J7**
Tucson, *U.S.A.*, **26 D4**
Tucupita, *Venezuela*, **32 F2**
Tucurui Reservoir, *Brazil*, **33 J4**
Tugela Falls, *South Africa*, **74 E5**
Tuguegarao, *Philippines*, **47 H4**
Tula, *Russia*, **58 D3**
Tulcea, *Romania*, **65 J2**
Tulsa, *U.S.A.*, **27 G3**
Tumaco, *Colombia*, **32 C3**
Tumbes, *Peru*, **32 B4**
Tunduma, *Tanzania*, **73 F5**
Tunduru, *Tanzania*, **73 G6**
Tunis, *Tunisia, national capital*, **68 D1**
Tunisia, *Africa, country*, **68 C2**
Tunja, *Colombia*, **32 D2**
Tupelo, *U.S.A.*, **27 J4**
Tupiza, *Bolivia*, **34 E4**
Turbat, *Pakistan*, **53 H6**

Turbo, *Colombia*, **32 C2**
Turin, *Italy*, **64 C2**
Turkana, Lake, *Africa*, **73 G3**
Turkey, *Asia, country*, **52 C4**
Turkistan, *Kazakhstan*, **50 B2**
Turkmenabat, *Turkmenistan*, **52 H4**
Turkmenbasy, *Turkmenistan*, **52 F3**
Turkmenistan, *Asia, country*, **52 G4**
Turks and Caicos Islands, *North America*, **29 K3**
Turku, *Finland*, **60 G3**
Turpan, *China*, **50 F2**
Turpan Depression, *China*, **50 G2**
Tuscaloosa, *U.S.A.*, **27 J4**
Tuvalu, *Oceania, country*, **38 E5**
Tuxtla Gutierrez, *Mexico*, **28 F4**
Tuzla, *Bosnia and Herzegovina*, **65 F2**
Tuz, Lake, *Turkey*, **65 K4**
Tver, *Russia*, **58 D2**
Twin Falls, *U.S.A.*, **26 D2**
Tynda, *Russia*, **55 G3**
Tyrrhenian Sea, *Europe*, **64 D3**
Tyumen, *Russia*, **59 K2**

U

Ubangi, *Africa*, **72 C3**
Uberaba, *Brazil*, **34 J3**
Uberlandia, *Brazil*, **34 J3**
Ubon Ratchathani, *Thailand*, **46 D4**
Ucayali, *Peru*, **32 D5**
Udaipur, *India*, **51 C6**
Uddevalla, *Sweden*, **60 D4**
Udon Thani, *Thailand*, **46 D4**
Uele, *Democratic Republic of Congo*, **72 D3**
Ufa, *Russia*, **59 H3**
Uganda, *Africa, country*, **73 F3**
Uitenhage, *South Africa*, **74 E6**
Ujung Pandang, *Indonesia*, **45 E5**
Ukhta, *Russia*, **54 C2**
Ukraine, *Europe, country*, **58 C4**
Ulan Bator, *Mongolia, national capital*, **48 G1**
Ulanhot, *China*, **49 K1**
Ulan Ude, *Russia*, **55 F3**
Ulm, *Germany*, **62 G4**
Uluru, *Australia*, **40 F5**
Ulyanovsk, *Russia*, **59 F3**
Uman, *Ukraine*, **61 J6**
Ume, *Sweden*, **60 F2**
Umea, *Sweden*, **60 G3**
Umnak Island, *U.S.A.*, **25 C3**
Umtata, *South Africa*, **74 E6**
Unalaska Island, *U.S.A.*, **25 C3**
Ungava Bay, *Canada*, **25 N3**
Ungava Peninsula, *Canada*, **25 M2**
Unimak Island, *U.S.A.*, **25 C3**
United Arab Emirates, *Asia, country*, **53 F7**
United Kingdom, *Europe, country*, **62 D3**
United States of America, *North America, country*, **26 F3**
Upington, *South Africa*, **74 D5**
Uppsala, *Sweden*, **60 F4**
Ural, *Asia*, **59 G4**
Ural Mountains, *Russia*, **59 H2**
Uray, *Russia*, **59 J1**
Urganch, *Uzbekistan*, **50 A2**
Urmia, *Iran*, **52 E4**
Uruapan, *Mexico*, **28 D4**
Urucui, *Brazil*, **33 K5**
Uruguaiana, *Brazil*, **34 G5**
Uruguay, *South America, country*, **34 G6**
Urumqi, *China*, **50 F2**
Usak, *Turkey*, **65 J4**
Ushuaia, *Argentina*, **35 E10**
Uskemen, *Kazakhstan*, **54 E3**
Utah, *U.S.A., internal admin. area*, **26 D3**
Utsjoki, *Finland*, **60 H1**
Utsunomiya, *Japan*, **49 N3**
Uy, *Asia*, **59 J3**
Uyuni, *Bolivia*, **34 E4**
Uzbekistan, *Asia, country*, **54 D3**
Uzhhorod, *Ukraine*, **61 G6**

GENERAL INDEX

Acknowledgements

Cover design by Hannah Ahmed   Managing editor: Gillian Doherty   Managing designer: Mary Cartwright

Every effort has been made to trace the copyright holders of the material in this book. If any rights have been omitted, the publishers offer to rectify this in any subsequent edition, following notification. The publishers are grateful to the following organizations and individuals for their contributions and permission to reproduce material (t=top, m=middle, b=bottom, l=left, r=right, bg = background):

© Agripicture 57br (Peter Dean). © Air Photographics, Inc., CNOVS-969-20 4tr. © Courtesy CIA 84-97. © Craig Asquith 11 projections, 14b, 15, 82. © Corbis 6tr (Dan Guravich), 7tr (W. Perry Conway), 10 (Christopher Cormack), 12–13(Raymond Gehman), 12tr (Owen Franken), 13tr (Adam Woolfitt), 14tr (Bill Ross), 22bl (Richard Cummins), 23br (W. Perry Conway), 30b (Galen Rowell), 31tr (Eye Ubiquitous), 37br (Bates Littlehales), 42–43b (Michael S. Yamashita), 43br (Keren Su), 66–67b (Tom Brakefield), 67br (Gallo Images), 76bl (Galen Rowell), 78b (Wolfgang Kaehler). © Digital Vision 1, 2–3, 4bl, 8–9bg, 16bg, 18–21bg, 24–29bg, 32–35bg, 38–41bg, 44–55bg, 56–57bg, 58–65bg, 68–75bg, 76br, 80–81bg, 84–97bg. © European Map Graphics Ltd 5t, bm & br, 7bl, 16–21, 22–23 map, 24–29, 30–31 map, 32–35, 36–37 map, 38–41, 42–43 map, 44–55, 56–57 map, 58–65, 66–67 map, 68–75, 77, 79. © Stephen Moncrieff 4ml simple map, 6bl globes, 11 globes. © NERC Satellite Station, University of Dundee www.sat.dundee.ac.html 9tl. © PHOTO ESA 8mr. © Science Photo Library 9br (European Space Agency), 76tr (Worldsat International), 78mr (NASA). © Still Pictures 36–37t (Pascal Kobeh). © UN/Mark Garten 97b.

This edition first published in 2010 by Usborne Publishing Ltd, 83–85 Saffron Hill, London EC1N 8RT, England. www.usborne.com